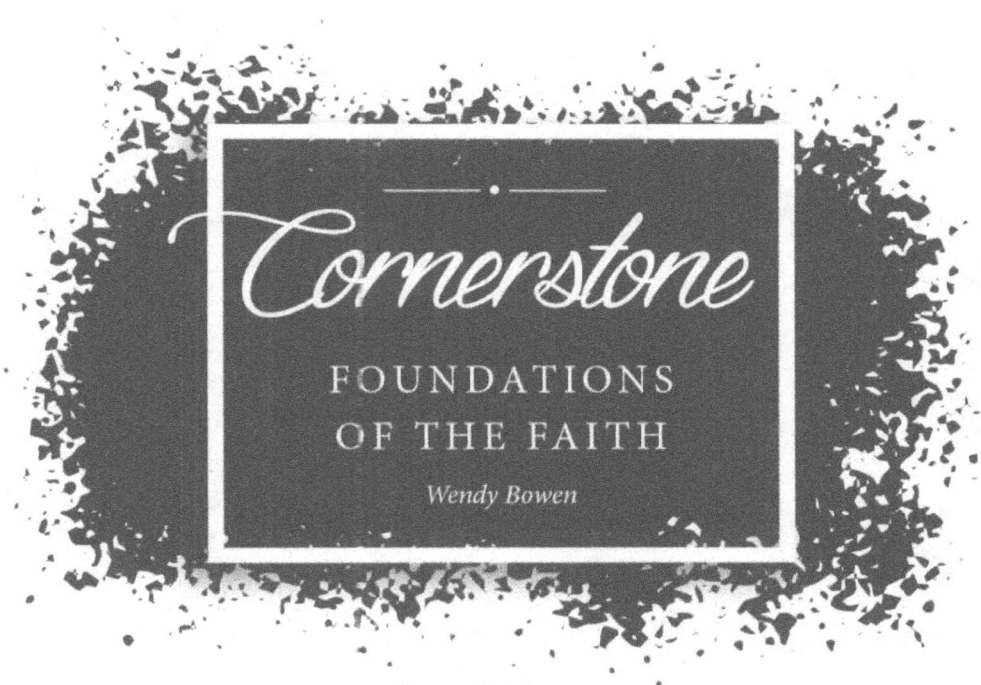

Cornerstone
FOUNDATIONS OF THE FAITH
Wendy Bowen

CORE CURRICULUM COURSE

Manifest INTERNATIONAL
We Live to Manifest Our King

Cornerstone: Foundations of the Faith

Copyright © 2020 Wendy Bowen

ALL RIGHTS RESERVED WORLDWIDE

Manifest International, LLC

ISBN: 978-1-951280-12-3

Scripture references in this book are from the New International Version of the Bible unless otherwise noted. Emphasis added by author for teaching purposes.

Scripture taken from the HOLY BIBLE, NEW INTERNATIONAL VERSION ® NIV ® Copyright © 1973, 1978, 1984, 2011 by Biblica, Inc. Used by permission of Biblica, Inc. All rights reserved worldwide. – Scripture quotations are taken from the Holy Bible, New Living Translation, copyright © 1996, 2004, 2007 by Tyndale House Foundation. Used by permission of Tyndale House Publishers, Inc. Carol Stream, Illinois 60188. All rights reserved. – Scripture taken from the New King James Version ®. Copyright © 1982 by Thomas Nelson, Inc. Used by permission. All rights reserved.

All Biblical definitions in this book are from Strong's Hebrew and Greek Lexicon, Gesenius' Hebrew-Chaldee Lexicon, and Thayer's Greek Lexicon

Some excerpts and adaptations from other books by Wendy Bowen, including: ACTS © 2015, Paul's Prayers © 2016, Biblical Healing © 2016

Cover Image Credit: Designed by kues1 / Freepik

DEDICATION

To Jesus. The one and only cornerstone.

Contents

Guide to the Course		1
Course Introduction		2
Pre-Course Examination		3
UNIT ONE	**THE GOSPEL OF JESUS CHRIST**	**5**
Class 1.1	It Is Finished!	6
Class 1.2	Established by Faith	17
Class 1.3	No More Religion	19
Class 1.4	Serving From Love	24
Key Questions & Group Exercises		31
UNIT TWO	**THE HOLY SPIRIT**	**33**
Class 2.1	Holy Spirit Poured Out	34
Class 2.2	New Heart & New Spirit	40
Class 2.3	Repentance & Fruit	48
Class 2.4	How to Hear God	50
Key Questions & Group Exercises		56
UNIT THREE	**COMMUNITY OF GOD**	**59**
Class 3.1	A Holy Kingdom	60
Class 3.2	A Called Out People	69
Class 3.3	Fellowship of One Family	76
Class 3.4	One Another	82
Key Questions & Group Exercises		87
UNIT FOUR	**MIRACLES**	**91**
Class 4.1	Power from Heaven	92
Class 4.2	Power & Authority	97
Class 4.3	Walking Like Jesus	105
Class 4.4	Gifts & Gathering	112
Key Questions & Group Exercises		114
UNIT FIVE	**SUFFERING & PERSECUTION**	**117**
Class 5.1	Godly Suffering	118
Class 5.2	Trials, Testings, & Tribulation	126
Class 5.3	Sovereignty & Thorns	132
Class 5.4	Persecution to the End	137
Key Questions & Group Exercises		138
UNIT SIX	**CHRISTLIKENESS & COMMISSION**	**141**
Class 6.1	Living by Faith	142
Class 6.2	Christlikeness (Being)	148
Class 6.3	Commission (Doing)	153
Class 6.4	Maturity (Fullness)	161
Key Questions & Group Exercises		165

Guide to This Course

This course is designed to firmly establish your faith in the truth of Jesus Christ and the reality of following Him in your daily life. You will learn all of what Jesus accomplished for us and how to walk with Him in the power of the Holy Spirit. You will learn about God's design for Christian community and how to endure victoriously through trials. You will learn to experience God's wonderful miracle power and keep your focus on God's purposes for your life.

Six Units, Four Classes Each, Plus Group Exercises

Each Unit of the Cornerstone Curriculum digs deeply into a specific element of life with God. Each Class contains various readings and spiritual exercises to help you KNOW the Word and DO what it says through practical application. Lord willing, we will soon have video teachings to supplement each class. Check for videos at www.manifestinternational.com/videos

Each Unit offers Key Questions and a Group Exercise for churches, home groups, or gatherings of believers who are taking the course together. The whole Curriculum can be completed in six weeks or at your own pace.

We pray that God will pour out His Spirit of wisdom and revelation to you as you grow in your knowledge of Him and that you are richly edified in your walk with Jesus as you build your faith in Christ alone.

Notes:

***Book Format Notes**: Please note that this course was initially assembled as an online course. It consists of writings, exercises, inspections, and other tools created for fostering spiritual growth. This book was created to make it easier for participants who desire the full course pre-assembled, rather than downloading each element individually.

Foundations and Maturity: This course can be taken again and again to set and re-set your faith in the foundations of Jesus Christ and Him crucified. It was also designed to prepare participants for the Perfection Course, a course focused on developing disciples to spiritual maturity.
The Perfection Course can be found at www.manifestinternational.com/perfection

Introduction

In my life before Jesus, I trained as a ballerina. At four years old, little aspiring ballerinas learn how to do plies, tendues, degages, and other exercises at the barre to develop their bodies and skill. Later in life, when a ballerina attains the professional level, she is at the barre every day doing plies, tendues, degages and the same exercises that the four year olds are doing. The exercises that develop the ballerina's body and skills are the same no matter what level of performance the dancer has attained.

When the Lord told me to put together this curriculum, He reminded me of my ballet days. In the Lord, we never grow too mature for the basics. No matter how established we think we are spiritually, even the most advanced follower of Christ can learn and grow from refreshing and restoring diligent practice of the essential elements of the faith. At any stage of spiritual life, it is important that we not just KNOW what Jesus taught but that we DO it... and keep doing it consistently...until He returns.

> *Matthew 7:24: Therefore everyone who **hears these words of mine and puts them into practice** is like a wise man who built his house on the rock.*

Therefore, in the six units of this course, we will dig into six essential elements of the Christian life, both in knowing what Jesus taught and also putting it into practice through spiritual exercises. The units are:

1) The Gospel of Jesus Christ: There is no other foundation for our faith. We must know and believe who Jesus is and what He did for us.

2) The Holy Spirit: One of the primary reasons Jesus came was so that He could put His Sprit inside of us to guide us into God's will and ways. We are His sheep and we can hear His voice!

3) Community of God: The Biblical design for community is for believers to be a royal priesthood and holy Kingdom. We have to learn to love one another as Christ loved us to make this a reality.

4) Miracles: God is still working miracles today. We have to believe God to work miracles for us as we walk with Him and understand the authority He has given us in Christ to work miracles according to His will.

5) Suffering & Persecution: Jesus made it clear that those who truly follow Him will suffer and be persecuted for doing so. When we understand what suffering for righteousness entails and what kind of suffering is not from God, we are better equipped to respond correctly in our trials.

6) Christlikeness & Commission: God's desire is for us to be like Jesus. Jesus gave us the great commission to make disciples. Our aim is spiritual maturity so that God's will is fulfilled in our lives.

My hope is to lay a solid foundation for you in each of these elements to give you a strong faith which will not be shaken by trials and tests. This course was designed to be taken again and again as we grow. We attain maturity through becoming like a child so, we never grow too big for the basics!

May you be richly blessed as you grow in your knowledge of Him!

PRE-COURSE EXAMINATION & QUESTIONS
Do You Know What You Believe?

Answer the following questions. Examine your beliefs about these aspects of the Christian faith and life with Jesus.

What is the purpose/point of the Christian life?	What does success look like for a follower of Jesus?

What is the Gospel of Jesus Christ?	How do we live our lives with the Holy Spirit?	What is God's design for Christian Community?

How do we access God's power for miracles?	What is the role of Christian suffering?	What does spiritual maturity look like?

What season or stage of the walk of faith are you in?	What is one thing you are hoping to learn through this course?

UNIT ONE:
THE GOSPEL OF JESUS CHRIST

KEY SCRIPTURE VERSE FOR UNIT ONE
For no one can lay any foundation other than the one already laid, which is Jesus Christ. - 1 Corinthians 3:11

CLASS 1: IT IS FINISHED!
1 Reading, 1 Exercise
Jesus Christ is the only begotten Son of God. He is the promised Messiah of Israel who fulfills the prophecies of Scripture and the seed of Eve who crushes the head of the serpent. Through faith in Him, we are saved from sin, redeemed from the curse, and granted eternal life with God. Learn who Jesus is and what He did for us!

CLASS 2: ESTABLISHED BY FAITH
1 Exercise
By grace through faith in Jesus, we receive His perfect record of righteousness. We can stand before God free of guilt, shame, and accusation, ready to receive all of His blessings!

CLASS 3: NO MORE RELIGION
1 Readings, 1 Visual Aid, 1 Exercise
We receive salvation and all of its benefits by grace through faith, not by what we do or do not do. Either Jesus finished it or we have to. Our only job now it to receive God's grace freely by faith.

CLASS 4: SERVING FROM LOVE
1 Reading, 1 Worksheet, 1 Exercise
We worship God by offering our lives in service to Jesus, not to earn anything from Him but out of gratitude for what He has done for us and a willful desire to partner with His purposes.

KEY QUESTIONS

GROUP EXERCISES

CORNERSTONE – UNIT 1.1 READING

It Is Finished!

Jesus Christ, the one and only begotten Son of God, was born of a virgin into the lineage of King David of Israel. He was crucified, died and was buried, He descended into hell and was resurrected from the dead on the third day by the power of God. He ascended into heaven and is now seated at the right hand of God with all power and authority in heaven and on earth and under the earth. After ascending to heaven, He poured out the Holy Spirit into all who believe in Him so that Jesus Christ now dwells in us by faith. He is coming back to judge the living and the dead, to avenge all evil, and to restore all things to God's design.

The Gospel is more than just Good News. The Gospel changes everything. Through the life, death, and resurrection of Jesus Christ, God established a new people in a right-standing relationship with Him. To know how something has changed, we need to know how it began. So let's start at the beginning.

Adam in Eden (Genesis 1-2)

In the beginning, God created everything: the heavens, the earth, and every living thing. Then, God made man in His own image, like a son bears the image of his father so that man could rule over everything that He had created. In Hebrew, the word for *man* is *Adam*. God formed Adam out of dust. Adam was not born, he was formed as a grown man in the same way that a potter or an artist forms something of clay. Then, God breathed the breath of life into Adam's nostrils, and he became a living being. Adam lived in paradise, and there was only one rule. While Adam was still alone, the Lord commanded him not to eat of the tree of the knowledge of good and evil. (See Genesis 2:16-17.)

But it was not good for Adam to be alone. He needed a helper for ruling over God's creation, so God put Adam into a deep sleep and made a woman from his rib. Adam's wife was not born, she was built out of Adam's rib in the same way that a building or a temple is built from raw materials. Adam could tell that this woman was made just like him – bone of his bone and flesh of his flesh. (See Genesis 2:23.)

Adam and Eve were completely innocent, unashamedly naked, and shared unhindered fellowship with each other and with God. They were one flesh – male and female of the same kind of species on the earth. They lived in paradise, in perfect bodies, in a perfect creation, where everything worked exactly as God designed it. God's purpose for creating man was for him to rule over His creation as God's appointed king and queen.

> *Genesis 1:28: God blessed them and said to them,* "**Be fruitful and increase in number; fill the earth and subdue it. Rule over** *the fish in the sea and the birds in the sky and over every living creature that moves on the ground.*"

In Hebrew, the word used for *subdue* in this passage is the word *kabash*. It means *to tread with the feet, to put into subjection, to make subservient*. You may have heard the expression *put the kabash on it* pertaining to getting a situation under control, or according to Urban Dictionary, *To squash something from a position of strength*. So to paraphrase, God told the man and Eve to fill the earth with people like them and *put the kabash* on all of creation. Moreover, the word for *rule over* in this passage also means *to tread with the feet* or *to have dominion*. In no uncertain terms, God was telling them that He had given them all authority over everything that He had created. Because of their innocence, they wouldn't abuse this authority and because they had an unhindered relationship with God, they would rule things exactly the way God wanted them. At least this was the plan.

Adam's Disobedience (Genesis 3)

But along came the serpent, who is the Devil, and God's adversary. (See Revelation 20:2.) He was a part of God's creation which Adam and Eve had complete authority over. The serpent deceived the woman and she ate from the tree of the knowledge of good and evil, even though she knew that God had said not to eat of this tree. She then handed some to Adam who also ate. As soon as Adam ate from the forbidden tree, everything changed. By not exerting their God-given authority over the serpent, they became subject to him. When explaining to God what they had done, the woman admitted that the serpent had deceived her. The Hebrew word for *deceived* in this passage means *to put into debt, to become a creditor, to lend with interest and usury*, stemming from a Hebrew root word for deceptive practices. Essentially, like being trapped by a loan shark with astronomical interest rates, Adam and Eve were now slaves to the devil. (See Proverbs 22:7.) There was no hope of paying their way out.

Adam sinned by disobeying the one command God had given him. The consequence was exactly what God had said from the beginning – death. However, this did not mean instantaneous death of the body as we would think of it but more an explanation of death coming about. When God said, "you will surely die," die or death is the same expression that would be used to say that someone is *dying of thirst* except in this case, Adam and Eve are dying of sin. Through disobedience, they separated themselves from fellowship with God, who is the source of life and consequently, their bodies would eventually die because of it. This death also denotes premature death, something that was not originally intended or, like the example of dying of thirst, could be remedied if only a drink of water were available. The bottom line is that because of their sin and without a God-given remedy, physical death was going to happen to both of them and everyone who descends from them, which includes all of us.

I say again, as soon as Adam ate from the forbidden tree, everything changed. Their eyes were opened, and their entire consciousness was changed from innocence to shame. They immediately knew that they were naked, and they tried to hide from each other and from God. There was no remedy for what had happened, there was no drink of water for this thirst, and there was no way for them to pay their way out of debt to the evil one or the consequence of death. They were stripped of their authority in the earth because they had now become the subjects of a new master. They lost their position of unhindered fellowship in the presence of God, and they and all of their descendants were now under a curse. Instead of freedom, authority and life, there was fear, subjection, and death. Through his choice, Adam went from innocent to guilty. His nature or his "internal operating system" so to speak, proved not to be good but evil, not righteous but sinful, and not blameless but rebellious against God.

Adam was now cursed to die and return to the dust out of which God had formed him. In fact, because of Adam's error, all of creation was placed under a curse. However, in spite of all this, we do see the first glimmer of some good news to come. Because the serpent had deceived the woman, God cursed the serpent and promised that someday the offspring of the woman would crush the adversary forever.

> *Genesis 3:15: And I will put enmity between you and the woman, and between your offspring and hers;* **he will crush your head**, *and you will strike his heel.*

Jesus' Obedience

Fast forward to the days of Jesus. Jesus was not formed by God like Adam, and He was not built by God like Adam's wife. Rather, He was born of a woman, a descendant of Eve, just like you and me. After Jesus was born, He grew from infancy, to boyhood, to manhood in the same way that you and I grow up. Later, in the days of His ministry, Jesus' favorite way to refer to Himself was the Son of Man. Since the word for man in Hebrew is Adam, Jesus called Himself the son of Adam.

However, Jesus was not conceived by a man of natural descent or in the natural way. Jesus was born to a young woman named Mary who was a virgin. Moreover, He was conceived by the power of the Holy Spirit of God. Therefore, Jesus' nature from conception in His mother's womb was the perfect nature of God Himself. His "operating system" was the same as God's because He was the Son of God. By the miracle working power of God, Jesus was both the Son of Man and the Son of God in one package.

> *Luke 1:30-35: But the angel said to her, "Do not be afraid, Mary; you have found favor with God. You will conceive and give birth to a son, and you are to call him **Jesus**. He will be great and will be called the **Son of the Most High**. The Lord God will give him the **throne of his father David**, and he will reign over Jacob's descendants forever; **his kingdom will never end**." "How will this be," Mary asked the angel, "**since I am a virgin**?" The angel answered, "The **Holy Spirit will come on you**, and the power of the Most High will overshadow you. **So the holy one to be born will be called the Son of God.***

Mary was engaged to marry a man named Joseph. Both Mary and Joseph could trace their family lineage directly back to King David of Israel, the one whom God had promised a descendant to sit on the throne for eternity. (See 2 Samuel 7:11-16.) This also means that Jesus was Jewish, born into the people of Israel, the only people on earth in covenant with the God who is the Creator of heaven and earth.

The Jewish people all have one common ancestor, a man named Abraham. God promised Abraham that He would make a special nation out of Abraham's descendants and that they would own a special land – the land we know of today as the land of Israel. Abraham believed God in spite of the fact that even one descendant was totally unlikely because his wife was barren. Then, God did exactly what He promised, and Abraham's wife gave birth to a son named Isaac. Isaac was the only son of Abraham who inherited God's special promise. In due course, Isaac had a son named Jacob, and Jacob inherited God's promise of a nation made of his descendants. Jacob proceeded to have twelve sons, and after that, God changed Jacob's name to Israel. Jacob's sons had families which became tribes and were collectively known as the twelve tribes of Israel. After a while, there was famine in the land, so they moved to Egypt. (see Genesis 12–50) Over the course of time, all the people of Israel became subjected to harsh and oppressive slavery by the Egyptians and this went on for about four hundred years. But God appointed a man named Moses, an Israelite from the tribe of Levi, to confront the king of Egypt and lead the people of Israel to freedom. After they were freed from the Egyptians, Israel had become a nation of people descended from Abraham, just as God had promised. (see Exodus 1–15) At that time, God gave Moses and the nation of Israel His Law; the perfect standard of conduct, obedience, and sacrifice which He required for maintaining a right relationship with Him. Israel was the only nation on earth with God's Law and commands which, if obeyed, resulted in God's abundant blessing. In fact, the promises obtained through obedience to these laws are righteousness, blessing, and life from God. (See Deuteronomy 6:25, 11:26-28, 30:19, 32:47.)

Read in your Bible, from the Book of Deuteronomy, Chapter 28, verses 1-14, which describes the blessings promised by God for obedience to His commands.

Unfortunately, no one in history has ever been able to live up to God's perfect standard. Why? Because, regrettably, ever since Adam rebelled against God, his rebellious nature has been inherited by all of his descendants, meaning all of mankind, including Abraham and his descendants. This inherited internal operating system of Adam is completely opposed to the Law of God with its underlying pride, selfishness, and evil desires which lures each and every one of us into sin. Nobody has ever been able to obey God's Law perfectly, and everyone has fallen short of God's standard. (See James 1:14; Romans 3:23.)

However, recall that Jesus was born by the power of the Holy Spirit. Because of this, Jesus had the nature of God within Him. Therefore, everything Jesus thought and did was a perfect demonstration of God's thoughts and actions. Because of this, Jesus lived a perfect life and fulfilled the requirement of God's Law. Jesus was never lured into sin because He did not have the nature of Adam. Although His divine nature was tested in every possible way, Jesus never sinned. He did everything the way that God wanted it done.

> *Matthew 4:1: Then Jesus was led by the Spirit into the wilderness to be **tempted** by the devil. (See also Mark 1:13; Luke 4:2.)*
>
> *Hebrews 4:15: For we do not have a high priest who is unable to empathize with our weaknesses, but we have one who has been **tempted in every way, just as we are--yet he did not sin**. (See also 1 Peter 2:22; 1 John 3:5.)*

During His years of ministry, Jesus did many things which proved that He was sent by God and the Son of God living in human flesh. He performed many miracles that no one on earth had ever performed. He healed the sick, opened the eyes of the blind and the ears of the deaf, caused the lame to leap, cast demons out of people, and every funeral that He attended, He raised the dead. He had authority over all creation including the weather, the seas, and multiplication of food. Everything about Him brought life, peace, wholeness, and restoration. He taught the Word and ways of God with authority and demonstrated the power of God through miracles. Jesus revealed the life and authority which God had intended for all of mankind to have when He created Adam way back in the beginning. It was like heaven on earth.

Jesus' Suffering and Death

In spite of this, the religious leaders of Israel and the rulers of the world rejected Jesus. They planned and plotted and arrested Jesus because of false accusations, and sentenced Him to death through an illegitimate trial for a crime that He did not commit. They crucified Him.

Jesus knew in advance that this would happen, and He told His followers several times that He would have to suffer and die. In fact, this had been God's design since the earth was even formed. (See Revelation 13:8.) This means that Jesus' life was not taken from Him because neither man nor the devil has any power or authority over Him. (See John 14:29-31, 19:11.) Jesus laid His life down willingly to do the will of God and in order to fulfill the Scriptures concerning the Messiah of Israel. (See Matthew 21:42, 26:53-54; Mark 12:10; Luke 20:17; Psalm 118:22.) This was the only way to remedy the problem that Adam had created at the beginning. Jesus, the only one who had earned through His obedience the right to righteousness, blessing, and life, would instead willingly suffer exile, curse, and death.

> *Matthew 16:21: From that time on Jesus began to explain to his disciples that **he must go** to Jerusalem and **suffer many things** at the hands of the elders, the chief priests and the teachers of the law, and that **he must be killed** and on the third day be raised to life. (See also Mark 8:31-9:1; Luke 9:21-27.)*
>
> *Matthew 20:18-19: "We are going up to Jerusalem, and the Son of Man will be delivered over to the chief priests and the teachers of the law. **They will condemn him to death** and will hand him over to the Gentiles **to be mocked and flogged and crucified**. On the third day he will be raised to life!" (See also Mark 10:32-34; Luke 18:31-34.)*
>
> *John 10:17-18: The reason my Father loves me is that **I lay down my life**--only to take it up again. No one takes it from me, but **I lay it down of my own accord**. I have authority to lay it down and authority to take it up again. This command I received from my Father.*

God's Law requires a blood sacrifice to atone, forgive, and cleanse from sin. This sacrifice must be unblemished without any defects as a substitute for the defects of the person who had fallen short of

God's standard. Without going into too much detail, the Law required an animal sacrifice of a bull, a lamb, or birds, depending on what the person could afford. Through the shedding of the animal's blood, the sin of the human offender was forgiven. The sacrifice of an innocent life restored an individual person or the whole community of Israel to right standing with God.

Because of Jesus' perfect, unblemished life, He was completely without defect by God's standard. As such, He offered Himself as a sacrifice to pay for all of our sin. He offered a sacrifice of the highest value, far beyond the value of any animal. Jesus sacrificed human life, the life of a Son of Man, which has more value than a bull or a goat. He also sacrificed the life of the Son of God which has infinite inexplicable worth. This makes the value of His sacrifice incalculable. Through this, He paid our debt and created a way for the whole world to be restored to right standing with God.

> *John 1:29: The next day John saw Jesus coming toward him and said, "Look, the **Lamb of God, who takes away the sin of the world!**" (See also Hebrews 10:5-10.)*
>
> *Hebrews 9:22: In fact, the law requires that nearly everything be cleansed with blood, and **without the shedding of blood there is no forgiveness [of sin.]** (See also Leviticus 17:11.)*

But that's not all. By hanging on a tree, according to God's Law, Jesus also became a curse. The curse of God's Law is written out in great detail in Deuteronomy 28:15-68 and Leviticus 26:14-46. The curse includes every form of sickness and disease, every kind of lack and hunger, all relational problems between people and nations, all forms of oppression by every kind of enemy, and separation or exile from God. On the cross, Jesus received the full punishment and consequence for every disobedient act of all of mankind throughout the course of history.

> *Galatians 3:13: Christ redeemed us from the curse of the law **by becoming a curse** for us, for it is written: "Cursed is everyone who is hung on a pole." (Quoting Deuteronomy 21:23.)*

But that's not all. When Jesus died, we also died with Him. In another passage Jesus said:

> *John 12:32-33 NASB: "And I, if I am lifted up from the earth, will **draw all men to Myself**." But He was saying this to indicate the kind of death by which He was to die.*

Let's consider what Jesus, who was a Hebrew, was really saying. Remember that *man* in Hebrew translates as *Adam*, so when Jesus said *I will draw all men unto me*, He meant that He drew all of Adam, meaning every single one of Adam's descendants, the whole of mankind onto Himself on the cross. This includes me, you, and everyone we know who has been afflicted by our inherited sinful nature. He was the Son of Adam, embodying each and every one of us in His death. Like a giant magnet, Jesus drew the soul of every person ever born into His death with Him. Like pin-the-tail on the donkey, every descendant of Adam was pinned up with Jesus in this miraculous working of God's power.

> *Romans 6:6: For we know that our **old self was crucified with him** so that the body ruled by sin might be done away with, that we should no longer be slaves to sin--*
>
> *Galatians 2:20: **I have been crucified with Christ and I no longer live**, but Christ lives in me. The life I now live in the body, I live by faith in the Son of God, who loved me and gave himself for me.*
>
> *Colossians 3:3: **For you died**, and your life is now hidden with Christ in God. (Also Colossians 2:20; 2Corinthians 5:14.)*

Read in your Bible from the Book of Isaiah, chapter 52, verses 13-15, and all of Isaiah chapter 53. You will see in this passage Isaiah's description of God's Suffering Servant. This Isaiah passage begins with the very phrasing Jesus used to describe to His followers the way He would suffer and die. Jesus' words were:

*John 8:28: So Jesus said, "When you have **lifted up** the Son of Man, then you will know that I am he and that I do nothing on my own but speak just what the Father has taught me. (See also John 3:14-15, 12:32-33.)*

Read in your Bible, all of Psalm 22. You will see that the first and last verse of Psalm 22 are the "bookends" of what Jesus uttered when His time on the cross began and finished.

*Matthew 27:46: About three in the afternoon Jesus cried out in a loud voice, "Eli, Eli, lema sabachthani?" (which means "**My God, my God, why have you forsaken me?**")*

*John 19:30: When he had received the drink, Jesus said, "**It is finished.**" With that, he bowed his head and gave up his spirit.*

But that's not all. Here is the best part! In both Isaiah 53 and Psalm 22, there is a shift from suffering to praise. Why? Because this has all been God's plan from the beginning and in spite of the most upside down looking circumstances, the will of the Lord is being put into effect! Jesus knew that God had accepted His sacrificial offering and had heard His cry for help. It was FINISHED!

RESURRECTION AND ASCENSION

Jesus died on the cross and at His death, His soul descended into the pit of Hell while His body went into the grave. But God had indeed accepted Jesus' sacrifice. Therefore, God raised Jesus from the dead.

*Acts 2:24: But **God raised him from the dead**, freeing him from the agony of death, because it was impossible for death to keep its hold on him.*

*Acts 13:32-34: "We tell you the good news: What God promised our ancestors he has fulfilled for us, their children, by raising up Jesus. As it is written in the second Psalm: 'You are my son; today I have become your father.' **God raised him from the dead** so that he will never be subject to decay. As God has said, 'I will give you the holy and sure blessings promised to David.' (See also Romans 1:4.)*

In resurrection, Jesus was not formed out of dust like Adam, and He was not born of a woman as He had been before. When God raised Jesus from the dead, Jesus was begotten again by God, as His Son. In the genealogies of Scripture, you will read things like "Abraham *begot* Isaac," meaning Isaac was Abraham's son, produced by Abraham's seed. Jesus had already been born by the seed of God into human flesh and God had already acknowledged Him as His begotten Son. (See Matthew 3:17, 17:5; Mark 1:11, 9:7; Luke 3:22, 9:35.) However, this time, instead of being born by God through a virgin, Jesus was begotten again by God out of the pit of Hell and by God's absolute miracle working power. Jesus' soul returned to His body, and the life giving power of the Spirit of holiness transformed His perishable body to an incorruptible body which will never perish.

But that's not all. Through His death and resurrection, Jesus crushed the head of the serpent. Recall the promise God made to Eve back in the beginning. The resurrection proves that mankind's cruel oppressor could not keep Jesus captive in death. Jesus conquered the evil one, stomped on the serpent's head, trampled him with His feet, and *put the kabash* on him. Jesus is now alive eternally, never to die again. Death has been overcome and the enemy has been defeated. Hallelujah!

After the resurrection, Jesus revealed to hundreds of people that He was indeed alive. Then, clouds lifted Jesus into heaven where He is seated at the right hand of God. Jesus now has all power and authority to rule, reign, *put the kabash* on all of God's creation, and to be its King forever.

*Mark 16:19: After the Lord Jesus had spoken to them, **he was taken up into heaven** and he sat at the right hand of God. (See also Luke 24:51; Acts 1:9.)*

> *Philippians 2:9-11: Therefore **God exalted him to the highest place and gave him the name that is above every name**, that at the name of Jesus every knee should bow, in heaven and on earth and under the earth, and every tongue acknowledge that Jesus Christ is Lord, to the glory of God the Father.*

A NEW ADAM

Undoubtedly, Jesus is King. But yet, it is equally true that evil still exists in the world. This is because even though the benefits of Jesus' sacrifice are available to everyone, only those who know that Jesus is Lord and believe in their hearts that God raised Jesus from the dead are included in relationship with God. When we believe Jesus, we become part of a new people, a new generation, a new Adam. This means that on the earth today, there are only two kinds of people: First Adams and Second Adams.

All of us were born the first time by our natural mother and biological father, descendants of the First Adam. For those of you who do not yet believe that Jesus Christ is Lord, you are still part of the First Adam. You are still spiritually separated from God, in darkness, and dead. Whether you believe it or not, apart from faith in Jesus, there is no form of religious observance or spirituality that can give you access to the Most High God, and no amount of good deeds can give you right standing with God.

But when you believe that Jesus is Lord and that God raised Him from the dead, you are born again, begotten again by God who is now your Father. The seed of God (the Holy Spirit) comes to dwell in your heart. When you believe, you are spiritually transferred from death to life, from the kingdom of darkness to the kingdom of light, and from separation from God to restored fellowship with Him. You become part of the Second Adam and one of God's beloved children.

> *John 1:12-13: Yet to all who did receive him, to those who believed in his name, he gave the right to **become children of God**-- children born not of natural descent, nor of human decision or a husband's will, but **born of God**. (See also 1 John 5:1.)*

> *John 3:3-6: Jesus replied, Very truly I tell you, no one can see the kingdom of God unless they are **born again**. ... no one can enter the kingdom of God unless they are **born of water and the Spirit. Flesh gives birth to flesh, but the Spirit gives birth to spirit.***

> *1Peter 1:3, 23: Praise be to the God and Father of our Lord Jesus Christ! In his great mercy he **has given us new birth** into a living hope through the resurrection of Jesus Christ from the dead, ... For **you have been born again**, not of perishable seed, but of imperishable, through the living and enduring word of God.*

When we are baptized, we demonstrate what we believe in our hearts, and we are symbolically entering into the death and resurrection and ascension of Christ, being begotten again by God.

> *Colossians 2:12-13: having been **buried with him in baptism**, in which you were also **raised with him through your faith in the working of God**, who raised him from the dead. When you were dead in your sins and in the uncircumcision of your flesh, **God made you alive with Christ**. He forgave us all our sins, (See also Romans 6:4.)*

> *Colossians 3:1: Since, then, **you have been raised with Christ**, set your hearts on things above, where Christ is, seated at the right hand of God.*

> *Ephesians 1:3, 13: Praise be to the God and Father of our Lord Jesus Christ, who has **blessed us in the heavenly realms with every spiritual blessing in Christ**... For he has rescued us from the dominion of darkness and **brought us into the kingdom of the Son he loves**,*

But that's not all. There are some obvious realities that haven't been addressed yet. Even people who believe Jesus still live in bodies that die, on earth and not in heaven, and still make mistakes and fall short of God's perfect standard.

When Jesus was on earth, He functioned in flesh like ours but with the operating system of God's nature. After Jesus ascended into heaven, He poured out the Holy Spirit. (See Acts 2:33.) When we believe Jesus, the Holy Spirit dwells in our hearts and becomes our new nature. We now have the Holy Spirit in us as our new operating system even though we are still in our earthly bodies. When we allow the Holy Spirit to direct our lives, we live the way that Jesus did when He was in flesh. Through faith and obedience to the Holy Spirit within us as our new operating system, we can live in constant and unbroken communion and communication with God, and we can demonstrate the perfect will of God.

> *2Peter 1:4: Through these he has given us his very great and precious promises, so that through them **you may participate in the divine nature**, having escaped the corruption in the world caused by evil desires.*

Think of it this way: God formed the first man out of dust and breathed life into him – a natural Adam – and his wife was in him when he was formed. Then, God built Adam's wife out of his rib to be just like him, to be one flesh with him, and to help him fulfill God's purpose in the earth. When Jesus was born again in resurrection, God breathed again the Holy Spirit into Him, forming a whole new type of Adam – a spiritual Adam – and his Bride was in Him when He was born again. Now, God is building Jesus' Bride, which is us who believe, aka the Church. God is building Jesus' Bride out of His own spiritual substance, His Body, to be just like Him, to be one flesh with Him, so that God will have made male and female of the same kind of species, to fulfill God's purposes in the earth. Everyone who believes that Jesus is Lord is a new species, a born again species, a spiritual species, a heavenly species even though we still live in earthly bodies. God formed the first Adam like a potter or artist forms a vessel of clay, and the first Adam's wife was taken out of him. God made the second Adam like an artist or a poet creating a masterpiece, and we who believe are part of this new creation. (See Ephesians 2:4-10.)

> *2Corinthians 5:17: Therefore, **if anyone is in Christ, the new creation has come**: The old has gone, the new is here!*

But, let's be real. We all still sin and make mistakes and fall short of perfection. Yes, this is true, but this is where the news gets really good! Through faith in what Jesus did on our behalf, we receive His perfect record as if we had never sinned. By faith, the blood of Jesus purifies us and we are perfect in God's sight.

> *1John 1:7 AMP: But if we [really] walk in the Light [that is, live each and every day in conformity with the precepts of God], as He Himself is in the Light, we have [true, unbroken] fellowship with one another [He with us, and we with Him], and **the blood of Jesus, his Son, cleanses us from all sin [by erasing the stain of sin, keeping us cleansed from sin in all its forms and manifestations]**.*

Therefore, no matter what we may have done in our past, no matter what we may have done an hour ago, no matter what we may do tomorrow or next week or five years from now, Jesus' blood and death has already paid for it. There is no reason for us to ever hide from God as Adam and Eve did, there is no reason for shame, and there is nothing which can keep us from having unbroken fellowship with God who is our Creator and our Heavenly Father.

Think of it this way: when God made the rule about eating from the wrong tree, it was a rule between Him and Adam when Adam was alone. Adam's wife had not been built yet. Eve was the first one who ate from the wrong tree, but nothing actually changed for them until Adam ate it because God had made the rule with Adam. It was Adam's disobedience which caused the change in their position before God. In the same way, but reversing this error, Jesus re-established our right standing with God through His perfect obedience to God's Law. Therefore, in the same way that Eve eating from the wrong tree did not change their status with God, our errors against the Law of God do not change our status with God. We stay in right relationship with God no matter how much we mess up because the rule was established between God and Jesus who never sinned.

That's really good news!

Jesus is Coming Back

Jesus died to save us from death. He became sin to save us from sin. He became a curse to save us from the curse. He became man to save us from ourselves. He's coming back to save us from God's wrath.

> *Hebrews 9:27-28: Just as people are destined to die once, and after that to face judgment, so Christ was sacrificed once to take away the sins of many; and **he will appear a second time, not to bear sin, but to bring salvation to those who are waiting for him**.*

When Jesus comes back, everyone who believes in Him will be clothed with an imperishable resurrection body just like His. Those whose bodies have already died will be raised from the grave, and those who are still alive when He returns will be instantly transformed. We will all be taken up into the air to meet Him and be with Him forever. (See 1 Corinthians 15:52; 1 Thessalonians 4:17.) But those who do not believe Jesus is Lord will be subject to eternal judgment, condemnation, and hell. The wrath of God will be poured out on the earth to avenge all evil. We don't want anyone we know to be subject to this. Importantly, we don't know when He is coming back. Therefore, we do everything that we can to share Jesus and the hope of salvation with everyone we know. (See 2 Peter 3:9-10; 2 Corinthians 5:10-11.)

Think of it this way: God told the first Adam and Eve to be fruitful and multiply in the natural way, through giving birth to natural children. Now, God through Jesus tells us to be fruitful and multiply in a spiritual way, by making disciples of Christ.

> *Matthew 28:18-20: Then Jesus came to them and said, "All authority in heaven and on earth has been given to me. **Therefore go and make disciples** of all nations, baptizing them in the name of the Father and of the Son and of the Holy Spirit, and **teaching them** to obey everything I have commanded you. And surely I am with you always, to the very end of the age."*

In fact, to complete our assignment, Jesus gave us authority in the same way that Jesus had authority when He was on the earth. The Holy Spirit gives us power to do miracles, heal the sick, cast out demons, raise the dead, and command creation the same way that Jesus did when He was on the earth.

> *John 14:12: Very truly I tell you, **whoever believes in me will do the works I have been doing, and they will do even greater things** than these, because I am going to the Father.*

But that's not all. Jesus came in the flesh the first time to make reparation for the First Adam's error. Jesus is coming back to fulfill man's assignment to *put the kabash* on all evil for the rest of eternity. After that, all of creation will be restored to God's design. It will be like Eden all over again and we will live with God in our perfect bodies for all eternity. (See 1 Corinthians 15:25-26.)

> *Revelation 21:1-8: Then I saw "**a new heaven and a new earth**," for the first heaven and the first earth had passed away, and there was no longer any sea. I saw the Holy City, the new Jerusalem, coming down out of heaven from God, prepared as a bride beautifully dressed for her husband. And I heard a loud voice from the throne saying, "Look! God's dwelling place is now among the people, and he will dwell with them. They will be his people, and God himself will be with them and be their God. '**He will wipe every tear from their eyes. There will be no more death**' or mourning or crying or pain, for the old order of things has **passed away**." He who was seated on the throne said, "**I am making everything new!**" Then he said, "Write this down, for these words are trustworthy and true." He said to me: "It is done. I am the Alpha and the Omega, the Beginning and the End. To the thirsty I will give water without cost from the spring of the water of life. **Those who are victorious will inherit all this, and I will be their God and they will be my children**."*

We want everyone we know and love to be with us in heaven and on the new earth in the age to come. Therefore, until Christ returns, we have an assignment. We take the Gospel of Jesus Christ to the ends of the earth with signs and wonders following so that everyone may come to know Jesus is Lord and receive their eternal inheritance.

Ok, that's all… for now.

INVITATION

If you have not yet placed your faith in Jesus Christ as your Lord and Savior and you desire to be included in the salvation you've just learned about, then all that you need to do is believe. If you are ready for the Gospel to change your life and make you new, then pray this prayer out loud and from your heart.

> **Prayer:** *God, I am by nature a sinner and I believe that you sent Your Son, Jesus, to die for my sins. I believe that You raised Jesus from the dead to everlasting life. I repent of my sins and I make Jesus Christ my Lord. Send the Holy Spirit into my heart and make me a new creation. In Jesus' name, Amen.*

Hallelujah! Jesus is King! Welcome to the family and salvation of God!

Basic Training Exercise

FAITH

Proverbs 3:5-6 NIV – Trust in the LORD with all your heart and lean not on your own understanding; in all your ways submit to him, and he will make your paths straight.

DESCRIPTION

Faith is what we do when we believe that God is real and true to His word. God's desire is for us to trust Him with our whole heart in every aspect of our lives. In fact, Jesus said that the only work God requires of us is to believe in the One that God sent.

It is not always easy to trust in a God we cannot see in favor of reliance on our own ideas, abilities, money, resources, or remedies for our situations and problems. Furthermore, our lives are multifaceted and while we may have great faith in one area we may be weak in faith in another. This said, whatever we truly believe in and depend upon is revealed by the actions we take.

The practice of Faith is about trusting God with our lives, our situations, our relationships, until every facet of our being relies upon Christ alone.

TALK WITH GOD

In your life, what has been your experience of trusting God rather than your own understanding?

There is a saying that, "God helps those who help themselves." Do you believe this is true? Why or why not? What is God sharing with you about his?

Are there areas of life that you find it easier or more challenging to trust God? Talk to Him about this.

How is God inviting you trust Him more or in new areas of your life?

PRAYER

Father, I believe, help my unbelief. I want to trust you more and in more aspects of my life. Show me how to trust you more, and how to make reliance upon you my way of life. In Jesus' name, Amen.

Category: Basics

PURPOSE:

To grow in faith and application of trusting God in our lives.

To increase in obedience and understanding of God's will and ways.

To identify and prune our lives of areas of faithlessness.

SPIRITUAL FRUIT:

Faith and faithfulness.

Repentance from self-reliance over trust in God.

Purified motives.

Reduced manipulation of situations (i.e. trying to control outcomes.)

Experience of God's ways and work on our behalf.

PRACTICE

1. Invite the Holy Spirit to highlight an aspect of your life in which God desires for you to walk in greater faith. Examples include:

Finances	Family
Work/Career	Marriage/Romance
Social/Friends/Fun	Health/Sickness
Location/Living Place	School/Education

2. As you move forward in faith in this area, commit to doing the following:

   - Ask God what He wants you to do rather than telling Him what you want Him to do.
   - Release back to God things you have initiated or are sustaining in your own strength. Allow God to prune you.
   - Listen to God in prayer and do what He says.
   - Place your faith in the power of God and not the wisdom of this world.

3. As you walk by faith in this area, take note of the following:
   - What is your typical response when faced with an issue?
   - In what ways might you be presuming you know what God's will is rather than asking Him?
   - In what ways are you relying on your own abilities rather than trusting in God's ability on your behalf?
   - In what ways are you trusting in other people's counsel rather than personal prayer and revelation from the Lord?
   - In what ways do you need to let go and let God?
   - What feelings come up in you as you begin to trust God?
   - What doubts come up in you as you begin to trust God?
   - How does the truth of the Gospel of Jesus Christ dispel your doubt? How is God calling you to trust Him more?

4. Praise God for His faithfulness even as you grow in faith.

NOTES:

_____

ADDITIONAL SCRIPTURES:

Hebrews 11:1, 6
James 2:17-18
Colossians 2:8
1 Corinthians 1:24, 2:5
Romans 1:16-17
Genesis 15:6
Habakkuk 2:4
John 6:29

CORNERSTONE – UNIT 1.2

ESTABLISHED BY FAITH

By grace through faith in Jesus, we receive His perfect record of righteousness. We can stand before God free of guilt, shame, and accusation, ready to receive all of His blessings!

Use the worksheet on next page as a guide for this chart.

CORNERSTONE COURSE
Transformed through Faith in the Gospel

The Old You	Forgiven & Set Free by Christ's Death & Resurrection	New Creation
Nature of Sin Generations from Adam	Anything you were born into. Examples: Race, nationality, tribe, gender, genes, height, age, family patterns, selfishness, depravity, etc.	**Divine Nature** The Holy Spirit Born Again in Resurrection
Acts of Sin Trespasses Iniquities	Anything have done, including motives. Examples: Lying, cheating, moral failures, addictions, sexual immorality, slander, covetousness, hatred, etc.	**Righteousness** Purity, Holiness Spiritual Fruit
Curse Afflictions Exile from God	Any limitation on your ability to receive blessing. Examples: Lack, defeat, sickness, inability to get ahead, subjugation, broken relationships, miscarriages, etc.	**Blessings** Victory, Health Access to God
Kingdom of Darkness False Spirituality Religion	Any participation with works of darkness. Examples: The occult, idol worship, curses, consulting spirits and the dead, witchcraft, astrology, religious legalism, karma, vows, wisdom of man, tradition, etc.	**Kingdom of Heaven** Light of the World Total Freedom
Personal Attributes Advantages/ Disadvantages	Anything that you have going for you or against you. Examples: Birthrights, experiences, marital status, wealth or poverty, education, successes or failures, strengths/weaknesses, the way that you were raised, etc.	**Child of God** Living Hope Eternal Inheritance

ALL RIGHTS RESERVED © 2016 Wendy Bowen · Scriptures NIV · www.manifestinternational.com

www.manifestinternational.com

TRANSFOMRED THROUGH FAITH WORKSHEET
Accompanies Transformed through Faith Chart

To me this is like the days of Noah, when I swore that the waters of Noah would never again cover the earth. So now I have sworn not to be angry with you, never to rebuke you again. ... In righteousness you will be established: Tyranny will be far from you; you will have nothing to fear. Terror will be far removed; it will not come near you. If anyone does attack you, it will not be my doing; whoever attacks you will surrender to you. - Isaiah 54:9, 14-15

1. In your life so far, what has been your biggest struggle area? Find it below and in **Column One**.

    Sin Nature, Generational Curse   Cursed Life, Can't Get Ahead   Pride in Personal Strength

    Sinful Acts and Behavior   Darkness and False Spirits   Self-Pity in Personal Weakness

2. In what ways do you still need to repent or turn from wrong ways/ideas in this area? Use **Column Two** to prompt your reflection.

    _____
    _____
    _____
    _____

3. Submit these things to God and ask for God's forgiveness and cleansing.

    _____
    _____
    _____

4. Select a Scripture from the Scripture list to pray for yourself on this issue. Slowly read this Scripture out loud three times. What does this say about what Jesus did for you? How does this impact your life?

    _____
    _____
    _____

5. How is God asking you to walk in freedom from sin, the curse, flesh, and darkness?

    _____
    _____
    _____

6. What does this mean about your new identity as a New Creation? **Use Column Three** to aid reflection.

    _____
    _____
    _____

7. Praise God for what He has done for you. Jesus is King!

NO MORE RELIGION: LAW TO GRACE*

After being raised form the dead, Jesus explained to His disciples that through His life, death, and resurrection, He fulfilled the Old Covenant. He also established and sealed the New Covenant with His blood. He opened their minds to understand the Scriptures, which we know of as the Old Testament, particularly the writings of Moses, the Psalms, and the Prophets, to reveal what had been accomplished by God's power through His suffering, death, and resurrection. Jesus also told His followers to wait for power from heaven which would institute a whole new way of doing things. (See Luke 24:45-49.)

> *Matthew 5:17:* Do not think that I have come to abolish the Law or the Prophets; **I have not come to abolish them but to fulfill them**.
>
> *Matthew 26:28:* This is **my blood of the covenant**, which is poured out for many for the forgiveness of sins.
>
> *Hebrews 8:13:* **By calling this covenant "new," he has made the first one obsolete**; and what is obsolete and outdated will soon disappear.

FROM OLD TO NEW

The Old Covenant is the Law of God which required measuring up to God's standard through perfect obedience to God's requirements in order to earn right standing with God and access to God. The Law of God is called the Torah and is found in the first five books of the Bible, also known as the Pentateuch. It contains God's requirements for obedience, righteous behavior, and the blood sacrifices to atone for sin and errors. If God's standard was not met, the community or individual remained under a curse and deserved the death penalty for rebellion against God.

Without Jesus, we are spiritually living in the kingdom of darkness which is the domain of the evil one. The only way to regain access to God is through perfect obedience to His required standard which He expressed in the Law. Without Jesus, the only blessings we have access to are the ones God chooses to bestow upon us out of His own good will towards us because we are incapable of deserving them through our own attempts at righteousness.

> *Matthew 5:45b:* He [God] **causes his sun to rise on the evil and the good, and sends rain on the righteous and the unrighteous**.

However, Jesus' perfect obedience to God's Law makes Him the only person ever in history to measure up to God's standard of perfection. Jesus' sacrifice paid the price for all of our errors, mistakes, and rebellion against God. Therefore, when we believe Jesus, we are transferred from the kingdom of darkness to the Kingdom of Light – the Kingdom of Heaven where we are already spiritually seated with Christ.

> *Colossians 1:13-14:* **He has rescued us from the dominion of darkness and brought us into the kingdom of the Son he loves**, in whom we have redemption, the forgiveness of sins.
>
> *Ephesians 2:6:* And God raised us up with Christ and **seated us with him in the heavenly realms in Christ Jesus**

The New Covenant is the way of God's grace through faith in Jesus Christ. Believers receive right standing with God as a free gift and access to Him along with all the blessings this entails. In other words, when we believe in our hearts that God raised Jesus from the dead, we are no longer required to measure up to God's standard because Jesus measured up for us. In the New Covenant of Christ, we are not blessed or cursed because of our own obedience or lack thereof. We are blessed by God because of Christ's obedience which satisfied the Old Covenant requirement completely.

> *Romans 5:1-2: Therefore, since **we have been justified through faith, we have peace with God through our Lord Jesus Christ**, 2 through whom **we have gained access by faith into this grace** in which we now stand. And we boast in the hope of the glory of God.*

By faith, we enter into the cleansing from our own unrighteousness and by faith, we receive Jesus' perfect record as if it were our own. We have been set free from the Law of sin and death!

SET FREE FROM STRIVING

Think of it this way: have you ever parked your car in a parking garage where there is a fee for parking? If so, then you know that there is a difference between when you have to pay to leave the parking garage and when you have visited the right person who can offer parking validation. When your parking ticket is validated, you do not have to pay because your ticket has been stamped PAID by the person you visited. This is what happens through faith in Jesus. Everyone since Adam has had an un-payable parking fee and has been stuck in the oppressive and miserable "parking lot" of the evil one's domain. Under the Old Covenant, the Law was the fee schedule for paying our way out of the parking garage and perfect obedience was the only way be released. Nobody in all of history had ever been able to pay the fee and leave. However, through the New Covenant in Christ, we receive a PAID stamp on our lives because Jesus' perfect obedience PAID the fee for everyone who will believe. Therefore, we are free to leave the "parking garage" of the evil one's control over our lives once and for all. Jesus PAID for our freedom forever from all oppression of any sort including everything we may have done in our past, bad circumstances, sickness, poor relationships, poor self-image, all demonic oppression through evil spirits, and everything else included in the curse of the Law of God. (see Deuteronomy 28:15-68; Leviticus 26:15-39.) We stand justified before God as if we never had a parking fee at all because our ticket is stamped PAID. We are totally free in Christ.

This transfer from Law to grace could also be called graduating from Romans chapter 7 to Romans chapter 8. In Romans 7, the apostle Paul described how, when he lived under the Law, the Law invoked in him an uncanny war between what he knew was the right thing to do and what he actually did. It seemed that the more he tried to do what was right, the more wrong he did. He said, in effect, "I do what I don't want to do, and I don't do what I do want to do." Finally, in exasperation, he gave up and denounced himself as a wretched man. (See Romans 7:15-24.) I call this getting stuck in the *do do*, pronounced *doo doo*. For those of you who don't know, in my culture *doo doo* is an expression used for excrement, like the kind from a dog that we might accidentally step in from time to time. Getting stuck in the *do do* is no fun for anyone much like life under the Law because we can never measure up by what we *do do*. But Paul used this demonstration from his own life to guide us into the glorious freedom from the Law which we now have through faith in Christ. He graduated from Law-mindedness in Romans 7 to grace and Holy Spirit-mindedness in Romans 8. He then boldly declared that those who have placed their faith in Christ are not in the *do do* anymore. Why? Because we no longer live as those who are measured by what we *do* but as those who have direct access to God because of what Jesus *did*. Accordingly, we no longer strive to obey God's Law to be good or to measure up through our conduct. Rather, now we strive to rest in Jesus' perfect obedience on our behalf and to obey the Holy Spirit within us.

> *Romans 8:1-2: Therefore, there is now **no condemnation for those who are in Christ Jesus**, 2 because through Christ Jesus the law of **the Spirit who gives life has set you free from the law of sin and death**.*

Significantly, this will also change the way we live and the way we pray. When we live according to the Law, the only thing to pray for is God's mercy because we can never and will never measure up and deserve curse over blessing. Typically, this leaves us looking for new methods or techniques of prayer or piety in order to attain what we seek and we are never quite sure of God's goodness or willingness to fulfill His promises.

However, when we live as those who have been established in the righteousness of Christ, we know that God's mercy is never failing because Jesus took the penalty we deserve. Therefore, we can pray boldly and confidently for God, our Father, to bring His kingdom to earth *as it is in heaven* as an extension of God's grace, mercy, and fulfilled promises to everyone who will receive it by faith.

> *Hebrews 4:16: Let us then **approach God's throne of grace with confidence**, so that we may **receive mercy and find grace to help us in our time of need**.*

GRACE TO LOVE

Thayer's Greek Lexicon definition of God's grace includes the fact that we receive favor and preferential treatment from God that we do not deserve but also describes God's grace as, "the merciful kindness by which God, exerting his holy influence upon souls, turns them to Christ, keeps, strengthens, increases them in Christian faith, knowledge, affection, and kindles them to the exercise of the Christian virtues." This means that through the transfer from Law to grace, not only does God not hold our imperfections and weaknesses against us – His grace gives us power to do His will.

This is important because the commands of the New Covenant are slightly different than the Law. Under the Old Covenant, the Law commands us to "Love the Lord your God with all your heart with all your soul with all your mind and with all your strength and to love your neighbor as yourself." (See Matthew 22:36-40; Mark 12:29-31; Luke 10:27; quoting Deuteronomy 6:4-5; Leviticus 19:18.) When we function from a Law mindset, we are constantly trying to prove our love by working really hard in our own strength to show off our righteousness or try to do enough good deeds to earn His blessing. Our focus remains entirely on ourselves and developing our own righteousness, no matter how much we try to convince ourselves that we are loving and serving other people.

However, Jesus gave us a new command in the New Covenant: to love others as He has loved us.

> *John 13:34: **A new command I give you**: Love one another. As I have loved you, so you must love one another.*

> *John 15:12, 17: **My command is this**: Love each other as I have loved you. ... **This is my command**: Love each other. (See also 1 John 3:23, 4:10)*

Now instead of striving, we can rest in Christ's love for us. Then, we can love others the way that He loves us by the power of God's grace working within us and through the Holy Spirit dwelling inside of us. Our focus shifts off of ourselves and on to Jesus who gives us what we do not deserve and guides us in loving others with grace that they do not deserve.

In short, if we are working to be good or to prove our love for God or for others, then we are not truly doing good works for Christ. In fact, if we are working with a motive of attaining right standing with God, it means that we are still operating under the old way of doing things rather than the new way which Christ established for us. Christ followers have been transferred from old to new, from the Old Covenant to the New Covenant, from darkness to light, and from Law to grace.

TRANSFERRED
Post Card Handout

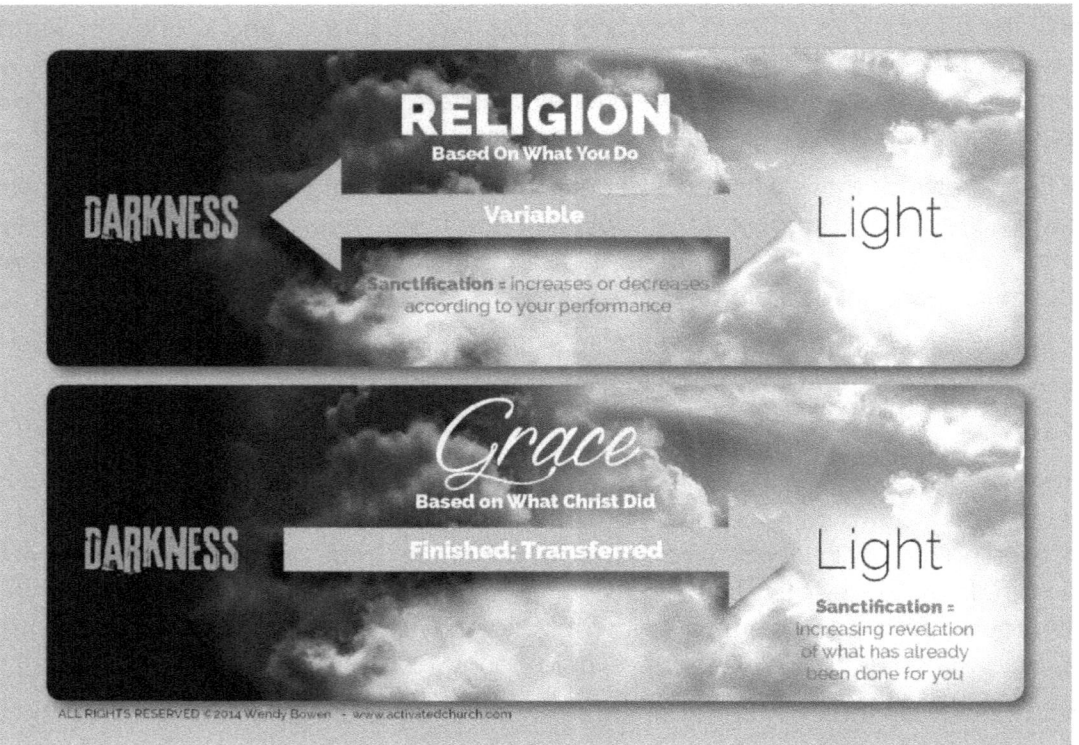

He has delivered us from the domain of darkness and transferred us to the kingdom of his beloved Son, in whom we have redemption, the forgiveness of sins.

Col 1:13-14

For by a single offering he has perfected for all time those who are being sanctified.

Heb 10:14

And you, who once were alienated and hostile in mind, doing evil deeds, he has now reconciled in his body of flesh by his death, in order to present you holy and blameless and above reproach before him

Col 1:21-22

For I am not ashamed of the gospel, for it is the power of God for salvation to everyone who believes, to the Jew first and also to the Greek. For in it the righteousness of God is revealed from faith for faith, as it is written, "The righteous shall live by faith."

Rom 1:16-17

For at one time you were darkness, but now you are light in the Lord. Walk as children of light

Eph 5:8

Scriptures are ESV translation

www.activatedchurch.com

Basic Training Exercise

REST & REMEMBER

Deuteronomy 5:15 NIV – Remember that you were slaves in Egypt and that the LORD your God brought you out of there with a mighty hand and an outstretched arm. Therefore the LORD your God has commanded you to observe the Sabbath day.

DESCRIPTION

Rest is very important to God. Even God rested on the seventh day after He finished all of His work. Through faith in Christ, God invites us to enter His rest because Jesus finished all of the work of our salvation and redemption.

The Israelites had been slaves in Egypt, subjugated and driven by harsh task-masters. But by the blood of the Passover lamb, God delivered them out of slavery. Their historical reality gives us a beautiful prophetic picture of how we were slaves to sin, to this world, and to the evil one. But now by the blood of Jesus, we have been set free.

God called the Israelites to rest as a way of remembering that His leadership is not like the slave-masters they had experienced in Egypt. In fact, He had rescued them from that kind of abuse.

Therefore, practicing Rest & Remember is about stopping to rest from our tasks in order to remember the ways that God has redeemed us and set us free from the bondage of this world, from our own nature, and from the evil one.

MEDITATION

Invite the Holy Spirit to speak to you and read the Deuteronomy passage above and the Additional Scriptures listed on the next page.

What stands out to you in these passages? How do these passages give you freedom for rest?

How have you viewed God as a harsh task-master? How is serving Him supposed to be different than this?

What else do you sense the Lord speaking to you?

PURPOSE:

To enter into the rest that Jesus provides for our souls.

To recognize in our own lives how God has delivered us from the world, the flesh, and the devil.

To deepen our understanding of what Jesus has accomplished for us.

SPIRITUAL FRUIT:

Deeper rest in Christ.

Greater trust in God.

Increased peace in our hearts.

Genuine thankfulness and joy for what God has done for us.

More recognition of the work of Jesus.

PRAYER

Father, thank you sent Jesus to be my Passover Lamb who delivers me from the flesh, the world, and the devil. Help me to remember the ways that I was in bondage and the ways that you have rescued me and changed my heart since the day I first placed my faith in you. Fill me afresh with wonder at your mercy and grace. In Jesus' name, Amen.

PRACTICE

1. Stop and rest (literally) from the demands of life including business, community, household, family, and even ministry or church-related duties. If needed, schedule a time.

2. Consider your life before Jesus (i.e. your way of life, behavior, trusts, addictions, the path your life was on, etc.) Use the following questions as a guide for reflection:
   - What or who were you enslaved to before Jesus entered your life? How has God rescued you from this?
   - In what ways are you different now than your former life? How has life with God changed you?
   - How has God delivered you from subjugation to evil? Addictions? Oppression? Demons?
   - How has God delivered you from over-working or the burden of providing, performing, or producing to take care of yourself?
   - How has God saved you from the need to be busy or task-driven to feel accomplished or useful?
   - How has God freed you from finding your legitimacy in your work or in your ability to meet certain standards?

3. Take time to praise God for His mercy and kindness towards you. Praise God that He is a kind and loving leader, not a harsh task-master. Thank God for your new life with Him.
   - Begin afresh and enter into the rest (physical and spiritual) that God has provided for us in Jesus. Trust Him to continue His work in your life.
   - Considering your answers to these questions, in what areas is God calling you a deeper level of rest, trust, deliverance, and freedom in Him?

ADDITIONAL SCRIPTURES:

Genesis 2:2

Hebrews 4:1-11

Romans 4:1-8

Matthew 11:28-30

Philippians 1:6

Psalm 127:1-2

Isaiah 55:1-3

Revelation 21:6

Mark 6:31-32

Psalm 23

Psalm 81

Matthew 25:24-25

NOTES: _____

New Covenant Worship: Serving from Love

When Jesus first called His disciples, they were going about their ordinary lives, working in their normal jobs to make a living like regular people. It was what they had always done and most likely, what their father's and families had done for generations. But Jesus beckoned them to follow Him.

> *Matthew 4:18-20: As Jesus was walking beside the Sea of Galilee, he saw two brothers, Simon called Peter and his brother Andrew. They were casting a net into the lake, for they were fishermen.* **"Come, follow me," Jesus said, "and I will send you out to fish for people." At once they left their nets and followed him.**

> *Matthew 4:21-22: Going on from there, he saw two other brothers, James son of Zebedee and his brother John. They were in a boat with their father Zebedee, preparing their nets.* **Jesus called them, and immediately they left the boat and their father and followed him.**

> *Matthew 9:9: As Jesus went on from there, he saw a man named Matthew sitting at the tax collector's booth.* **"Follow me," he told him, and Matthew got up and followed him.**

These ordinary men immediately dropped everything right in the middle of their work day. Without ifs, ands, or buts, their lives changed in an instant as they received a new purpose – to follow Jesus. Three years later after Jesus was crucified and raised from the dead, some of the disciples figured they would return to normal life and go back to their family business. But Jesus explained to them why His suffering had been necessary to fulfill the Scriptures, atone for sin, and pay for the redemption of mankind. They worshiped Jesus in awe of all God had done for their salvation. Then before Jesus ascended to heaven, He commanded His disciples to go into all the world to tell people about what God had done for them. A second time, Jesus was beckoning them to give up their plans and everything they had ever known in order to fulfill the plan of God. Nothing about their lives would ever be ordinary again.

Living Sacrifice

What the first disciples did is our example of New Covenant worship. They recognized that nothing on earth could possibly compare in significance, value, or appeal to the privilege of knowing Jesus and walking with Him. The same is still true for us today because Jesus is still worthy of our worship, our devotion, our love, and our lives.

> *Romans 12:1: Therefore, I urge you, brothers and sisters,* **in view of God's mercy, to offer your bodies as a living sacrifice, holy and pleasing to God--this is your true and proper worship.**

In this verse, *worship* is defined as "service rendered for hire including ministry in service to God and sacred services according to His will." Another word used to describe *worship* means to "kiss the hand in token of reverence or to kneel or prostrate oneself to express respect."

In the Old Testament, worship service to God very literally consisted of priestly service in the Tabernacle or Temple which fulfilled God's regulations for sacrifice and consecration. In those days, only specially designated people were anointed to serve God, enter into His presence, and hear His voice. Priests were set apart from everyone else and dedicated exclusively to their God-assigned duties. They worshiped God by serving Him. Through serving Him, they served others.

Now, in the New Covenant, we are called by God to bow our knee to Jesus and lay down our lives for Him in order to fulfill God's Kingdom purposes. Sometimes, like the first disciples, this means we have to drop everything we are doing and leave behind life as we know it in order to follow Him fully.

A heart positioned towards God in adoration that is ready and willing to do whatever He may ask of us is the very heart that God has been seeking from the beginning of mankind. Unfortunately, this was impossible for any human to achieve. Adam bowed his knee to the deceiver by eating from the wrong tree because Adam did not love God more than he loved himself. He selfishly wanted to be exalted rather than showing honor and reverence for God who had created the whole world for him. The love of the Old Testament priests grew cold because they did not love God more than self-righteousness, ritual, and status. They selfishly wanted to benefit from their position rather than being awed at God's kindness in choosing them. No one in history has ever been able to love God more than they love themselves.

Except for Jesus. He never bowed His knee to the tempter, and His love for God never grew cold. He willingly offered all of Himself in obedience to God in order to give God what He desired most – mercy. He loved God more than His own life. This was His form of worship, even unto death.

> *Hebrews 10:5-7: Therefore, when Christ came into the world, he said: "Sacrifice and offering you did not desire, **but a body you prepared for me**; with burnt offerings and sin offerings you were not pleased. **Then I said, 'Here I am**--it is written about me in the scroll-- **I have come to do your will, my God.'"** (Quoting Psalm 40:6-8.)*

> *Hosea 6:6: For **I desire mercy**, not sacrifice, and **acknowledgment of God** rather than burnt offerings. (See also Proverbs 21:3; 1 Samuel 15:22; Isaiah 1:11.)*

The Hebrews passage above is quoting Psalm 40. In the original Psalm, the verbiage used is, "sacrifice and offering you did not desire, *but my ears you have opened."* Jesus lived His life in absolute devotion to God, acknowledging God through everything He did and every word He said. (See John 5:19-20.) His ears were open to hear what God wanted Him to do and He loved God enough to do what God said.

Now that we are indwelt with the same Spirit that Jesus had, we can worship God the way that Jesus did. Our spiritual ears have been opened so that we can listen to the Holy Spirit and obey God's guidance for our lives. Each one of us is a priest called by God to worship Him, stand in His presence, and hear His voice. (See 1 Peter 2:9; Revelation 5:10; Hebrews 4:16.) If we truly appreciate what Jesus has done for us, then like Him, we will say, *"Here I am – I have come to do your will, my God."* We will offer God our bodies to be used for His purposes no matter what He might call us to do. We will not waver in double-mindedness or selfish thoughts for our own provision or exaltation in order to make God and His Kingdom the first and highest priority of our life.

> *Romans 6:13: Do not offer any part of yourself to sin as an instrument of wickedness, but rather **offer yourselves to God as those who have been brought from death to life; and offer every part of yourself to him as an instrument of righteousness**.*

> *1Corinthians 6:19-20: Do you not know that **your bodies are temples of the Holy Spirit**, who is in you, whom you have received from God? **You are not your own; you were bought at a price. Therefore honor God with your bodies**.*

> *Matthew 6:25, 33: Therefore I tell you, **do not worry about your life**, what you will eat or drink; or about your body, what you will wear. Is not life more than food, and the body more than clothes? ... But **seek first his kingdom and his righteousness**, and all these things will be given to you as well.*

Worship and Love

Typically when we think of worship, we think of singing songs of praise and adoration and exaltation. This is also valid and true. Jesus is our King. If we were to worship and exclaim our praise for a king of this world, we would pay our respects to him out of reverence for his majesty, his position of power and authority, and out of any thankfulness we felt for how well and justly he ruled us or the kindness he showed us. We worship King Jesus this way, it's just that His throne is in heaven rather than on earth. This said, heaven has been worshipping Jesus for a very long time.

Worship in heaven sounds like this:

> *Revelation 4:8b: Day and night they never stop saying:* " **'Holy, holy, holy is the Lord God Almighty,' who was, and is, and is to come.**"

> *Revelation 4:11:* "**You are worthy**, *our Lord and God,* **to receive glory and honor and power**, *for you created all things, and by your will they were created and have their being.*"

> *Revelation 5:9: And they sang a new song, saying:* "**You are worthy** *to take the scroll and to open its seals,* **because you were slain, and with your blood you purchased for God persons from every tribe and language and people and nation.**

> *Revelation 5:12: In a loud voice they were saying:* "**Worthy is the Lamb, who was slain, to receive power and wealth and wisdom and strength and honor and glory and praise!**"

> *Revelation 5:13: Then I heard every creature in heaven and on earth and under the earth and on the sea, and all that is in them, saying:* "**To him who sits on the throne and to the Lamb be praise and honor and glory and power, for ever and ever!**"

If we truly believe these exclamations of God's worthiness and glory then our lives must be altered from what they were before we knew Jesus. For example, believers in the Book of Acts were singularly devoted to the Lord Jesus Christ and their lives were consumed with worship for their eternal King. Nothing else mattered. They devoted their lives to prayer and eagerly waited for His prompting through the Holy Spirit to direct their hearts and their lives. They willingly fasted to humble themselves before Him, increase their sensitivity to His Spirit, and to become vessels of His power. They studied the Scriptures night and day to receive new revelation of all that He had accomplished for them. They took communion together to celebrate their bond with one another in Him as a special people of God.

> *Acts 1:14: They all* **joined together constantly in prayer**, *along with the women and Mary the mother of Jesus, and with his brothers.*

> *Acts 2:41-42: Those who accepted his message were baptized, and about three thousand were added to their number that day.* **They devoted themselves to the apostles' teaching and to fellowship, to the breaking of bread and to prayer.**

> *Acts 4:32:* **All the believers were one in heart and mind. No one claimed that any of their possessions was their own**, *but they shared everything they had.*

This is because worshipping Jesus in heaven and serving His Body on earth are inextricably intertwined. As the Old Covenant priests demonstrated, when we worship God by serving Him then, through serving Him we serve others. When we offer our lives to God in worship as His New Covenant priests, He will, undoubtedly, lead us to reach out to those who do not know Him and love other believers deeply from the heart. Jesus said, "If you love me, you will keep my commands." His command is to love one another the way Jesus loved us – by living selflessly for God as we open our ears to stay in step with His voice.

> *Philippians 2:3-8:* **Do nothing out of selfish ambition or vain conceit.** *Rather, in humility* **value others above yourselves, not looking to your own interests but each of you to the interests**

*of the others. In your relationships with one another, have the same mindset as Christ Jesus: Who, being in very nature God, **did not consider equality with God something to be used to his own advantage; rather, he made himself nothing by taking the very nature of a servant**, being made in human likeness. And being found in appearance as a man, he **humbled himself by becoming obedient to death--even death on a cross!***

We do not worship for show, or sacrifice to pay our way into blessing. We do not serve others out of obligation to God. The only reason to worship, sacrifice, and serve God is out of genuine love for Him. If we do not love Him, our priestly service has grown cold and is worth nothing.

SURRENDER & TRANSFORMATION

The Apostle Paul's transformation story is probably the most dramatic conversion in the New Testament. Interestingly, Paul, who had been called Saul, did not receive the Gospel message the first time that he heard about Jesus. Quite the contrary, it infuriated him. He had been the most aggressive religious zealot in his day against Jesus and all of His claims of Lordship and had persecuted Christians, approved of their assassinations, and tried to force Christ's witnesses to deny that Jesus is the Messiah. But then, when Paul was on his way to Damascus on a mission to find, imprison, and kill more Christians, he had an encounter with the Jesus, and his life was changed forever.

> *Acts 26:14-15: We all fell to the ground, and I heard a voice saying to me in Aramaic, **'Saul, Saul, why do you persecute me? It is hard for you to kick against the goads.'** Then I asked, 'Who are you, Lord?' 'I am Jesus, whom you are persecuting,' the Lord replied.*

"Kicking against the goads" was a proverbial expression for resisting the obvious to the point of self-destruction. A *goad* is an iron tool used to prod cattle along in the way that their masters want them to go. The Scriptures and prophecies of Scripture all point to Jesus as the Messiah of Israel, but Paul resisted.

When Paul finally became a believer, he had to rethink everything he had ever known about God in order to actually know Him. As Paul's approach to life was completely renovated to follow Jesus, he was rejected by almost everyone, lost almost everything he had, and forfeited the status he had attained for his zeal and expertise. For about ten years, Paul became a nobody. But Paul considered all of this a small price to pay because of the price Jesus had paid for him. This was his mindset:

> *Philippians 3:7-9: But **whatever were gains to me I now consider loss for the sake of Christ**. What is more, **I consider everything a loss because of the surpassing worth of knowing Christ Jesus my Lord, for whose sake I have lost all things. I consider them garbage**, that I may gain Christ and be found in him, not having a righteousness of my own that comes from the law, but that which is through faith in Christ--the righteousness that comes from God on the basis of faith.*

God changed Paul's heart. He no longer resisted God but instead, went on to be the most influential advocate for Christianity the world has ever known. Paul proclaimed Jesus, established many churches, wrote a large portion of what we know of as the New Testament, and endured through persecution, and chronic near death experiences. Paul offered his life as a living sacrifice to serve King Jesus. Eventually, he gave his life for Jesus and was martyred, beheaded for proclaiming a King other than Caesar.

Not everyone is called to martyrdom, but every believer is called to take up their cross and follow Jesus. Not everyone is called to give away everything that they own, but every believer is called to love nothing more than Jesus and to cling to nothing of this world. Not everyone is called to be like the Apostle Paul but every believer is called to be like Jesus. Each one of us has a role and a purpose in God's Kingdom. Will you fulfill yours?

PROCESS WORKSHEET
ALIGNING WITH GOD

www.manifestinternational.com

INSTRUCTIONS

Sometimes, we find ourselves wanting or needing to align or re-align our lives with God and His purposes. It is important to seek God's guidance and be willing to do whatever is required of us to get in step with Jesus.

Use the following as a guide to help you pray and seek God. Write down a summary of your perception of God's responses of each of the following questions/prayers.

What is God's purpose for you?

> **Prayer:** God, show me Your purpose for me. Show me where my life is out of alignment with Your purposes and help me to align with Your will for me. Guide me, protect me, and give me the strength and courage to submit myself to Your will for me, no matter what it takes.
>
> *Philippians 2:13 - For it is God who works in you to will and to act in order to fulfill his good purpose.*
>
> *Psalm 37:23 NLT - The LORD directs the steps of the godly. He delights in every detail of their lives.*

How has your unique journey/history prepared you for God's purpose?

> **Prayer:** God, show me how You can use the experiences I have had so far for Your Kingdom. Thank You that You are redeeming my past to bring You glory. Thank You that nothing is ever wasted with You and You are always moving forward.
>
> *Romans 8:28 - And we know that in all things God works for the good of those who love him, who have been called according to his purpose.*

How has God designed you? What has He designed you for?

> **Prayer:** God, You created me and You know me better than I know myself. Show me what You designed me for and what You have called me to be and to with my life.
>
> *Psalm 139:13-16 - For you created my inmost being; you knit me together in my mother's womb. I praise you because I am fearfully and wonderfully made; your works are wonderful, I know that full well. My frame was not hidden from you when I was made in the secret place, when I was woven together in the depths of the earth. Your eyes saw my unformed body; all the days ordained for me were written in your book before one of them came to be.*

Where does God want you to be?

> **Prayer:** God, where do You want me to be in this stage of my life? Is there anywhere You want me to go short-term, long-term or permanently?
>
> *Isa 30:21 - Whether you turn to the right or to the left, your ears will hear a voice behind you, saying, "This is the way; walk in it."*

How does God want you to interact with your family, spouse, children, etc?

Prayer: God, show me how to be a better spouse and parent. Show me how to honor my parents.

Colossians 3:18-21 - Wives, submit yourselves to your husbands, as is fitting in the Lord. Husbands, love your wives and do not be harsh with them. Children, obey your parents in everything, for this pleases the Lord. Fathers, do not embitter your children, or they will become discouraged.

Ephesians 6:2 - "Honor your father and mother"--which is the first commandment with a promise.

What are the recurring difficulties in your life? How does God want to stop this cycle?

Prayer: God, show me my unique pattern of temptation and my areas of weakness. Forgive me for my errors and sins. Break me free from myself. Strengthen me to make new choices to honor You.

1 Corinthians 10:13 - No temptation has overtaken you except what is common to mankind. And God is faithful; he will not let you be tempted beyond what you can bear. But when you are tempted, he will also provide a way out so that you can endure it.

How does God want to release you from burdens, bitterness, or wounds from the past?

Prayer: God, help me to forgive those who have hurt me. Help me not to hold a grudge. Wash me so I can be clean. Heal my heart and heal my body.

Psalm 34:18 - The LORD is close to the brokenhearted and saves those who are crushed in spirit.

1 Peter 2:23-24 - When they hurled their insults at him, he did not retaliate; when he suffered, he made no threats. Instead, he entrusted himself to him who judges justly. "He himself bore our sins" in his body on the cross, so that we might die to sins and live for righteousness; "by his wounds you have been healed."

How does God want you to balance work/tasks and rest?

Prayer: God, show me the rhythm You want for my life and how to fulfill my responsibilities. Help me to say "no" to things You do not want me to do and "yes" to things You want me to do.

Matthew 11:28-30 - "Come to me, all you who are weary and burdened, and I will give you rest. Take my yoke upon you and learn from me, for I am gentle and humble in heart, and you will find rest for your souls. For my yoke is easy and my burden is light."

How will God provide for this?

Prayer: God, give me the faith to know that You will provide for me when I am aligned with You.

Matthew 6:33 - Seek first his kingdom and righteousness, and all these things will be given to you.

Romans 13:8 - Let no debt remain outstanding, except the continuing debt to love one another.

What is the next step God wants you to take?

Basic Training Exercise

WHERE YOUR TREASURE IS

Mat 6:19-21 NIV - Do not store up for yourselves treasures on earth, where moths and vermin destroy, and where thieves break in and steal. But store up for yourselves treasures in heaven, where moths and vermin do not destroy, and where thieves do not break in and steal. For where your treasure is, there your heart will be also.

DESCRIPTION

Jesus was not afraid to talk about money. In fact, He said that how we spend can reveal what we love, prioritize, and esteem as important. How we handle our finances can also be an indication of how much we truly trust God's ability or desire to provide for us and how much we truly involve Him in our daily lives. At times, our spending might be heavy in a certain category because we are obeying God's will. But at other times, we have given high priority to something that God does not value as highly as we do. All the same, where our treasure is reveals where our heart is. The practice if Where Your Treasure is examines our spending to shed light on how we are using our money and if it accurately represents our heart for God.

CONSIDERATIONS

What has been your experience with money? Did you grow up rich or poor? How has your financial life changed over the years?

What challenges you most about the subject of money? What "issues" do you have about it?

How involved do you think God wants to be in your finances? How involved do you want Him to be?

PRAYER

Father, I want my heart to be with you in every aspect of my life. Show me where my treasure is and how it is a reflection of the state of my heart towards you. Help me to align my heart and my treasure with your will and purposes, in Jesus' name, Amen.

Category: Basics

www.manifestinternational.com

ALL RIGHTS RESERVED © 2019 Wendy Bowen

Basic TRAINING
SPIRITUAL EXERCISES

PURPOSE:

To grow in trusting God in our finances.

To discern and align our priorities with God and His purposes.

To turn our financial decisions over to God.

SPIRITUAL FRUIT:

Repentance from self-reliance and the love of money.

Proper stewardship of the resources God has given us.

Increased trust in God's provision for our needs.

PRACTICE

1. Look back on the past week (or month) of your spending and prepare an outline of what you spent money on.
   - If this information is not readily available, journal or write down everything you spend for one week.
   - If you had any major and/or irregular expenses in the past week (or month) do not include them in this exercise.

2. Group your spending into major categories.
   - For example, categories might be Food, Household Bills, Education, Debt Repayment, Offerings, Ministry, etc.

3. Where is your treasure?
   - Calculate your total spending in each category.
   - Put the categories in order from most spending to least.
   - What category did you spend the most in? The least?

4. Where is your heart?
   - What does this snapshot of your spending reveal about what is important to you?
   - Do you feel that this spending snapshot demonstrates how important God is to you? His Kingdom? Ministry?
   - Do you think that this spending snapshot accurately represents the season or stage of life you are in? How so?
   - If a stranger were to look at your spending, what would they see as your highest priority? Would that be an accurate assessment of your heart? Why or why not?
   - How much did you involve God in your spending?

5. Ask God to help you align your spending with His will for you
   - Ask Him if there to reveal any "obligations" you have entangled yourself with that were not His will for you. Ask Him to begin to show you how to untangle it.
   - Repent from the ways you have not involved God in your spending or justified your spending apart from Him.
   - Receive the Lord's forgiveness. Listen to His voice. Do what He says.

NOTES: _____

ADDITIONAL SCRIPTURES:

Matthew 13:22

1 Timothy 6:9-10

Luke 16:13

Luke 12:13-21

Matthew 7:9-11

Philippians 4:11-19

Hebrews 13:5

Proverbs 23:4

Proverbs 19:17

Proverbs 28:27

www.manifestinternational.com

UNIT ONE – KEY QUESTIONS
The Gospel of Jesus Christ

Use this worksheet to test your grasp of the material and exercises of Unit One.

What is the Gospel of Jesus Christ? (in your own words)	

Who is Jesus?	What did Jesus do for us?

What are some examples of the benefits of faith in Jesus?	How do we receive the benefits of what Jesus did for us?

What do we have to do to continue in God's blessing?	Why do we serve Jesus? How do we serve Jesus?

What is one thing you learned that you did not know before?	What questions do you still have about this subject?

UNIT ONE: GROUP EXERCISES

Using the Transformed through Faith Chart and Worksheet, have each person in the group share a personal and specific testimony of how Jesus saved or delivered them.

AND/OR

Using the Aligning with God Worksheet, have each person in the group share how God is aligning their lives with His purposes.

UNIT TWO:
THE HOLY SPIRIT

KEY SCRIPTURE VERSE FOR UNIT TWO
In the last days, God says, I will pour out my Spirit on all people. Your sons and daughters will prophesy, your young men will see visions, your old men will dream dreams. Even on my servants, both men and women, I will pour out my Spirit in those days, and they will prophesy. - Acts 2:17-18

CLASS 1: HOLY SPIRIT POURED OUT
1 Reading, 1 Exercise
Fifty days after the resurrection, Jesus poured out the Spirit of the Lord from heaven. Now, the Holy Spirit dwells in the hearts of all who believe in Jesus.

CLASS 2: NEW HEART & NEW SPIRIT
1 Reading, 1 Worksheet, 1 Visual Aid
The Holy Spirit dwells inside of each believer to communicate according to God's will and execute its multifaceted job description.

CLASS 3: REPENTANCE & FRUIT
1 Reading, 1 Exercise
As we lay aside the desires of our flesh, the Holy Spirit works in our lives to produce certain characteristics which prove our participation in divine nature.

CLASS 4: HOW TO HEAR GOD
1 Reading, 1 Exercise
God sent the Holy Spirit to dwell within each believer so that we can live our lives in constant communication with Him, guided by his direction.

KEY QUESTIONS

GROUP EXERCISES

The Holy Spirit Poured Out*

After Jesus was raised from the dead, He showed Himself to His disciples as eternally alive in a glorified resurrection body. Then, before ascending to heaven, Jesus told His disciples to wait for the Holy Spirit before they did anything in His name. Even though He had already commanded them to GO into all nations to make disciples, He first told them to WAIT until the Holy Spirit had been poured out. The Holy Spirit is of supreme significance to God's plan for our redemption through His Son.

Prophetic Foreshadows

Jesus was crucified on the day of Passover, the exact anniversary of the day that God had delivered Israel from four hundred years of slavery. In the first Passover, the Israelites slaughtered an unblemished male lamb and painted its blood on their doorposts so that the destroyer could not touch them. (See Exodus 12.) These events were a picture of Jesus, the eternal Lamb of God, whose blood was shed so that by His blood, we who believe Him are set free from slavery to sin and death. When Jesus was crucified, He was slaughtered as the eternal Passover Lamb to take away the sins of the world. (See John 1:29; 1 Peter 1:8-19; 1 Corinthians 5:7.)

On the third day after the original Passover, early in the morning, the waters of the Red Sea were rolled away and the Israelites walked through the Red Sea on dry ground. Their enemies, Pharaoh and the world's most powerful army, were overcome and the Israelites rejoiced and worshipped God. (See Exodus 14-15.) Every year after this on the third day after Passover, early in the morning, the appointed priest would wave the first sheaf of the spring harvest in an observance of the Feast of First Fruits. (See Leviticus 23:9-14.) This was typically a bundle of grain from the first and best portion as a representation of dedicating the whole harvest to the Lord, even though the full harvest was still yet to come.

These events were a picture of Christ's resurrection. It was early in the morning on the third day after His crucifixion that the stone of His tomb was rolled away and Jesus walked out in a resurrection body of eternal life! He had defeated the evil one, overcome death, and triumphed over the enemies of mankind. He became the wave offering of the First Fruits of resurrection harvest – the first and best portion – wholly dedicated to God in anticipation of the harvest yet to come. We who believe are that harvest and we will be resurrected when He returns.

> *1 Corinthians 15:23 NLT: But there is an order to this resurrection:* **Christ was raised as the first of the harvest; then all who belong to Christ will be raised when he comes back.**

All of this is to say that the events of the Old Testament, particularly the Feasts of the Lord, serve as prophetic foreshadows of the work of Christ. (See Leviticus 23; Colossians 2:17; Hebrews 8:5, 10:1.) Three of these Feasts were fulfilled through Jesus' crucifixion, resurrection, and the outpouring of the Holy Spirit, which we are discussing in this unit. Here is a chart of them:

Nation of Israel	Feast of God	Fulfilled in Christ
Passover	Passover	Crucifixion
Red Sea Crossing	Feast of First Fruits	Resurrection
Law Given at Sinai	Feast of Weeks	Pentecost

THE FIFTIETH DAY

In the original Passover, on the fiftieth day after the Israelites had walked through the Red Sea, God met with His people in power and with fire at Mount Sinai and gave them the Ten Commandments. (See Exodus 19:1-16.) On the fiftieth day after leaving Egypt, God descended on the mountain in a great pillar of fire with billowing smoke, thunder which shook the earth, and a great trumpet blast. All of the Israelites standing at the base of the mountain trembled at the power of their God.

> *Exodus 19:16-19:* **There was thunder and lightning, with a thick cloud over the mountain, and a very loud trumpet blast.** *Everyone in the camp trembled. Then Moses led the people out of the camp* **to meet with God,** *and they stood at the foot of the mountain.* **Mount Sinai was covered with smoke, because the LORD descended on it in fire. The smoke billowed up from it like smoke from a furnace, and the whole mountain trembled violently.** *As the sound of the trumpet grew louder and louder, Moses spoke and the voice of God answered him.*

At Sinai, God spoke to His people and the fiery finger of God wrote His Laws on tablets of stone. (See Exodus 31:18.) To commemorate this event every year on the anniversary of God's powerful Sinai visitation, all Israelite men were required to gather in Jerusalem for the Feast of Weeks. This is a holy day for worshipping the Lord and rejoicing in the abundance of the Promised Land and another offering of the First Fruits is brought before the Lord. Everyone is included in this feast, even foreigners, and the poor are remembered with mercy and grace. (See Deuteronomy 16:1-17; Leviticus 23:15-22.)

These events were a picture of the work of Jesus. On the fiftieth day after His resurrection, Jesus poured out the Holy Spirit to His disciples. The day is now known as Pentecost, which literally means fiftieth day.

PENTECOST OUTPOURING

After His resurrection, Jesus appeared to His disciples for forty days and then, He ascended to heaven. Before He left, He told them to wait in Jerusalem for power from heaven which He would send soon.

> *Acts 1:3-5: After his suffering, he presented himself to them and gave many convincing proofs that he was alive. He appeared to them over a period of forty days and spoke about the kingdom of God. On one occasion, while he was eating with them, he gave them this command:* **"Do not leave Jerusalem, but wait for the gift my Father promised,** *which you have heard me speak about. For John baptized with water, but* **in a few days you will be baptized with the Holy Spirit."**

> *Acts 1:8:* **But you will receive power when the Holy Spirit comes on you; and you will be my witnesses** *in Jerusalem, and in all Judea and Samaria, and to the ends of the earth."*

120 disciples of the risen Lord Jesus waited for Him to send the Holy Spirit so that they could be empowered for their global assignment of proclaiming His Kingdom. They devoted themselves to prayer while they waited for the Lord to pour out the Holy Spirit. They gathered together every day at the Temple to praise God and they stayed at night in an upper room nearby in Jerusalem.

> *Luke 24:49-53:* **I am going to send you what my Father has promised;** *but* **stay in the city until you have been clothed with power from on high."** *When he had led them out to the vicinity of Bethany, he lifted up his hands and blessed them. While he was blessing them, he left them and was taken up into heaven. Then they worshiped him and returned to Jerusalem with great joy.* **And they stayed continually at the temple, praising God.**

> *Acts 1:12-15: Then the apostles* **returned to Jerusalem** *from the hill called the Mount of Olives, a Sabbath day's walk from the city. When they arrived,* **they went upstairs to the room where they were staying.** *Those present were Peter, John, James and Andrew; Philip and Thomas, Bartholomew and Matthew; James son of Alphaeus and Simon the Zealot,*

*and Judas son of James. They **all joined together constantly in prayer**, along with the women and Mary the mother of Jesus, and with his brothers... among the believers (a group numbering about a hundred and twenty.)*

These 120 disciples waited in prayer and rejoicing in Jerusalem for ten days after Jesus ascension. Then, the fiftieth day arrived – the day of Pentecost.

Because it was required for all Jewish men to make pilgrimage to Jerusalem to observe the Feast of Weeks, the city was packed. Jewish men from all the nations of the world were gathered in Jerusalem and were heading to the Temple to celebrate the feast to the Lord.

*Acts 2:5: Now there were staying in Jerusalem **God-fearing Jews from every nation under heaven**.*

The disciples of Jesus were gathered together at the Temple, as per was their usual routine. They were most likely at the main entrance of the Temple near the Southern Steps. Then suddenly, a mighty wind blew through the place and the followers of Jesus were filled with the Holy Spirit.

*Acts 2:1-4: **When the day of Pentecost came**, they [120 disciples of Christ] were all together in one place. Suddenly **a sound like the blowing of a violent wind came from heaven and filled the whole house** where they were sitting. They saw what seemed to be **tongues of fire that separated and came to rest on each of them. All of them were filled with the Holy Spirit** and began to speak in other tongues as the Spirit enabled them.*

On the exact anniversary of the day God had descended to His people in a consuming fire at Mount Sinai, the fire power of God descended into the hearts of Christ's disciples in Jerusalem. The gigantic fire which was on top of Mount Sinai was now divided into smaller segments and rested upon each of them. At Sinai, the fiery finger of God which had written the Ten Commandments on tablets of stone but now at Pentecost, God wrote His laws on hearts of stone and transformed them into hearts of flesh. (See Ezekiel 11:19, 36:26-27; Jeremiah 24:7.)

Not Drunk - Witnesses

At Sinai, as the trumpet sound grew and Moses spoke to God, the Hebrew word used to describe that God "answered" is a word that means "to testify, speak, or respond as a witness." You could say that God testified with His own voice to His people about Himself and His requirements for them to remain in relationship with Him. This testimony was given to all the Israelites and the mixed multitude that had come out of Egypt with them. (See Exodus 12:38.)

At Pentecost, as soon as the Holy Spirit was poured out, the 120 disciples of Jesus were supernaturally empowered by God and began to testify as witnesses about the wonders of God and faith in Jesus Christ. In fact, the disciples were empowered by the Holy Spirit to supernaturally declare the works of God in every language under heaven, which they did not otherwise know how to speak. You could say that God testified by His Spirit through the voices of those who believed Jesus. Because of this, all the Jewish people who had gathered together in Jerusalem for the Feast of Weeks could hear the testimony about Jesus in their own language, in addition to whoever else was in Jerusalem at that time.

Needless to say, onlookers were perplexed by this and wondered, "What can this mean?" Some even concluded that Christ's disciples must be drunk. (See Acts 2:6-13.) But Peter stood up to explain what was happening and, filled with the Holy Spirit, gave an inspired and empowered proclamation of the Gospel of Jesus Christ. He explained that what the people in Jerusalem were witnessing with their own eyes and ears was the fulfillment of the promises that God made to the Jewish people centuries before.

*Acts 2:14-21: Then **Peter stood up with the Eleven**, raised his voice and addressed the crowd: "**Fellow Jews and all of you who live in Jerusalem**, let me explain this to you; listen carefully to what I say. **These people are not drunk**, as you suppose. It's only nine in the*

> *morning! No, this is **what was spoken by the prophet Joel**: 'In the last days, God says, **I will pour out my Spirit on all people**. Your **sons and daughters will prophesy**, your young men will see visions, your old men will dream dreams. Even on my **servants, both men and women, I will pour out my Spirit in those days**, and they will prophesy. I will show wonders in the heavens above and signs on the earth below, blood and fire and billows of smoke. The sun will be turned to darkness and the moon to blood before **the coming of the great and glorious day of the Lord**. And **everyone who calls on the name of the Lord will be saved**.' (Quoting Joel 2:28-32.)*

Peter went on to tell the crowd about how Jesus had come and had been confirmed by God with miracles and wonders only to be crucified in fulfillment of the Scriptures of the Suffering Servant but how God had raised Jesus from the dead to everlasting life in fulfillment of the Scriptures of His chosen one not being trapped in the decay of death! Peter assured them that what they heard was God's confirmation of Jesus as the Messiah of Israel and Savior of mankind through the fulfillment of even more Scriptures pertaining to God's plan of redemption.

> *Acts 2:32-33: **God has raised this Jesus to life, and we are all witnesses of it**. Exalted to the right hand of God, he has received from the Father **the promised Holy Spirit and has poured out what you now see and hear**.*

At Peter's anointed proclamation, those who heard were cut to the heart and asked what they needed to do to be saved. Peter instructed them to repent and be baptized to have their sins forgiven so that they could also receive the gift of the Holy Spirit. Right then and there, three thousand people gave their lives to Jesus Christ and were baptized in the pools at the Southern Steps where the ritual baths for cleansing before entering the Temple area were located (the ruins of which are still there today.)

> *Acts 2:37-41: When the people heard this, they were cut to the heart and said to Peter and the other apostles, "**Brothers, what shall we do?**" Peter replied, "**Repent and be baptized, every one of you, in the name of Jesus Christ for the forgiveness of your sins. And you will receive the gift of the Holy Spirit**. The promise is for you and your children and for all who are far off--for all whom the Lord our God will call." With many other words he warned them; and he pleaded with them, "Save yourselves from this corrupt generation." **Those who accepted his message were baptized, and about three thousand were added to their number that day**.*

At Sinai, God had given His Law and three thousand people died. (See Exodus 32:28.) At Pentecost, God poured out His Spirit, and three thousand people were brought into everlasting life! The old has passed and the new has come. The old gave commands leading to condemnation and death, the new gives empowerment from the Spirit for a righteous and holy life!

> *2Corinthians 3:6-9: He has made us competent as **ministers of a new covenant**--not of the letter but of the Spirit; **for the letter kills, but the Spirit gives life**. ...**If the ministry that brought condemnation was glorious, how much more glorious is the ministry that brings righteousness!***

Inclusion in the Outpouring

Once the Holy Spirit was poured out to the initial believers in Jerusalem, they continued to testify of God's grace and goodness through Jesus. As they proclaimed the Gospel of Jesus Christ to the ends of the earth, events similar to the original outpouring of the Holy Spirit occurred in various places to demonstrate without a doubt that God included Samaritans, Gentiles, and disciples of John the Baptist who believed Jesus. (See Acts 2-Jews; Acts 8-Samaritans; Acts 10-11-Gentiles; Acts 19-disciples of John the Baptist.) Just like the Feast of Weeks included foreigners and remembrance of the poor, all types of people are able to participate in God's gift of the Holy Spirit through faith in Jesus.

Of course, this also served to fulfill the promises and prophecies (of which there are many) of the Messiah of Israel who would save not only Israel but the Gentiles as well. For example:

> Isaiah 42:6: "I, the LORD, have called you in righteousness; I will take hold of your hand. I will keep you and will **make you to be a covenant for the people and a light for the Gentiles**,
>
> Isaiah 49:6: he says: "It is too small a thing for you to be my servant to restore the tribes of Jacob and bring back those of Israel I have kept. **I will also make you a light for the Gentiles, that my salvation may reach to the ends of the earth.**"

However, sharing the Gospel of the Jewish Messiah with Gentiles was extremely controversial at that time. In fact, it was bizarre and offensive for God to break through the cultural barriers in order to include Gentiles in salvation through Christ. This is part of why God's initial outpourings of the Holy Spirit were so powerful. It was undeniable that salvation through Jesus Christ was available to anyone from any nation, tribe, or tongue who placed their faith in Jesus for salvation. (See Revelation 5:9.)

Even today, when we place our faith in Jesus Christ as our Lord and Savior, the Holy Spirit marks us with the seal of God for our inclusion in the promise of Abraham, and gives us a deposit guaranteeing our inclusion in the heavenly inheritance, no matter what nation or ethnicity we may originate from.

> Ephesians 1:13: And you also were included in Christ when you heard the message of truth, the gospel of your salvation. When you believed, **you were marked in him with a seal, the promised Holy Spirit**,
>
> 2Corinthians 1:21-22: Now it is God who makes both us and you stand firm in Christ. **He anointed us, set his seal of ownership on us, and put his Spirit in our hearts as a deposit**, guaranteeing what is to come.
>
> 2Corinthians 5:5: Now the one who has fashioned us for this very purpose is God, who has **given us the Spirit as a deposit**, guaranteeing what is to come.
>
> Galatians 3:14: He redeemed us in order that the blessing given to Abraham might come **to the Gentiles through Christ Jesus, so that by faith we might receive the promise of the Spirit**.

Sometimes, we have powerful experiences when the Holy Spirit first comes into our lives, almost as if God is granting us our own little Pentecost outpouring. However, we do not always feel the Holy Spirit so powerfully and we can't base our faith in Jesus on what we feel or don't feel. Let's keep it simple. If you believe Jesus Christ is Lord and that God raised Him from the dead, then you received the Holy Spirit when you believed. (See Ephesians 1:13.) If you do not believe Jesus, then you do not have the Holy Spirit in you, and you do not belong to Christ. (See Romans 8:9.) (Note: We will discuss the various functions of the Holy Spirit in later chapters.)

Therefore, if you want more of the Holy Spirit, ask for more, and commit to living your life by following His direction, allowing the power of God to help you carry out His work as His witness who brings Him glory.

> Luke 11:9-13: **So I say to you: Ask and it will be given to you; seek and you will find; knock and the door will be opened to you.** For everyone who asks receives; the one who seeks finds; and to the one who knocks, the door will be opened. "Which of you fathers, if your son asks for a fish, will give him a snake instead? Or if he asks for an egg, will give him a scorpion? If you then, though you are evil, know how to give good gifts to your children, **how much more will your Father in heaven give the Holy Spirit to those who ask him!**

Basic Training Exercise

URIM & THUMMIM

Exodus 28:30 NIV – Also put the Urim and the Thummim in the breastpiece, so they may be over Aaron's heart whenever he enters the presence of the LORD. Thus Aaron will always bear the means of making decisions for the Israelites over his heart before the LORD.

DESCRIPTION

Under the regulations of the Old Covenant, the High Priest wore a breastpiece which contained special stones called the Urim & Thummim. Urim means "lights" and Thummim means "perfections." These stones were used as a way of obtaining revelation from the Lord regarding the perfect will of God.

For example, the Urim & Thummim were used to inquire of the Lord for military movements – to move or to stay. (Numbers 27:21) They were used to single out a person within a group – this one or that one. (1 Samuel 14:41) They were also used to determine who was admitted or not – yes or no. (Ezra 2:63; Nehemiah 7:65)

Scripture is not exactly clear how these stones worked. Some say it was like casting lots like a spiritual coin toss. Others say that when a specific question was asked of the Lord, either the Urim or the Thummim would supernaturally illuminate.

Today, in the New Covenant, we have the Holy Spirit. The Holy Spirit gives us access to guidance from God through direct revelation from our High Priest, Jesus.

Therefore, practicing the Urim & Thummim today is a spiritual exercise about presenting the Lord with a simple question. Yes or no? This one or that one? Which one of these? This way or that way? To go or to stay? Right or left?

He will answer us by the Holy Spirit dwelling in our hearts. It is as if He presses the answer onto our hearts or illuminates our heart and mind with revelation of God's perfect will for our situation. Then, we can proceed by faith with whatever guidance He supplies, trusting that we are walking in His will for us.

Basic TRAINING
SPIRITUAL EXERCISES

PURPOSE:

To listen to God for His guidance in all situations.

To submit our lives to God's ever-present direction.

To increase in discernment given by the Holy Spirit.

To function in God-given wisdom.

SPIRITUAL FRUIT:

Increased focus on God's voice.

Developing skill in hearing God's voice.

Greater surrender and obedience to God.

Alignment with God's will, perspective, and purpose.

Advancement in God's path for your life.

Wisdom from above.

Category: Listening to God

ALL RIGHTS RESERVED © 2018 Wendy Bowen

www.manifestinternational.com

PRACTICE

1. Think about a situation in your life that you would like God to speak to you about.

2. Narrow the issue down to a simple question.
   - Questions such as: Yes or no? This one or that one? Which one of these?, etc.

3. Ask the Lord your question.
   - Say something like, "Jesus, I ask for your response to: _____."

4. Listen with your heart for what Jesus replies. Be still and wait patiently until you sense that you have received an answer, as if you were standing in front of the High Priest watching for the response of the Urim & Thummim.
   - You might sense a pull or a leaning in your heart towards "yes" or "no" or "none of these."
   - You might have a Scripture verse flash into your mind.
   - You might sense a direction or something the Lord wants you to do other than what you inquired about.

5. Implement whatever Jesus speaks to you.

6. Throughout your day, continue to check in with the Lord to be certain that you are staying in step with Him. The Urim & Thummim exercise can be done anytime and anywhere.

PRAYER

Father, thank you for sending Jesus to be my High Priest who sits at your right hand and knows your perfect will. Thank you that you have put your Spirit within me to receive guidance from you. Help me to seek your guidance continually every moment of the day and to develop the habit of asking for your direction and wisdom with each step I take. Speak to me even now. In Jesus' name. Amen.

NOTES:

_____

_____

_____

ADDITIONAL SCRIPTURES:

Proverbs 3:5-6

Hebrews 3:7, 15

John 10:3-5

John 16:13

Mark 4:24

Isaiah 30:21

Urim & Thummim

Numbers 27:21

1 Samuel 14:41

1 Samuel 28:6

Ezra 2:63

Nehemiah 7:65

Category: Listening to God

ALL RIGHTS RESERVED © 2018 Wendy Bowen

www.manifestinternational.com

A New Heart & A New Spirit*

From the beginning of mankind, it was God's design to have a heart to heart relationship with us so that we could be and do all the things He intended for us. Unfortunately, Adam messed this up for all of us by eating from the wrong tree because of his nature of rebellion against God. As descendants of Adam, we are just like him because we were born with the same rebellious heart. In our human minds, we can never figure out what God would do or what He wants us to do in any given situation. No matter how godly we try to be, our Adam-like hearts are selfish, deceived, wicked, and constantly in error against God.

> *Jeremiah 17:9:* The **heart is deceitful above all things and beyond cure**. Who can understand it?

> *Genesis 6:5:* The LORD saw how **great the wickedness of the human race** had become on the earth, and that **every inclination of the thoughts of the human heart was only evil all the time.**

Even if we managed to figure it out God's will in any given situation, it would not be in our nature to do it the way God wanted. As such, even if we tried to do it to the best of our ability, we would eventually fail. We are totally unable to do the will of God with our own mind, will, and heart.

God knew this about humanity. He foresaw the solution and promised to bring it to fruition.

> *Ezekiel 36:26:* I will **give you a new heart** and put a **new spirit in you**; I will remove from you your heart of stone and give you a heart of flesh.

> *Jeremiah 24:7:* I will **give them a heart to know me, that I am the LORD.** They will be my people, and I will be their God, for they will return to me with all their heart.

> *Ezekiel 11:19:* I will **give them an undivided heart and put a new spirit in them**; I will remove from them their heart of stone and give them a heart of flesh.

God fulfilled these promises through Jesus Christ. The Holy Spirit is the new heart and the new spirit which God has given us and places within us when we believe Jesus. The Holy Spirit is the Spirit of the Lord, the Spirit of Jesus, whose only desire and agenda is to see the will of God fulfilled. When we believe Jesus, we are born again as a new type of people on the earth who have the very nature of God inside of us. In generations past, God kept this hidden as a mystery but now, the promise is revealed and realized in us. Jesus is inside of us!

> *2Peter 1:4:* Through these [God's power, glory, and goodness] he has given us **his very great and precious promises**, so that through them **you may participate in the divine nature**, having escaped the corruption in the world caused by evil desires.

> *Colossians 1:26-27:* the mystery that has been kept hidden for ages and generations, but is now disclosed to the Lord's people. To them God has chosen to make known among the Gentiles the **glorious riches of this mystery, which is Christ in you, the hope of glory.**

The Holy Spirit gives us direct and constant connection to God at all times to know His will and also supplies the strength for us to do it. The Holy Spirit gives us the very life of God in our mortal bodies and the same power which raised Christ from the dead. Therefore, when we allow the Holy Spirit to work in our hearts and follow the guidance of the Holy Spirit over our own inclinations and preferences, we become like Jesus. This is how God transforms our hearts, renews our minds, changes our character, and gives us moral fortitude to walk in righteousness as our own genuine response in whatever situation we face. Christ is in us!

In fact, the work of the Holy Spirit in the lives of Christ's first followers made them so much like Christ that this is how they became known as Christians, which means little Christ's. The word Christ is the Greek equivalent used to express that Jesus is the "Messiah" or anointed King, and also means "Anointed or Anointed One." To anoint means "to smear," typically with oil, and it is symbolic of consecration or being set apart for a special assignment from God. In the same way that Jesus was God's Anointed One, now, we are His anointed ones. He has anointed us with the Holy Spirit. I like Thayer's Greek Lexicon definition of Christ: "who by His holy power and Spirit lives in the souls of His followers, and so moulds their characters that they bear His likeness giving them a mind conformed to the mind of Christ."

THE SPIRIT OF THE LORD

Let's take a deeper look at the Spirit of the Lord which now dwells inside of us because we believe Jesus.

> *Isaiah 11:2-3a: The Spirit of the LORD will rest on him--* **the Spirit of wisdom and of understanding,** *the Spirit of* **counsel and of might,** *the Spirit of the* **knowledge and fear of the LORD**-- *and he will* **delight in the fear of the LORD.**

This passage describes the Spirit of the Lord that rested upon Jesus and now dwells within each one of us who believe. This is the Spirit of the Lord, the self-existent one who has no beginning and no end, and the only one Creator of the Universe. The Spirit of the Great I AM dwells inside of us. The God whose unapproachable presence and power caused sinners and men to be struck down in an instant can now dwell inside of us because the sacrifice of Jesus cleanses our sin to give us access to God. Amazing!

The Holy Spirit gives us wisdom and understanding. Wisdom could be defined as is the right application of knowledge at the right time and understanding could be defined as the accurate perception of circumstances, people, and the dynamics involved in whatever situation we face.

The Holy Spirit gives us counsel and might. When Jesus was with His disciples, He counseled them in the will of God but now that He has ascended to God, He sent the Holy Spirit to guide us from within as our Counselor who reminds us of all that Jesus taught and demonstrated so that we stay in alignment with God's will. (See John 14:26.) Along with the counsel, the Holy Spirit gives us the might, meaning the strength, bravery, moral fortitude, or supernatural power, to put the counsel into practice.

The Holy Spirit gives us knowledge. This includes the knowing God directly and experientially for ourselves; plus the knowledge of God's will and ways in order to do what He desires; and the knowledge of things which are to come. (See Ephesians 1:17; Colossians 1:9-10; John 16:13.) Without this knowledge, we perish. (See Hosea 4:6.) Moreover, with the intelligence of the Creator of all things and the author of all truth, the Holy Spirit can give us a higher level of intelligence than we could ever attain in our own natural minds.

The Holy Spirit gives us the fear of the Lord. At the end of the age, every person will stand before God and give account for what they have done – good or bad. The fear of the Lord is to live today with reverent recognition of God's supremacy and authority in our lives by following His ways and turning away from evil. (See Proverbs 8:13; Job 28:28; Psalm 11:10.)

CHOOSING THE TREE OF LIFE

Now that the Spirit of the Lord dwells inside of us, we should be the wisest, most intelligent, powerful, and honorable people on earth, right? Well...yes! The problem is that we do not always choose to listen to the Holy Spirit and even if we listen, we do not always do what He says. Hmmm... This sounds like the problem of all mankind from the beginning.

God has given us freewill to choose to obey Him or not. Back in the Garden of Eden, Adam and Eve had constant access to the Tree of Life at any time they desired in addition to eating from any other fruit bearing tree. All things were permitted for them, except for one tree: The Tree of the Knowledge of Good and Evil. This tree was very appealing to look at and seemed to promise great rewards of strength, wisdom, and prosperity. But it had no ability to give life and, in fact, brought only death. Adam and Eve chose to eat from the forbidden tree and were subsequently banished from the Garden of Eden, losing their access to the Tree of Life in the process.

Interestingly, Biblical references to the Tree of Life can only be found in the Genesis, the beginning, the book of Revelation, the end, and the book of Proverbs, which is a collection of God's wisdom right in the middle. In the beginning, God gave humans full access to the Tree of Life and in the end, after God has judged the earth and restored it, we will again have full access to the Tree of Life. But in the meantime as we wait for total restoration, through faith in Christ and the indwelling Holy Spirit, God has given us spiritual access to the Tree of Life again.

> *Proverbs 3:18:* **She [wisdom] is a tree of life** *to those who take hold of her; those who hold her fast will be blessed.*
>
> *1Corinthians 1:30: It is because of him that* **you are in Christ Jesus, who has become for us wisdom from God**--*that is, our righteousness, holiness and redemption.*

God's wisdom is a Tree of Life. Jesus Christ is the wisdom of God. Therefore, with the Spirit of God's wisdom dwelling inside of us, we have Tree of Life is within us! The life of God gives us wisdom and vitality from within to know God's will and to do it. Figuratively speaking, this means that we can choose every day to eat from the Tree of Life by obeying the Holy Spirit, or we can choose to eat from the Tree of the Knowledge of Good and Evil by following our own inclinations, desires, and fleshly passions.

Jesus is our example of one who lived this way. Jesus never did anything to try to be a good person or do good things. Jesus never did anything that was evil. He never functioned from a "principle" or "theology" or "teaching" about what was right/good and what was wrong/evil. He obeyed God by obeying the Holy Spirit that was within Him. He always did what the Father desired for Him to do and only said what God said. (See John 5:19, 8:48, 12:49.) For certain, Jesus could discern good and evil very clearly, but all of His actions were based on God's will and guidance in each situation because He was always being led by God, not by His flesh.

For us, this means submitting to the promptings of the Holy Spirit inside of us rather than caving into the cravings of our flesh. This includes dying to ourselves and our own ideas. If we are truly dead in Christ's death then, what right do we have to have thoughts of our own about what we should be doing? The truth is that even when we do "good" things, they can be wrong things when they are not God-directed things. Our aim is not to be "good" but to be like Jesus. To be like Him means to do it the way He did, by the indwelling Holy Spirit rather than the knowledge of good and evil that comes from principles, theologies, and our own ideas about things.

If we persist in living by our fleshly desires, we may as well be eating from the wrong tree, like Adam. We have a bad spiritual diet and it will show in our lives. Typically, this results in us becoming frustrated and having a wrong view of God because He didn't bless the mess that we chose to get ourselves into, or because we are dealing with the consequences of our own self-directed choices. (See Galatians 6:7.) This also evidences itself when we are always searching for the next great teaching that is going to fix our lives or the most anointed preacher or teacher who can solve all our problems. When we won't look to the Holy Spirit within, we will look for the Holy Spirit in others. Our spiritual growth will be stunted or stagnated and we will be confused.

> *Ephesians 4:13-14: until we all reach unity in the faith and in the knowledge of the Son of God and* **become mature**, *attaining to the whole measure of the fullness of Christ. Then*

> *we will **no longer be infants, tossed back and forth by the waves, and blown here and there by every wind of teaching and by the cunning and craftiness of people in their deceitful scheming**.*
>
> *Hebrews 5:14 NASB: But **solid food is for the mature**, who because of practice have their senses trained to **discern good and evil**.*

Part of the good news is that unlike Adam in the Garden of Eden, we do not lose our access to the Tree of Life (or Holy Spirit) if we choose to eat from the wrong tree. Jesus' sacrifice was sufficient for our mistakes and self-willed choices. His love covers over our errors as we grow but His grace is not an excuse for our willful disobedience.

When we cooperate with the Holy Spirit by allowing ourselves to be led by Him, we become the children of God. We no longer have to be enslaved to trying to earn good standing with God through trying to be good. Jesus purchased good standing with God for us so that we can be children of God. Now, we cry out to God as our Father who loves us and always leads us on the path of righteousness to the most blessing. Our heart to heart connection with God has been restored!

> *Romans 8:14-15: For **those who are led by the Spirit of God are the children of God**. The Spirit you received does not make you slaves, so that you live in fear again; rather, **the Spirit you received brought about your adoption to sonship. And by him we cry, "Abba, Father."***

If we truly appreciate what Jesus has done for us, we desire to grow up in Him by learning how to hear and obey God's voice. When we have a good spiritual diet through obedience to the Holy Spirit's guidance, we grow spiritually to maturity and Christ's likeness – the full measure of sonship. We also become like a Tree of Life. As we do the things that Jesus does and say the things that Jesus says, we become like branches of Christ and we produce life-giving fruit which supplies wisdom and strength to others while drawing them to Jesus.

> *Proverbs 11:30: **The fruit of the righteous is a tree of life**, and the one who is wise saves lives.*

ROLES OF THE HOLY SPIRIT

While we walk with God in deeper and deeper levels of dependence on Him, it can be helpful to know the job descriptions of the Holy Spirit. If the Holy Spirit does not do His job then God is a liar. Since God is not a liar, we can trust Him to do these things, especially when we cannot see with our eyes or in our circumstances that He is at work. For starters, Jesus said this about what the Holy Spirit does:

> *John 16:8-11 ESV - And **when he [the Holy Spirit] comes, he will convict the world concerning sin and righteousness and judgment**: concerning sin, because they do not believe in me; concerning righteousness, because I go to the Father, and you will see me no longer; concerning judgment, because the ruler of this world is judged.*

The Holy Spirit is the only one who can truly change a human heart. The Holy Spirit is the only one who can prove to anyone that Jesus is their Lord, Savior, and eternal Judge. The Holy Spirit is the only one who can convince anyone that they are a sinner in need of a Savior or that what they have been doing or believing is wrong. No matter how persuasive an evangelist or apologist is, they have no power to change anyone's heart. Only God can do that, and He does so by His Spirit.

Equally so, for those who do believe Jesus, the Holy Spirit is the only one who can expose the areas of unbelief in our lives in a way that brings lasting change and releases us to receive God's blessings. The Holy Spirit helps us to know that we have victory over the evil one who has been defeated through Jesus' death and resurrection.

Our salvation and growth to spiritual maturity is the Holy Spirit's job from start to finish. Our role is to believe God and let the Holy Spirit do His job by listening to Him and obeying Him when He speaks rather than resisting Him or thinking that we know better. This means that we can stop telling God how to do His job in our lives and we can stop bossing other people around and manipulating them to get our own way because we trust that our Father is working it all out for us and for them in His way, in His timing, and for His purposes. He has been God for a very long time and He knows what He is doing!

Here is a chart of the various roles and job description of the Holy Spirit.

ROLES AND FUNCTIONS OF THE HOLY SPIRIT	
Holy Spirit Job Description	**Scriptures**
Births us as children of God, cries out "Abba, Father" in our hearts. Gives us life, seals us for redemption.	John 3:5-8, 6:63 • Romans 8:11,16 • 1 Corinthians 12:13 • 2 Corinthians 1:22, 3:6, 5:5 • Galatians 4:6, 6:8 • Ephesians 1:13, 4:30
Regenerates, purifies, sanctifies, washes and transforms us. Gives us fruit of the spirit, the character of Christ, and joy.	John 16:8-11 • Romans 15:16 • 1 Corinthians 6:11 • 2 Corinthians 3:18 • Galatians 5:22-23 • 1 Thessalonians 1:6 • 2 Thessalonians 2:13 • 1 Peter 1:2 • Titus 3:5
Brings liberty from law of sin and death. Pours love into our hearts, dwells in us, fills us, and helps us know Jesus is in us.	John 14:17 • Acts 2:4, 4:8,31, 9:17 • Romans 5:5, 8:2,9 • 1 Corinthians 3:16 • 2 Corinthians 3:17 • Ephesians 5:18 • 2 Timothy 1:14 • 1 John 3:24, 4:13
Teaches, reveals mysteries of God, and reminds us of the teachings of Jesus.	Luke 12:12 • John 14:26, 16:13-15 • Acts 6:10 • 1 Corinthians 2:10-14 • Ephesians 1:17, 3:5 • 1 John 2:27
Speaks to us and through us. Confesses that Jesus is Lord who came in the flesh. Says "Come, Lord Jesus."	Matthew 10:20 • John 15:26-27, 16:13-14 • 1 Corinthians 12:3 1 Timothy 4:1 • Hebrews 3:7 • Revelation 2:11, 22:17 1 John 4:2 • Acts 2:4, 4:31, 8:29, 10:19, 11:12,28, 21:4,11
Comforts, encourages, and helps us. Intercedes for us teaches us to pray.	John 14:26 • Acts 9:31 • Romans 8:26-27 • 1 Corinthians 14:14 • Jude 1:20
Knows and guides us in the ways and will of God. Gives us access to God. Bears witness to truth.	Mark 1:12 • John 16:8,13 • Romans 8:14, 9:1 • 1 Corinthians 2:11 • Galatians 5:18 • Ephesians 2:18 • Acts 1:2, 8:29, 10:19, 11:28, 13:4, 16:6-7, 20:22-23
Gives power for life, to obey truth, in our bodies. Battles against flesh. Empowers for ministry, and with spiritual gifts, prophecy/dreams/visions, etc.	Matthew 12:28 • Luke 4:18-19, 24:49 • Acts 1:8, 2:4, 17-18 • Romans 1:11, 8:11, 15:19 • 1 Corinthians 2:4, 12:7-13, 14:2 • Galatians 5:16-26 • Ephesians 3:16 • Hebrews 2:4 • 1 Peter 1:12 • 2 Peter 1:21 • Revelation 19:10
Appoints and guides ministry. Unites and builds us into house of God.	Acts 13:2,4, 16:6-9, 20:28 • 1 Corinthians 4:21 • 2 Corinthians 1:17 • Ephesian 2:14-22, 4:3

All of this means that because you believe Jesus, God has given you a new heart and a new spirit. The Holy Spirit will change your life by changing your heart. You have nothing to fear because Christ is in you!

> 2 Timothy 1:7: For the **Spirit God gave us does not make us timid**, but **gives us power, love and self-discipline**.

HOLY SPIRIT ROLES WORKSHEET

www.manifestinternational.com

But very truly I tell you, it is for your good that I am going away. Unless I go away, the Advocate will not come to you; but if I go, I will send him to you. When he comes, he will prove the world to be in the wrong about sin and righteousness and judgment: about sin, because people do not believe in me; about righteousness, because I am going to the Father, where you can see me no longer; and about judgment, because the prince of this world now stands condemned. - John 16:7-1

Roles and Functions of the Holy Spirit

Holy Spirit Job Description	Scriptures
Births us as children of God, cries out "Abba, Father" in our hearts. Gives us life, seals us for redemption.	John 3:5-8, 6:63 • Romans 8:11,16 • 1 Corinthians 12:13 • 2 Corinthians 1:22, 3:6, 5:5 • Galatians 4:6, 6:8 • Ephesians 1:13, 4:30
Regenerates, purifies, sanctifies, washes and transforms us. Gives us fruit of the spirit, the character of Christ, and joy.	John 16:8-11 • Romans 15:16 • 1 Corinthians 6:11 • 2 Corinthians 3:18 • Galatians 5:22-23 • 1 Thessalonians 1:6 • 2 Thessalonians 2:13 • 1 Peter 1:2 • Titus 3:5
Brings liberty from law of sin and death. Pours love into our hearts, dwells in us, fills us, and helps us know Jesus is in us.	John 14:17 • Acts 2:4, 4:8,31, 9:17 • Romans 5:5, 8:2,9 • 1 Corinthians 3:16 • 2 Corinthians 3:17 • Ephesians 5:18 • 2 Timothy 1:14 • 1 John 3:24, 4:13
Teaches, reveals mysteries of God, and reminds us of the teachings of Jesus.	Luke 12:12 • John 14:26, 16:13-15 • Acts 6:10 • 1 Corinthians 2:10-14 • Ephesians 1:17, 3:5 • 1 John 2:27
Speaks to us and through us. Confesses that Jesus is Lord who came in the flesh. Says "Come, Lord Jesus."	Matthew 10:20 • John 15:26-27, 16:13-14 • 1 Corinthians 12:3 1 Timothy 4:1 • Hebrews 3:7 • Revelation 2:11, 22:17 1 John 4:2 • Acts 2:4, 4:31, 8:29, 10:19, 11:12,28, 21:4,11
Comforts, encourages, and helps us. Intercedes for us teaches us to pray.	John 14:26 • Acts 9:31 • Romans 8:26-27 • 1 Corinthians 14:14 • Jude 1:20
Knows and guides us in the ways and will of God. Gives us access to God. Bears witness to truth.	Mark 1:12 • John 16:8,13 • Romans 8:14, 9:1 • 1 Corinthians 2:11 • Galatians 5:18 • Ephesians 2:18 • Acts 1:2, 8:29, 10:19, 11:28, 13:4, 16:6-7, 20:22-23
Gives power for life, to obey truth, in our bodies. Battles against flesh. Empowers for ministry, and with spiritual gifts, prophecy/dreams/visions, etc.	Matthew 12:28 • Luke 4:18-19, 24:49 • Acts 1:8, 2:4, 17-18 • Romans 1:11, 8:11, 15:19 • 1 Corinthians 2:4, 12:7-13, 14:2 • Galatians 5:16-26 • Ephesians 3:16 • Hebrews 2:4 • 1 Peter 1:12 • 2 Peter 1:21 • Revelation 19:10
Appoints and guides ministry. Unites and builds us into house of God.	Acts 13:2,4, 16:6-9, 20:28 • 1 Corinthians 4:21 • 2 Corinthians 1:17 • Ephesian 2:14-22, 4:3

1. Why do you think Jesus said, "It is for your good that I am going away?"

   _____
   _____
   _____

2. **Read Column One** of the chart. Which of these categories do you desire to experience more in your life with the Holy Spirit?

New Birth	Regeneration	Liberty	Teach	Truth
Comfort	Guidance	Power for life	Ministry	Unity

3. **Use Column Two** of the chart. Look up the Scriptures listed beside the category you selected and write them down.

   _____
   _____
   _____
   _____
   _____
   _____
   _____
   _____

4. What do you sense the Lord highlighting for you out of these Scriptures? Is there any action you sense the Lord prompting you to take?

   _____
   _____
   _____

5. Ask the Holy Spirit to highlight one Scripture for you from your list. Slowly read and speak this Scripture out loud three times. What do you sense the Lord speaking to you through this Scripture?

   _____
   _____
   _____
   _____

6. In what ways is God asking you to walk and live with the Holy Spirit more?

   _____
   _____
   _____

7. How will you continue to walk in faith rather than slipping back into old patterns?

   _____
   _____
   _____

8. Praise God for what He has done for you. Jesus is King!

LOVE
Post Card Handout

LAW & FLESH

GOD'S LOVE — SEPARATION

Love the Lord your God with all your heart.
Deuteronomy 6:5

GOD'S LOVE — SEPARATION

Love your neighbor as yourself.
Leviticus 19:18

LAW: Striving to please God and earn His love and blessings through our own efforts. Functioning without faith in Christ from our old nature. Leads to frustration, exhaustion, and religion.

GRACE & HOLY SPIRIT

GOD'S LOVE *for me in Christ.*

As the Father has loved me, so have I loved you. Now remain in my love.
John 15:9

GOD'S LOVE *through me to others.*

My command is this: Love one another as I have loved you.
John 15:12

GRACE: Receiving God's love freely through faith in Christ. Loving others freely from our new nature, the Holy Spirit. Leads to freedom from all fear, genuine love for others, and Christlikeness.

CORNERSTONE – UNIT 2.3

Repentance & Fruit
Scripture Reading & Worksheet

Read each of the following passages and then use the chart below for study and reflection.
- The Book of Matthew, Chapters 5-7
- The Book of Romans, Chapter 8
- The Book of Galatians, Chapter 5

Main Themes & Common Message:	God's Commands:
Key Verses/Highlights:	**Questions I Have about this:**

What is God's definition of spiritual fruitfulness? Is this different than you expected? How so?

List some characteristics or evidence of the work of the Holy Spirit in someone's life.

Fruit of the Holy Spirit in your life:	Areas in my life in need of repentance/more fruit:

Notes & Lessons Learned:

Basic Training Exercise

CONVICTION OF SIN

Psalm 32:5 NIV - Then I acknowledged my sin to you and did not cover up my iniquity. I said, "I will confess my transgressions to the LORD." And you forgave the guilt of my sin.

DESCRIPTION

God already knows how we have sinned against Him through our actions (transgressions) and even in our thoughts (iniquities.) Sin is anything we do or think that is not like God. We were created to be like Him but we have all fallen terribly short.

Conviction is not a ritual self-assessment of how we find ourselves to be faulty. We are not God. Instead, one of the roles of the Holy Spirit (who is God) is to bring conviction of sin by making us aware that we are in violation of God's will and ways. He does this even as we are in the act of doing or thinking it!

Before the Holy Spirit enters our lives, we may not think that the things we do, think, or feel are wrong. But once we place our faith in Jesus and receive the Holy Spirit in our inner man, He begins to reveal our ungodliness so that we can confess our sins and be free. This is God's way of purifying our hearts, choices, and behaviors from the inside out.

In the Old Testament, when an Israelite became aware that they had sinned, the brought a sacrifice to the Priest, confessed their sins over the sacrifice, and trusted that the blood cleansed away their sin.

In the New Covenant, Jesus is our only High Priest and ultimate sacrifice for our sins. When the Holy Spirit convicts us of sin, we can confess our sins to Jesus, trusting that His blood washes us clean.

The practice of Conviction of Sin is about inviting the Holy Spirit to bring conviction of sin in areas where we are falling short of the glory of God. Then, we can acknowledge how we are out of alignment with God and His ways, receive His forgiveness, and move forward into new life.

Basic TRAINING
SPIRITUAL EXERCISES

PURPOSE:

To invite the Holy Spirit to work in our hearts to bring conviction of sin.

To come into agreement with God about our sin so that we may receive His forgiveness.

To be purified from sin through the blood of Jesus and the work of the Holy Spirit.

SPIRITUAL FRUIT:

Honesty and integrity before God.

The development of Christlike character.

Deeper submission to and alignment with God.

Clear conscience from our failures in order to live new life in Christ.

TALK WITH GOD

Consider the fact that Jesus never sinned, from childhood to manhood, even in His heart. How does this increase your respect and awe for Him? Tell Him about it.

Consider the fact that the same Holy Spirit who dwelt in Jesus now dwells in you to empower you to resist sin. How does this strengthen you to live a new life with God's power? Talk to God about this.

PRAYER

Father, thank you that you sent Jesus to be the sacrifice for my sins. Thank you for sending the Holy Spirit to convict me of sin. Examine my life and my heart so that I can be more like you. In Jesus' name, Amen.

PRACTICE

1. Invite the Holy Spirit to reveal some areas where your thoughts and actions are out of alignment with God.

2. Ask God to reveal to you why these thoughts or behaviors are unlike Him or not what He desires for you. For example:
   - Are they unloving, hypocritical, arrogant, selfish, or unbecoming?
   - Are they contradictory to how God sees you – His child?
   - Are they rooted in trusting in something other than God?
   - Are they harmful, damaging, or dangerous to you or others?
   - Are they part of pattern of choices from your old life?
   - Do they stem from a wrong motive?
   - Are they unwise? Do they lead to unfortunate consequences or poor choices?

3. When you feel a genuine recognition of how you have been in error, acknowledge your faults to God. This is confession of sin.

4. Receive total forgiveness as a free gift because of the blood of Jesus. You are now clean. Praise God!

NOTES:

ADDITIONAL SCRIPTURES:

John 16:8
Acts 2:37
Luke 18:13
1 John 1:9
Proverbs 28:13
James 5:16
Leviticus 5:5
Acts 19:18
1 John 1:10
Hebrews 9:14

Hear My Voice: How to Hear God

Living by the guidance of the Holy Spirit does not have to be complicated. It starts with simply trusting that you do indeed hear His voice. Sometimes at first, it doesn't seem like a voice speaking. Actually, it seems more like an inner knowing about something, usually about something that you have no rational way of knowing but somehow, you just know. You might call it an impression or a sense of what is really happening underneath the surface of a situation or of what you are supposed to do about something.

We begin living by the Holy Spirit by trusting that this inner knowing is, in fact, the voice of God. Begin by trusting that Jesus does speak to you because you are His sheep.

> *John 10:14, 27:* "I am the good shepherd; I know my sheep and **my sheep know me**-- ... **My sheep listen to my voice**; I know them, and **they follow me**.

No More Casting Lots

When Jesus ascended into heaven and told His disciples to wait in Jerusalem for the promise of the Holy Spirit, they obeyed His order and went into the city. However, while they were waiting, they took some Kingdom business into their own hands. Without the Holy Spirit, they still regarded the Kingdom of God in an earthly manner and were anticipating that Jesus was going to return imminently as a warrior King to restore great power and dominion to Israel. (See Acts 1:7.) They read the Scriptures (without the Holy Spirit) and concluded that it must be God's will for them to appoint someone to replace Judas who had betrayed Jesus and hanged himself. They created criteria for this person's qualifications (without the Holy Spirit) and chose between two prospective candidates in the most godly manner they could think of – they cast lots. (See Acts 1:12-26.)

In essence, this is a spiritual coin toss. To us this seems foolish but to them, it was a scripturally approved and proven methodology for settling differences. (See Joshua 7:14; 1 Chronicles 24; Nehemiah 10:34.) God even controlled the lot casting of Gentiles. (See Jonah 1:7; Ezekiel 21:21.)

> *Proverbs 16:33:* The lot is cast into the lap, **but its every decision is from the LORD**.

> *Proverbs 18:18:* **Casting the lot settles disputes** and keeps strong opponents apart.

However, let us learn from the example of the pre-Holy Spirit disciples and not do what they did. It can be tempting for us, even with the Holy Spirit, when we perceive and believe that we understand the will of God, to rush ahead and try to bring it to pass using our own way of doing things. This is especially true when we have good ways of doing things and even "Biblical" ways of approaching situations based on our theology or understanding of God's principles.

The problem is that our logical, practical, common sense methods may not be at all the way that God has designed to bring His will to pass. Like the first believers, there are times when God tells us to wait for Him and instead, we busy ourselves doing things that He did not ask us to do – and we base it on Scripture! There are times when we put all of our own criteria on something or someone even though that may or may not be the criteria that God has for that thing or person. There are times when, even though we are very prayerful, we are simply wrong because we are not waiting for God and listening for the Holy Spirit the way that we should. The disciples were told to wait for the Holy Spirit before they went anywhere or did anything for Jesus. In our walk with the Lord, we also must learn to wait for the Holy Spirit, both for His prompting and His power, before we go anywhere or do anything in Jesus name. Like them, we need a new guidance system to lead us into all truth and show us what to do and how to do it. Otherwise, we ourselves are no better than lot casters.

> John 6:63: **The Spirit [God's way] gives life; the flesh [our idea] counts for nothing**. *The words I have spoken to you--they are full of the Spirit and life.*
>
> Zechariah 4:6b: '**Not by might nor by power, but by my Spirit**,' *says the LORD Almighty.*

After the Holy Spirit was poured out, there is no record of disciples ever casting lots again. The Holy Spirit spoke to believers and directed their movements according to the will of God. Even for us today, if we want or need wisdom from God, all we have to do is ask.

> James 1:5-8: *If any of you lacks wisdom, you should ask God, who gives generously to all without finding fault, and it will be given to you. But when you ask,* **you must believe and not doubt, because the one who doubts is like a wave of the sea, blown and tossed by the wind**. *That person should not expect to receive anything from the Lord. Such a person is double-minded and unstable in all they do.*

Once we have asked and received wisdom from the Holy Spirit, all that is required of us is to believe that we have heard God. Then, we stand firm in what we have heard and obey the promptings of the Holy Spirit until what God told us becomes a reality.

WAYS TO HEAR GOD'S VOICE

When we think of talking to a person, we know that they can speak to us in a variety of ways. For example, they can speak to us face to face, call us on the phone, write us a letter, or send us a gift. When they are speaking, they might answer us with a yes or no, speak in plain terms, tell us what to do or where to go, tell us a story, or show us a picture in order to express their point.

Hearing from God is as simple as hearing from another person – as long as we do not overcomplicate it. Remember, God's design for mankind in the Garden of Eden was to be in constant open two-way communication with us. Jesus has restored us to spiritual access to God's guidance so that we can hear His voice and do what He says. You could say that having the Holy Spirit within us transfers us from an "external guidance system" to an "internal guidance system." No longer do we have to guess or try to interpret what God is saying through random events or seeming coincidences. God speaks to us.

Here is a brief snapshot of various ways that God speaks to us by the Holy Spirit.

Inner Impression: The primary way that God begins to speak to us as His children is through inner "impressions" in our hearts. As described above, it seems as if we know that we should or should not do something or go somewhere even if it might contradict what we think in our natural mind. As we begin to follow these impressions, God will guide us into deeper communication with Him.

Inner Urim & Thummim: In the Old Testament, the High Priest wore a breast piece which contained stones called the Urim & Thummim. These stones were used as a way of obtaining answers to important questions with a "yes" or "no," "this one" or "that one," "go to war" or "don't go to war." (See Numbers 27:21; 1 Samuel 14:41, 28:6; Ezra 2:63; Nehemiah 7:65.) Now that we have our High Priest, Jesus, dwelling inside of us through the Holy Spirit, it is like we have an inner Urim & Thummim. This means that we can consult God anytime about anything with a "yes or no" type of question and receive an answer in from Him.

Inner Direction: God also speaks to us with plain directive speech that we hear from the Holy Spirit within us. Jesus is our King and sometimes, He gives us instructions or guidance which He desires for us to follow. He also loves us and sometimes, He tells us to do or not do something for our own good. This happened frequently with the early believers in the Book of Acts.

Acts 8:29: **The Spirit told Philip,** "Go to that chariot and stay near it."

Acts 11:12a: **The Spirit told me** to have no hesitation about going with them.

(See also Acts 10:19, 11:28, 13:4, 16:6-7, 20:22-23, 21:4,11.)

In the days of the first followers of Jesus, the majority of the civilized world were illiterate. They had no access to the Holy Scriptures and even if they obtained access, they would not be able to read them. The letters of the New Testament were read out loud to the communities of believers that gathered together in homes to worship Jesus. They lived by the guidance of the Holy Spirit for everything they did and everywhere they went. This is the way Jesus lived and God desires for us to live this way too.

Dreams and Visions: When the Holy Spirit was poured out on the day of Pentecost, Peter quoted from the Book of Joel that God's sons and daughters would "see visions and dream dreams." (See Acts 2:17; Joel 2:28.) Dreams and visions are largely similar in that they are a visual image or a picture in motion that comes into our minds or plays across the stage of our consciousness. This does not mean that every picture we imagine or dream we have is from God. However, some dreams and visions are from God and should be taken seriously as God speaking to us.

When dreams and visions are from God, they can be subject to interpretation. We must seek the Lord and ask Him to help us interpret correctly. For example, when Peter had a vision of a sheet coming down from heaven, a voice also spoke to him with the interpretation. The interpretation was so far from what Peter anticipated that the Lord repeated it three times until Peter finally understood. (See Acts 10:9-17.) Therefore, we cannot be presumptuous that we automatically know what God is saying to us but must ask Him to help us. He will.

Through Scripture: God also speaks to us through His written Word. Even though the first disciples did not have access to the Scripture, in most cases, we do. The Word of God is the written record of God's communication with mankind from the beginning and shares with us what is still yet to come in the times ahead. When we read the Scripture with the Holy Spirit dwelling inside of us, it may seem as if certain words, phrases, stories, or passages are whispering to us, or standing out, or even shouting to us. This is the Lord communicating to us through His Word. This said, we cannot randomly select what parts of the Word of God we like to listen to and do not want to hear. We must approach the Scriptures with reverence for their holiness and authority in our lives. We stand upon the promises of God to us while also submitting ourselves under the authority of the One who authored it.

If we have access to the Word of God and are able to read, we must devote ourselves to studying it, meditating on it, and growing in our knowledge of God through understanding it correctly. This is the predominant way that we will grow in understanding God, His character, His ways and dealings with people, and what Jesus died to give us. This said, it is one thing to read a story about your best friend's interactions with other people but, it is another thing to spend time talking to and interacting with your best friend for yourself.

Scripture becomes our check and balance as we receive guidance and hear the Lord speaking to us to test whether or not they align with the Spirit of the Lord who wrote the Scriptures. This said, there are times when the Scriptures seem to contradict themselves (even though God is never actually contradictory.) For example:

Proverbs 26:4: **Do not answer a fool according to his folly**, or you yourself will be just like him.

Proverbs 26:5: **Answer a fool according to his folly**, or he will be wise in his own eyes.

Another example is how at the Red Sea, God told Moses to be still and lift his staff over the waters until they parted but at the Jordan River, God told Joshua to have the Israelites enter into the river so He could stop the flow. If Joshua had presumed based on the writings of Moses what Israel was to do when they encountered a body of water, they would still be waiting on the other side of the river!

All of this is to say that as supreme and overriding as the Word of God can be in our lives, it is only through relationship with God and hearing from the Holy Spirit that we will know which Scripture to apply at the right time.

Prophecy: God speaks to us today through the prophetic word. He can do this directly to us or He can send someone else to speak to us on His behalf about things that are happening in our lives, things God wants us to do, or things that are to come. There are many instances in the Old Testament of people who were used by God to deliver His Word to His people and there are several New Testament examples of this as well. Now that the Holy Spirit dwells in each one of us, according to the Scripture **all believers** can prophesy. This said, prophesying is a gift of God that we learn to function in. Like developing a skill, we grow in our accuracy, delivery, and interpretation of what God is saying. This said, like dreams and visions, not every prophesy is from the Lord. Therefore, we must seek the Lord for interpretation in order to respond correctly according to His will. (See 1 Thessalonians 5:20-21; 1 John 4:1.)

Audible Voice: God can and does sometimes speak in an audible voice. (See Matthew 3:17; John 12:28; Acts 9:3-7, 10:13.) This is like hearing the voice of a person in the room with you. This is rare but it does still happen today.

Circumstances: God does not actually speak through circumstances, but His hand upon our life can be evidenced through our circumstances. This can be challenging to interpret because sometimes we have walked ourselves into something that God never intended for us and yet, we are upset with God for it. (See Proverbs 19:3.) Other times, we think positive events prove that we are on the right path when in fact, it is the enemy leading us into a snare. Long story short, it is not the most accurate way of hearing from God or interpreting His will. Jesus died so that we can hear His voice.

Listening to the Lord: If we desire to hear the Lord more, we have to position ourselves to listen more to Him. This can be done through prayer, journaling, fasting, practicing His presence, and spending prayerful time with other believers. Regardless of how we choose to approach the Lord, the point is that we need to allow Him time to speak rather than filling the whole time with our own chatter.

Face to Face: Jesus calls us His friends. (See John 15:14.) What He desires is for us to have face to face communication with us, like a man speaks to His friend. This does not mean that Jesus will always appear to us but that we know His voice the way we know our best friend's voice. It is no longer riddles and mysteries but plain speech from one friend to another. This is the relationship Jesus had with the Father while He walked in a flesh like ours on the earth. This is the relationship He wants to have with us while we are still on this side of heaven so that we can know Him and move in step with Him. This is the language of love and spiritual maturity. (See 1 Corinthians 13:9-11.)

> *Numbers 12:6-8a: He [the Lord] said, "Listen to my words: "When there is a prophet among you, I, the LORD, reveal myself to them in visions, I speak to them in dreams. But this is not true of my servant Moses; he is faithful in all my house. **With him I speak face to face, clearly and not in riddles**; he sees the form of the LORD."*

NOT DOUBTING – ABIDING

One we have heard God, there are three primary ways we will be tempted to doubt His guidance. Jesus told the Parable of the Four Soils about a farmer who sowed seeds on 4 different kinds of soils. (See Matthew 13:1-23; Mark 4:1-24; Luke 8:4-18.) In this parable, the seed represents God's word, and the soil represents the condition of our hearts to receive and believe what God has said. We do not have time to dig fully into the Parable of the Four Soils but, instead, we're going to use it as a template for understanding how to stand firm in the Holy Spirit's guidance.

The first way we are tempted to doubt what God has said to us is through the enemy. The same serpent who tempted Adam and his wife to eat from the wrong tree in the Garden of Eden by saying to them,

Did God really say…?, will say the same thing to us. Of course, I am not referring to a literal serpent but a spiritual one who is constantly contradicting or twisting what God did indeed say. In fact, it seems that whenever God truly has said something, that contrary voice is right there saying, *Did God really say…?*, to get us to doubt and abandon God's guidance. Be alert for this, and don't allow the enemy to snatch away your confidence.

The second way we are tempted to doubt what God has said to us is through others misunderstanding us and the trials which arise in our lives between the time that God gives a promise and the time when the promise or purpose is fulfilled. We set out to obey God, and then our friends abandon us or pick on us or tell us that we've lost our mind to be doing such a thing. Then, everything seems to go wrong which would seem to prove our friends to be right…except they're not. It's just another way of testing our faith and causing us to question, *Did God really say…?* Be ready for this and be prepared to stand on God's promises through misunderstandings, persecution, trials, and attacks until His word is fulfilled.

The third way we are tempted to doubt what God has said to us is through our desire for other things, usually temporal things like comfort, money, status, or security. We set out to obey God and then, some other opportunity comes up that would pay us more money and/or we convince ourselves that God wants to bless us in ways that are, in truth, a distraction. Or, the responsibilities in our lives seem to take up all of our time so that we find ourselves unable to do what God has said. This includes even "good" or "godly" things like serving in the Church, taking care of our families, or working to make a living. Or, somehow, God's way just seems too hard, or it seems that we could have our desires fulfilled faster if we did it our own way or the world's ways. When these temptations come, we find ourselves asking, *Did God really say…?* This is why it is important to keep our hearts set on Christ and His Kingdom and things of eternal value so that these temporal things hold less value in our lives. God knows what we are eternally responsible for and He knows how to guide us in all of it.

But finally, there is a fourth soil in this parable and that is the soil that stands firm and endures through the questions, trials, confusion, and temptations all the way to receiving the promised outcome. This is the person who has remained or abided, in God's word and the things that He has promised.

> *John 15:4-8:* **Remain in me**, *as I also remain in you. No branch can bear fruit by itself; it must remain in the vine.* **Neither can you bear fruit unless you remain in me.** *"I am the vine; you are the branches.* **If you remain in me and I in you, you will bear much fruit**; *apart from me you can do nothing. If you do not remain in me, you are like a branch that is thrown away and withers; such branches are picked up, thrown into the fire and burned.* **If you remain in me and my words remain in you, ask whatever you wish, and it will be done for you.** *This is to my Father's glory, that you bear much fruit, showing yourselves to be my disciples.*

The word for remain in this passage means "to abide, continue, endure, keep, wait for, and not become different." While abiding can be challenging, it is not strained. All a branch has to do to remain in the vine is to allow the vine to fill it with sap and receive all that the vine has to give it.

Similarly, when we believe that we have heard God speak to us, we have to remain, continue, endure, and wait, receiving all that Jesus wants to share with us without hardening our hearts until what He says come to pass. Then, we will produce much fruit.

> *Hebrews 3:15: As has just been said:* **"Today, if you hear his voice, do not harden your hearts** *as you did in the rebellion."*

> *Proverbs 3:5-6: Trust in the LORD with all your heart and* **lean not on your own understanding; in all your ways submit to him,** *and he will make your paths straight.*

Basic Training Exercise

AT HIS FEET

Luke 10:38-42 NIV – As Jesus and his disciples were on their way, he came to a village where a woman named Martha opened her home to him. She had a sister called Mary, who sat at the Lord's feet listening to what he said. But Martha was distracted by all the preparations that had to be made. She came to him and asked, "Lord, don't you care that my sister has left me to do the work by myself? Tell her to help me!" "Martha, Martha," the Lord answered, "you are worried and upset about many things; but few things are needed—or indeed only one. Mary has chosen what is better, and it will not be taken away from her."

DESCRIPTION

Jesus said that only one thing was needed in our life with Him. This thing is time At His Feet.

Two sisters, Mary and Martha, provide a vivid example of how we sometimes approach our life with Jesus. Both sisters loved Jesus. Martha busied herself with much serving and Jesus loved her. But Mary sat at His feet, positioned to hear, receive, and partake of everything that He may convey to her. He said that she chose the better portion; and the one that would remain with her forever.

As we walk with and worship Jesus, placing ourselves At His Feet is essentially doing the same things that Mary did. We let go of control, set aside our concerns, anxieties, and even other forms of service to God in order to allow Jesus to speak to us and minister to us however He sees fit. When we do this, we will be refreshed in His presence and receive from Him things that will remain with us forever.

PRAYER

Father, thank you allow me and encourage me to take time to rest in your presence and sit at the feet of Jesus. Help me to still my heart and mind as I prioritize your desires over my own forms of serving you. Speak to me Lord, I am listening. In Jesus' name, Amen.

Basic TRAINING
SPIRITUAL EXERCISES

PURPOSE:

To sit in the presence of Jesus and receive from Him.

To take a time out from other forms of serving to be with God.

To grow in our relationship with Jesus by offering our time to Him over other things.

SPIRITUAL FRUIT:

Closer relationship with Jesus through drawing near to Him.

Deeper rest in Christ.

Fuller experience of God's peace and love.

Re-alignment to Christ-centered priorities.

CONSIDERATIONS

How and when can you make time to sit at Jesus feet? What is required for you to choose this over other demands of life?

How long can you sit At His Feet? (Recommendation: Start with at least 20 minutes.) If needed, set a timer so you can relax and not be anxious about exceeding the time allotted.

Where will you sit At His Feet so distractions are minimized? Will you turn off or silence electronics or leave them behind?

Will you play gentle worship music or not? There is value in music or silence. Ask God what He desires for your time.

Prayerfully consider your bodily position for being at the feet of Jesus. (For this exercise, I recommend being comfortable.)

Bring your Bible and a notebook to write down what Jesus reveals to you.

PRACTICE

1. Once you are in the place and position for your time:
   - Invite the Holy Spirit to minister to however He desires.
   - Be still and quiet in His presence.
   - Open your heart to receive from the Lord. Listen to Him and receive all that He reveals, heals, speaks, imparts to you, or instructs you to do. Watch with the eyes of your heart for any visions He may want to show you.
   - Don't worry if you fall asleep. He gives you rest as a gift.

2. After your time At His Feet, take a moment to write down any impressions you had about what Jesus was saying or doing during your time together.
   - What is one thing you sense Jesus spoke to you?
   - How do you feel different after time with Him compared to before time At His Feet?
   - Thank God for what He has done during your time.

3. Resume your regular duties rested and refreshed by Jesus.

NOTES: _____

ADDITIONAL SCRIPTURES:

Matthew 11:28-30

Psalm 16:11

John 15:1-1

James 4:8

Psalm 27:4

Genesis 2:2

Hebrews 4:1-11

Romans 4:1-8

Unit Two – Key Questions
The Holy Spirit

Use this worksheet to test your grasp of the material and exercises of Unit Two.

How do we live our lives with the Holy Spirit?	

Why did God send the Holy Spirit?	Where is the Holy Spirit?

What are some things the Holy Spirit does for us?	How does the Holy Spirit change us?

What is New Covenant obedience?	How do we hear God's voice?

What is one thing you learned that you did not know before?	What questions do you still have about this subject?

UNIT TWO: GROUP EXERCISES

Group Training Exercise

ABIDE IN ME – JOHN 15

PURPOSE:

Listen to God speak to you through the Scriptures.

Hear the promptings of the Holy Spirit for your life today.

GROUP SIZE:

Any size group.

DO THIS WITH OTHER SCRIPTURE PORTIONS:

Psalm 1
Psalm 23
Exodus 15
Isaiah 54
1 Corinthians 13
Romans 8
Matthew 5

DESCRIPTION

When we honor and approach the Scriptures as the Living Word of God, the Holy Spirit is free to speak directly into our lives today so that we are strengthened to know God's will for our lives and do it.

The origins of divine reading (Lectio Divina) date back to Christian monks who meditated on the Word of God in devotion in order to receive divine inspiration rather than theological knowledge. This practice engages with the Word of God in a way that is personal, relevant, and applicable.

To practice this, the same passage of Scripture is read three separate times out loud while listeners listen for the following:

- **First Reading:** One word or short phrase that stands out to you.
- **Second Reading:** What you sense God is speaking to you through this passage.
- **Third Reading:** What you sense God is telling you to do.

SCRIPTURE PORTION: JOHN 15:1-11

I am the true vine, and my Father is the gardener. He cuts off every branch in me that bears no fruit, while every branch that does bear fruit he prunes so that it will be even more fruitful. You are already clean because of the word I have spoken to you. Remain in me, as I also remain in you. No branch can bear fruit by itself; it must remain in the vine. Neither can you bear fruit unless you remain in me. I am the vine; you are the branches. If you remain in me and I in you, you will bear much fruit; apart from me you can do nothing. If you do not remain in me, you are like a branch that is thrown away and withers; such branches are picked up, thrown into the fire and burned. If you remain in me and my words remain in you, ask whatever you wish, and it will be done for you. This is to my Father's glory, that you bear much fruit, showing yourselves to be my disciples. As the Father has loved me, so have I loved you. Now remain in my love. If you keep my commands, you will remain in my love, just as I have kept my Father's commands and remain in his love. I have told you this so that my joy may be in you and that your joy may be complete.

GROUP PRACTICE

1. Pray and invite the Holy Spirit to speak to your hearts. Allow a moment of stillness before the first reading.
   - Keep in mind that since this is devotional, not intellectual, there are no right or wrong responses.

2. Have one person read the Scripture Portion out loud and slowly while others listen for one word or short phrase that stands out.

   _____
   _____
   _____

3. Have one person read the Scripture Portion out loud and slowly while others listen for what they sense God is speaking to them through this passage.

   _____
   _____
   _____

4. Have one person read the Scripture Portion out loud and slowly while others listen for what they sense God is telling them to do.

   _____
   _____
   _____

5. Share with one another the insights you received from the Lord.
   - Keep in mind that since this is devotional, not intellectual, there are no right or wrong responses.

Category: Listening to God

ALL RIGHTS RESERVED © 2019 Wendy Bowen

UNIT THREE: COMMUNITY OF GOD

KEY SCRIPTURE VERSE FOR UNIT THREE
You also, like living stones, are being built into a spiritual house to be a holy priesthood, offering spiritual sacrifices acceptable to God through Jesus Christ. For in Scripture it says: "See, I lay a stone in Zion, a chosen and precious cornerstone, and the one who trusts in him will never be put to shame." - 1 Peter 2:5-6

CLASS 1: A HOLY KINGDOM
1 Reading, 1 Exercise, 1 Scripture List
By faith, we have become a holy people who are included in the New Covenant and partake of the life of God. We are a new generation chosen by God to be His treasured possession. We are a holy Kingdom.

CLASS 2: SET APART PEOPLE
1 Reading, 1 Scripture Worksheet
Through faith, we have been set apart from this world in order to submit ourselves to the ways of God who has given authority to the Church.

CLASS 3: FELLOWSHIP
1 Reading, 1 Scripture Worksheet
In Christ, believers have been united as ONE body with many members. We belong to one another and partner together to see the plans of God fulfilled in us.

CLASS 4: ONE ANOTHER
1 Scripture Reading, 1 Exercise
More than a Kingdom, a Nation, or a partnership, believers are brothers and sisters in the household of God. We are called to love one another, giving preference to one another over others.

KEY QUESTIONS

GROUP EXERCISES

CORNERSTONE – UNIT 3.1 READING

A Holy Kingdom*

Thousands of years ago, the one and only God who created heaven and earth redeemed a kingdom for Himself. His design was for them to be holy, meaning special to Him, and unique among all the nations as His people. Through this kingdom, His goodness and power could be revealed to the rest of the world.

The events we read about in the Old Testament Scriptures are a prophetic shadow that reveals God's greater work of redemption and points us to His Son, Jesus Christ. In other words, what we see in the Old Testament in the natural is what we have spiritually in the New Covenant. For example, in the Old Testament we see literal battles and wars in earthly territories whereas in the New Covenant our fight is not against flesh and blood but against spiritual forces of evil in heavenly places. (See Ephesians 6:12.)

In light of this, in one event, the Passover is the most poignant example of the whole story God is telling about His eternal redemption of mankind through Christ, our eternal Passover Lamb.

*1 Corinthians 5:7b - For Christ, **our Passover lamb**, has been sacrificed.*

*1 Peter 1:18-19 - For you know that it was not with perishable things such as silver or gold that you were redeemed from the empty way of life handed down to you from your ancestors, but with the precious blood of Christ, **a lamb without blemish or defect**.*

*John 1:29 - The next day John saw Jesus coming toward him and said, "Look, **the Lamb of God**, who takes away the sin of the world!*

Understanding the original Passover story gives us insight into the eternal story God is telling about how He redeemed us to be His Holy Kingdom. Jesus was crucified on the anniversary of Passover in a parallel of events over one thousand years later. A whole new people of God was born in a day. In spite of the fact that we are all over the earth, we who believe Jesus are a special people, bound together like one nation united under the same King with the same God.

Read in your Bible, from the Book of Exodus, Chapters 12 through 14. You will read in these chapters about God's miraculous deliverance of the Israelites from four hundred years of slavery in the land of Egypt.

To recap: On the tenth day of the month, every family was ordered to select an unblemished lamb from their flock and bring it into their home. Then, on the fourteenth day of the month, they were to slaughter that lamb at twilight, paint the blood of the lamb on the doorpost of their home, and eat the lamb with unleavened bread. They did all of this as God had commanded through Moses, and then God sent the destroyer to bring judgment on Egypt by killing all their first born. God *passed over* the doors which were marked with the blood of the lamb so that the destroyer did not and could not touch the faithful Israelites. No foreigner was allowed to participate in it unless they were circumcised because circumcision was the symbol of the Israelite's special relationship with God and had been ever since God's covenant with their ancestor Abraham. In the middle of the night, the Israelites began walking out of Egypt and away from their lives as slaves. Then, on the third day, God parted the waters of the Red Sea and the Israelites walked through on dry ground. Finally, the waters closed back up to separate them from their enemies forever. There were most likely about two million of them, including a mixed multitude of gentiles who came with them. Those who believed made it through the waters of the Red Sea unscathed and they all rejoiced.

This was the birth of their nation. The Jewish people still celebrate Passover every year to commemorate what God did for them. It is also noted frequently throughout the Scriptures as the most significant day in the Israelite's history as God's people to remind them of His love, redemption, and power.

> *Exodus 19:5b-6a: Out of all nations* **you will be my treasured possession.** *Although the whole earth is mine,* **you will be for me a kingdom of priests and a holy nation.**

Fast forward to the week of the Passover celebration in the last days of Jesus' life on earth. On the tenth day of the month, Jesus rode into Jerusalem presenting Himself as the unblemished Lamb who was about to be sacrificed. Then, on the fourteenth day of the month, He was arrested and sentenced to be crucified/slaughtered. While He was on the cross, judgment was passed on Him in our place. Every enemy of mankind was placed upon Him including every sin, curse, sickness, punishment, and every oppression of the devil. The destroyer was allowed to destroy Jesus on the cross. He shed His blood and died, and He descended into the eternal fiery inferno, the pit of hell. But then on the third day, God raised Him from the dead. At daybreak, He walked out of the tomb in an imperishable resurrection body to live forever. He was once and for all separated from His enemies. This was the birth of a whole new kind of people: a spiritual people, an eternal people who will never die. The stone of the tomb had been rolled away just like the waters of the Red Sea had been for the people of Israel. Jesus walked out of the grave and all of us who believe were included with Him. This is the event we remember every time we take communion to celebrate forever what Jesus did for us and remember how because of God's great love and by His great power, He delivered us from sin and death forever.

THE NEW COVENANT & REMEMBRANCE

Jesus was Jewish. He knew the Passover symbolized what God required of Him and He tried to explain it to His disciples several times before it happened. Then, on the night of Passover, the night that Jesus was betrayed and handed over to be crucified, He showed His disciples the way to remember and celebrate the New Covenant which would be established through His death and resurrection.

> *Luke 22:15-20: And he said to them, "***I have eagerly desired to eat this Passover with you before I suffer***... And* **he took bread, gave thanks and broke it, and gave it to them, saying, "This is my body given for you;** *do this in remembrance of me." In the same way, after the supper* **he took the cup, saying, "This cup is the new covenant in my blood, which is poured out for you.** *(See also Matthew 26:26-28; Mark 14:17-25; John 13:21-30.)*

A covenant is a legally binding agreement between two or more parties where one or more of the parties become obligated to fulfill certain stated conditions. A covenant is an agreement of highest value, sealed with blood to symbolize that any party who does not meet the expressed terms and obligations of the covenant will pay with their own blood, usually meaning death.

In Jesus' day, all of Israel was expectantly waiting for their Messiah to arrive to institute a New Covenant which was better than the covenant of the Law. In this New Covenant, they would each know God for themselves and God would forgive all of their sins forever. Moreover, the Messiah would keep them constantly in God's good graces, so that God would always delight to bless them as His people and they would have total victory over their enemies.

> *Jeremiah 31:31-34: "The days are coming," declares the LORD, "when I will make a* **new covenant** *with the people of Israel and with the people of Judah. It will not be like the covenant I made with their ancestors when I took them by the hand to lead them out of Egypt, because they broke my covenant, though I was a husband to them," declares the LORD. "***This is the covenant** *I will make with the people of Israel after that time," declares the LORD. "***I will put my law in their minds and write it on their hearts. I will be their God, and they will be my people.** *No longer will they teach their neighbor, or say to one another,*

> *'Know the LORD,' because **they will all know me**, from the least of them to the greatest,"* *declares the LORD. "For **I will forgive their wickedness and will remember their sins no more.**" (Quoted in Hebrews 10:16-18.)*
>
> *Jeremiah 32:40-41: I will make **an everlasting covenant** with them: I will **never stop doing good to them**, and I will inspire them to fear me, so that they will never turn away from me. **I will rejoice in doing them good** and will assuredly plant them in this land **with all my heart and soul**.*
>
> *Jeremiah 33:15-16: In those days and at that time I will make a **righteous Branch sprout from David's line**; he will do what is just and right in the land... This is the name by which it will be called: **The LORD Our Righteousness**.*

Jesus fulfilled these promises and established the New Covenant. He is the Righteous One born in the line of David who gives us right standing with God because of His righteousness. Through His sacrifice in our place, our sins are forgiven and because of this, we are perpetually positioned for God's favor. Moreover, through the Holy Spirit, God's Laws are written upon our hearts and we can each know God for ourselves.

Now, when believers are assembled together, we take communion to remember that Christ's body was a sacrifice for us and His blood was shed for the forgiveness of our sins. It is a cup of blessing, thanksgiving, and celebration of the New Covenant which Jesus Christ established for us! (See 1Corinthians 10:16.)

THE BLOOD OF THE LAMB

In the original Passover, the Law of God had not yet been given to the Israelites and so, God did not hold them responsible for upholding the standard of the Law to be counted as righteous. They were delivered by faith. The only thing that was relevant in God's sight was whether or not they had painted the blood of the Passover lamb on their door.

For us as followers of Jesus, because Jesus fulfilled the Law and set us free from it, we are not required to meet the demands of the Law in order to have right standing with God. We are redeemed by faith. Jesus did not negate the Law of God for us through His blood but rather, He fulfilled it on our behalf so that we can receive the benefits of God's forgiveness and the blessings merited only by those who have a clean record before God. (See Romans 3:25-26.) Now, the only thing that is relevant in God's sight is whether or not we believe in the sufficiency of the shed blood of Jesus, our Passover Lamb.

This said, God knows His standard for atonement and it is expressed through His Law. Under the Law, at the Temple of God, when people brought their prescribed blood sacrifices of bulls, sheep, goats, or birds, they brought the greatest sacrifice they could afford to bring. (See Leviticus 5:7, 14:21.) When an offering was brought to God, all the sins of the person bringing the offering were transferred onto their sacrificial animal. Then, the animal was presented to God to shed its blood and give its life in the place of the person who had sinned so that the person could continue to live and be blessed as if they had never sinned.

> *Hebrews 9:22: In fact, the law requires that nearly everything be cleansed with blood, and **without the shedding of blood there is no forgiveness**.*
>
> *Leviticus 17:11: For **the life of a creature is in the blood**, and I have given it to you to make atonement for yourselves on the altar; **it is the blood that makes atonement for one's life**.*

Accordingly, in order for God's terms of payment for the forgiveness of every sin of every person since Adam to be satisfied, a sacrifice of infinite worth was required. God owns all of creation and could afford to give a priceless gift. He gave the best offering He could ever give by giving His one and only Son.

> *John 3:16: For **God so loved the world that he gave his one and only Son**, that whoever believes in him shall not perish but have eternal life.*

One drop of the blood of Jesus is more valuable in God's sight than millions of bulls, sheep, goats, and birds. Because of this, we can be fully assured that Jesus' sacrifice is completely sufficient to pay for all of our sins and errors and redeem us from sin and death forever.

ONE NEW MAN – A CHOSEN GENERATION

In the original Passover, Israel walked out of Egypt and was birthed as a nation out of another nation. (See Deuteronomy 4:34-35.) Since Israel's birth as a nation, there have been two kinds of nations on the earth in God's sight: Israel and all the other nations or, you could say, Jews and non-Jews. Anyone from any other nation who wanted to enter into relationship with the Most High God was required to be circumcised and convert to Judaism. God made no other way to be in relationship with Him. (Consider Ephesians 2:11-12.)

At the resurrection, Jesus walked out of the tomb and a whole new creation of humanity was birthed out of every nation, tribe, and tongue.

> *Ephesians 2:15b-19:* **His purpose was to create in himself <u>one new humanity</u>** *out of the two, [Jews & Gentiles] thus making peace, and* **in one body** *to reconcile both of them to God through the cross, by which he put to death their hostility... For through him we both have access to the Father by one Spirit. Consequently,* **you are no longer foreigners and strangers, but fellow <u>citizens with God's people</u> and also <u>members of his household</u>**,

Through the resurrection of Jesus, God created a new generation of humanity, a new species, out of an existing generation of humanity. The first generation includes all the natural descendants of Adam. The second generation includes everyone who believes that Jesus is Lord. We are a chosen generation and a new kind of people.

> *1Peter 2:9 NKJV: But you [are] a* **chosen generation, a royal priesthood, a holy nation, His own special people**, *that you may proclaim the praises of Him who called you out of darkness into His marvelous light;*

Through faith, we are transformed from the old type of humanity to the new type of humanity and we have the right to become sons and daughters of God. He pours the Holy Spirit out into our hearts so that by the Holy Spirit we cry out to Him as our Father.

> *Rom 8:15: The* **Spirit you received does not make you slaves**, *so that you live in fear again; rather, the* **Spirit you received brought about your adoption to sonship. And by him we cry, "Abba, Father."** *(See also Galatians 4:6.)*

This means that there are now only two kinds of people on the earth. First Adams and Second Adams. Anyone from the first generation of man who wants to be included in God's eternal covenant has to confess with their mouth that Jesus is Lord and believe in their heart that God raised Him from the dead. God has made no other way to be saved.

The truth is that it is God's desire for everyone to be saved through Christ. But until that day, we as fellow believers are a unique and peculiar people who share a bond that is eternally more significant than any other human bond, loyalty, ethnicity, or nationality. We are a new people.

INCLUSION IN THE NEW PEOPLE – BAPTISM

In the first Passover, the visible outward sign of inclusion in God's covenant promises to Abraham was circumcision. (See Genesis 17:10.) No Israelite or foreigner was allowed to participate in the Passover unless they were circumcised into the covenant. Then, when the Israelites literally walked through the Red Sea, they were figuratively baptized and emerged as the nation of Israel. (See 1Corinthians 10:1-2.)

But now, when we place our faith in Jesus, God gives us a *spiritual circumcision*. Our Adamic nature is rolled away as the Holy Spirit comes into our hearts. (See Romans 2:29; Ezekiel 36:26; Ephesians 1:13; 1 John 4:13-15.) Then, when we are baptized in water, we outwardly display the change in our hearts. As we are literally submerged into the waters of baptism, we figuratively include ourselves in the death of Jesus, and put to death the sinful nature we inherited from Adam. Coming up out of the waters of baptism signifies our participation in Jesus' resurrection. Our old life is rolled away and we emerge as a new creation.

> *Colossians 2:11-12:* **In him you were also circumcised with a circumcision not performed by human hands. Your whole self ruled by the flesh was put off when you were circumcised by Christ**, *having been buried with him in baptism, in which you were also raised with him through your faith in the working of God, who raised him from the dead.*

> *Romans 6:3-4: Or don't you know that all of us who were* **baptized into Christ Jesus were baptized into his death**? *We were therefore* **buried with him through baptism into death** *in order that, just as Christ was raised from the dead through the glory of the Father,* **we too may live a new life**.

Full submersion is the way that Christ's first followers understood the requirements and procedure for baptism. In fact, it is rooted in a practice ordained in God's Law for ritual cleansing, called a *mikveh* in Hebrew. Ritual cleansing like this was required of priests before they could serve God and was required of common people in order to remain clean before God.

When John the Baptist began his ministry in the Jordan River area, he was known as John the Immerser. John baptized people by submerging them in water as a demonstration that they had repented of their sins. (See Luke 3:3; Acts 13:24-25, 19:3-4.) Through John's baptism, repentant people were ceremonially cleansed as they awaited the arrival of the Messiah. But as soon as Jesus arrived, John immediately took second place to Jesus and pointed people exclusively to Him. (See John 3:26-30.)

Later, when Jesus commanded His disciples to baptize people from all nations, He was not referring to John's baptism. Through baptism in Jesus' name, we descend into a watery grave and rise again as a new creation. This is something that John's baptism did not include. In Jesus' baptism, we are repentant, cleansed of sin, and transformed into a new creation as the Holy Spirit makes His home in us. In fact, when John the Baptist prophesied of Jesus, he knew that Jesus' baptism would be more substantial and significant than his ritual washings. Jesus confirmed this before He ascended to heaven.

> *Luke 3:16-17: John answered them all, "***I baptize you with water***. But one who is more powerful than I will come, the straps of whose sandals I am not worthy to untie.* **He will baptize you with the Holy Spirit and fire**. *His winnowing fork is in his hand to clear his threshing floor and to gather the wheat into his barn, but he will burn up the chaff with unquenchable fire."*

> *Luke 24:49: I am going to send you what my Father has promised; but stay in the city until you have been* **clothed with power from on high**.

> *Acts 1:5: For* **John baptized with water**, *but in a few days* **you will be baptized with the Holy Spirit**.

For Christ's first followers in Jerusalem, the Holy Spirit had not yet been poured out. They eagerly awaited this "baptism" from heaven. For us today, since the Holy Spirit has already been poured out from heaven, we receive the Holy Spirit when we believe Jesus. There is only one baptism in Christ and it endues us with power from on high, as Jesus promised. (See Ephesians 4:5.) This said, the Holy Spirit functions in different ways to give us what we need to fulfill God's purposes. We will cover this more in a later chapter.

All of this is to say that we are included in God's New Covenant by grace through faith. Baptism reveals the change which has taken place in our hearts and our new commitment to God. The Holy Spirit marks us for ultimate redemption and gives us power for life until Jesus returns.

Heavenly Kingdom

Before Jesus ascended to heaven, His disciples expected Him to fulfill the Scriptures about the Messiah of Israel who will come with vengeance to destroy all of Israel's enemies and rule over all nations for eternity. They thought Jesus was going to establish His Kingdom in the ordinary way of earthly wars and kingdoms.

> *Acts 1:6-8: Then they gathered around him and asked him,* **"Lord, are you at this time going to restore the kingdom to Israel?"** *He said to them: "It is not for you to know the times or dates the Father has set by his own authority. But you will receive power when the Holy Spirit comes on you; and you will be my witnesses in Jerusalem, and in all Judea and Samaria, and to the ends of the earth."*

They were most likely expecting Jesus to lead them in political or military overthrow of their Roman oppressors to take dominion in the earth. This was a reasonable expectation on their part because of Scriptures pertaining to the rule of God's Messiah such as this one:

> *Daniel 7:21-22, 27: As I watched, this horn was waging war against the holy people and defeating them,* **until the Ancient of Days came and pronounced judgment in favor of the holy people of the Most High***, and the time came when* **they possessed the kingdom***. ...* **Then the sovereignty, power and greatness of all the kingdoms under heaven will be handed over to the holy people of the Most High***. His kingdom will be an everlasting kingdom, and* **all rulers will worship and obey him***.*

Assuredly, the day Christ's followers anticipated will come. However, until that day, Jesus' Kingdom is not of this world. Jesus establishes the Kingdom of God in the hearts of those who believe Him until He returns to reign on earth for eternity. Therefore, His purpose for us today is not political rebellion against the powers or governments of this world or taking dominion in the earth. God's priority is the salvation of souls. Therefore, we no longer regard it from an earthly point of view but from a heavenly one.

> *Luke 17:20-21: Once, on being asked by the Pharisees when the kingdom of God would come, Jesus replied,* **'The coming of the kingdom of God is not something that can be observed***, nor will people say, 'Here it is,' or 'There it is,' because the* **kingdom of God is in your midst [within you.]***"*

> *John 18:36-3: Jesus said,* **"My kingdom is not of this world.** *If it were, my servants would fight to prevent my arrest by the Jewish leaders. But now my kingdom is from another place." "You are a king, then!" said Pilate. Jesus answered,* **"You say that I am a king. In fact, the reason I was born and came into the world is to testify to the truth.** *Everyone on the side of truth listens to me."*

> *Revelation 1:5b-6: To him who loves us and has freed us from our sins by his blood, and has* **made us to be a kingdom and priests to serve his God and Father**--*to him be glory and power for ever and ever! Amen.*

Again, I say: Thousands of years ago, the one and only God who created heaven and earth redeemed a Kingdom for Himself. His design was for us to be holy, meaning special to Him, and unique among all the nations as His people. Through His Kingdom, God's goodness and power could be revealed to the rest of the world.

Jesus is our King. Our Kingdom is not of this world – it is holy. To be holy means to be set apart. Holy things are sacred, precious, and should be handled with special care unlike the way that common things are managed. In fact, one of the primary duties of the Old Covenant priests of God was to teach the people to distinguish between the holy and the common. (See Leviticus 10:10.) The way we make our decisions and live our lives reveals if we love the world and its ways or if we love God and His ways. (See 1John 2:15-17.) Our King's life does not conform to the pattern of this world and as we follow Him, our lives will reflect a holiness that is so peculiar that it becomes a sign and a wonder which brings God great glory.

*Revelation 12:10-11: Then I heard a loud voice in heaven say: "Now have come the **salvation and the power and the kingdom of our God**, and the authority of his Messiah. For the accuser of our brothers and sisters, who accuses them before our God day and night, has been hurled down. **They triumphed over him by the blood of the Lamb** and by the word of their testimony; they did not love their lives so much as to shrink from death.*

Basic Training Exercise

COMMUNION

Luke 22:15-20 NIV - And he said to them, "I have eagerly desired to eat this Passover with you before I suffer... And he took bread, gave thanks and broke it, and gave it to them, saying, "This is my body given for you; do this in remembrance of me." In the same way, after the supper he took the cup, saying, "This cup is the new covenant in my blood, which is poured out for you."

DESCRIPTION

On the night of the first Passover, God's people painted the blood of the lamb on the doorposts of their homes as an act of faith by which God would protect them from the destroyer. Even today when Passover is celebrated, it is done in remembrance of this great deliverance by the hand of God.

Jesus Christ is our eternal Passover Lamb. His blood was shed for the forgiveness of our sins so that we can be protected from the destruction of sin and the evil one. His body was broken so that we can freely enter into the presence of God to worship. When we take communion, we remember this great deliverance.

The first disciples of Christ took communion (or "broke bread") regularly. Consecrated bread and wine were made readily available for believers to serve themselves or take communion together. As a holy nation and a royal priesthood, (1 Peter 2:9) every believer is a priest of God and able to administer the body and blood of Christ with due reverence. This said, communion and the benefits of Christ's sacrifice are only available to those who believe that Jesus is Lord and that God raised Him from the dead. This means that if you do not yet believe in Jesus Christ as your Lord and Savior, you should abstain from communion or better yet, believe Jesus and partake.

Practicing the partaking of Communion is about commemorating Christ's sacrifice, renewing our faith in what He has done for us, and to looking forward to His return.

Basic TRAINING
SPIRITUAL EXERCISES

PURPOSE:

To honor and remember the sacrifice of Jesus.

To examine our faith in what Jesus did for us.

To rejoice in the forgiveness of our sins and our New Covenant access to God.

SPIRITUAL FRUIT:

Remembrance of Jesus.

Indwelling life of God.

Renewed faith.

Fresh start of forgiveness.

PRACTICE

1. Prepare the bread and wine.
   - Acquire bread and wine or juice to be consecrated to God for the purpose of Communion.
   - Consecrate the bread and wine to the Lord by praying over them something like, "I consecrate this bread and wine to the Lord."
   - Do not use this bread or wine for casual snacking.

2. Perceive the body and blood of Jesus.
   - Jesus said of the bread and wine, "this *is* my body" and, "this *is* my blood" even when He still had a natural body.
   - Read the Additional Scriptures about what the body and blood of Jesus have done for us.
   - Believe that these Scriptures apply to the body and blood you are about to partake of.

3. Examine yourself and your faith.
   - Do you believe that Jesus Christ shed His blood for the forgiveness of your sins?
   - Do you believe that you are totally forgiven?
   - Do you believe that you can receive all of the benefits of Christ body and blood through faith in Jesus?
   - Do you regard the communion bread and wine/juice as holy and consecrated to God?

4. Remember the Lord's death and proclaim His return.
   - Praise God that because of Jesus's sacrifice, you are protected from the destroyer until Jesus returns.

5. Partake.
   - As you eat the body and drink the blood of Jesus, be consciously strengthened with the life and power of God in your inmost being. The indestructible life of Christ and the same power that raised Christ from the dead is in you.

6. Praise God and rejoice in His salvation!

NOTES: _____

ADDITIONAL SCRIPTURES:

1 Corinthians 11:23-32

John 6:53-57

Luke 22:5-20

John 1:29

Hebrews 10:10

Colossians 1:22

Ephesians 1:7

Romans 5:9

1 John 1:7

Revelation 12:11

1 Corinthians 5:7

1 Peter 1:18-19

Passover Story:
Exodus 12-15

Category: Basics

Communion
Scripture List*

Jesus said to them, "Very truly I tell you, unless you eat the flesh of the Son of Man and drink his blood, you have no life in you. Whoever eats my flesh and drinks my blood has eternal life, and I will raise them up at the last day. For my flesh is real food and my blood is real drink. Whoever eats my flesh and drinks my blood remains in me, and I in them. Just as the living Father sent me and I live because of the Father, so the one who feeds on me will live because of me. – John 6:53-57

THE BODY OF CHRIST

We have been made holy through the sacrifice of the body of Jesus Christ once for all. Hebrews 10:10

But now he has reconciled you by Christ's physical body through death to present you holy in his sight, without blemish and free from accusation. – Colossians 1:2

"He himself bore our sins" in his body on the cross, so that we might die to sins and live for righteousness; "by his wounds you have been healed." – 1Peter 2:24

THE BLOOD OF JESUS

In him we have redemption through his blood, the forgiveness of sins, in accordance with the riches of God's grace. – Ephesians 1:7

Since we have now been justified by his blood, how much more shall we be saved from God's wrath through him! – Romans 5:9

Therefore, brothers and sisters, since we have confidence to enter the Most Holy Place by the blood of Jesus. – Hebrews 10:19

And so Jesus also suffered outside the city gate to make the people holy through his own blood. – Hebrews 13:12

How much more, then, will the blood of Christ, who through the eternal Spirit offered himself unblemished to God, cleanse our consciences from acts that lead to death, so that we may serve the living God! – Hebrews 9:14

But if we walk in the light, as he is in the light, we have fellowship with one another, and the blood of Jesus, his Son, purifies us from all sin. – 1John 1:7

And they sang a new song, saying: "You are worthy to take the scroll and to open its seals, because you were slain, and with your blood you purchased for God persons from every tribe and language and people and nation. – Revelation 5:9

They triumphed over him by the blood of the Lamb and by the word of their testimony; they did not love their lives so much as to shrink from death. – Revelation 12:11

A Called Out People

When God called the people of Israel out of Egypt, He set them apart from all other nations. Now, through our eternal Passover in Christ, God calls us out of every nation, tribe, and tongue to be His special people.

> *Revelation 5:9-10: And they sang a new song, saying: "You are worthy to take the scroll and to open its seals, because you were slain, and* **with your blood you purchased for God persons from every tribe and language and people and nation**. *You have made them to be* **a kingdom and priests to serve our God**, *and they will reign on the earth."*

> *Ephesians 3:10-11:* **His intent was that now, through the church, the manifold wisdom of God should be made known to the rulers and authorities in the heavenly realms**, *according to his eternal purpose that he accomplished in Christ Jesus our Lord.*

The word translated as "church" in the New Testament is the Greek word *ekklesia* which literally means "a called out people." God has called us out of this world to be His. We are a nation of people who have pledged our eternal allegiance to the same King – Jesus.

In the days of Jesus, Greek was the predominant language in the world. The word ekklesia was commonly used to describe the assembly of citizens in any given Greek city. In those days, citizenship was a special class of people with rights above those of non-citizens and slaves who were the property of their masters. Ekklesia was the word for the governmental assembly of the city, including officers who had authority over judicial matters for city politics and civil issues or disputes. For example, in Acts 19, the word ekklesia is used to describe the assembly in Ephesus of city leaders and citizens who wanted to put the Apostle Paul on trial for proclaiming Jesus and interfering with their idol making businesses.

For the first followers of Jesus, the concept of being a called out people of God with their own rights of governance was nothing new. Throughout the Old Testament, the word *qahal* is used to describe the whole assembly of the people of Israel who worshipped the same God, were governed by the same laws, and served the same king. (In today's Hebrew, congregations are referred to as *kehilla*, from this same word.) God's intent was that through the people of Israel following His laws, His righteousness and power would be displayed through their wisdom and justice. (See Deuteronomy 4:5-8.) Even when their land and lives were ruled or dominated by other nations, they sought diligently to maintain their right to govern themselves according to God's laws of worship and justice.

Now, when Jesus calls us to discipleship, He is calling us out of the world to belong to Him, to learn and live by His ways, and to follow Him with total loyalty to Him and His Kingdom. We have become the *ekklesia* of God, the New Covenant *qahal* of God, and citizens of heaven. (See Philippians 3:20.) We bow to no other king but Jesus. We are an autonomously governed body of people who have been delegated authority by our King to rule over judicial matters and disputes for those within His Body. We obey the rules of whatever land we live in as long as they do not conflict with our obedience to our King Jesus. We do not try to help the people of this world live better lives or be better people. We call them out of the kingdom of this world to be a part of the Kingdom of God. (Consider Acts 4:24-30.) Our goal is not to "start a church," "attend church" every weekend, or raise money for "church buildings." Jesus builds His church upon the fact that He is King.

> *Matthew 16:16-19: Simon Peter answered, "**You are the Messiah [King], the Son of the living God**." Jesus replied, "Blessed are you, Simon son of Jonah, for this was not revealed to you by flesh and blood, but by my Father in heaven. And I tell you that you are Peter, and **on this rock I will build my church [ekklesia]**, and the gates of Hades will not overcome it. **I will give you the keys of the kingdom of heaven; whatever you bind on earth will be bound in heaven, and whatever you loose on earth will be loosed in heaven**."*

The Church is built by Jesus. The Church is built upon the rock solid truth that Jesus is King – the Messiah who God promised for the redemption of mankind and who rules the earth for all eternity. Jesus died on a cross, descended into Hades [Hell] and was raised again to eternal life and freedom. The gates of Hell **did not** prevail against Him and they will not prevail against God's ekklesia. Hallelujah!

In His resurrection, Jesus attained the keys to the Kingdom of heaven. The gates of heaven had been locked shut due to man's sinfulness and the key to the lock was perfect righteousness. Jesus unlocked heaven for us through His righteousness according to God's Law so that we gain access to God through faith in Him. Hallelujah! Yet, Jesus did not keep the keys to Himself. In the passage above, He explicitly told His disciples ahead of time that He would give the keys to the Kingdom of Heaven to them, including authority to bind and to loose.

BINDING AND LOOSING

Binding and loosing was not a new concept for the first followers of Jesus and their understanding of being the ekklesia or called out people of God. Through the Old Covenant, it was the priests, scribes, religious leaders, and experts in God's Law who held the keys to the Kingdom of Heaven because they had the God-given right to determine what was allowed and what was forbidden.

Binding and loosing are legal terms for the establishment of that which is forbidden and that which is permitted. To *bind* is to impose a requirement and render it binding, meaning the people are bound to adhere to the requirement of face consequences. To loose is to allow/permit behaviors and render the people loosed from legal consequence and relieved from obligation.

God's intent and aim was always access to Him through righteousness so that His people could know Him and be His Kingdom. Unfortunately, the religious authorities enforced so many of their own binding regulations that they made it impossible for anyone to enter the Kingdom of God, including themselves. (See Matthew 23:13.) But now, we the Church have been given the keys to the Kingdom of Heaven through Christ-given authority to bind and to loose.

An example of this was demonstrated when the early apostles, elders, and disciples gathered together at the Jerusalem Council. The hot topic of theological debate in that day was whether or not a Gentile follower of Jesus should be required to be circumcised as evidence of their inclusion in God's people. To require circumcision would be to bind people in obligation to be circumcised, to not require circumcision would loose people from the obligation.

Significantly, the issues addressed at the Jerusalem Council all pertain to inclusion or expulsion from God's people. Circumcision was the sign of inclusion in God's Covenant since the days of Abraham and is included in the Law of Moses. However, under the New Covenant, to require obedience to one Law is equal to necessitating compliance with the entirety of the Law. (See James 2:10.) Any requirement other than faith in Jesus Christ is not the New Covenant which was sealed with the blood of Christ. We have been loosed from the legal obligation to obey the Law of Moses and all things are permitted for us. (See 1Corinthians 6:12, 10:23.) Righteousness and access to God is attained by grace through faith in Jesus Christ as a free gift not because of what we do or do not do. (See Ephesians 2:8.)

This said, the Law of God is good and explicitly details God's standard of purity in the event that there is any confusion about what is pleasing to Him. (See 1 Timothy 1:9-11; Romans 7:12.) Therefore, at the Jerusalem Council the apostles and elders agreed that in order to reveal God's holiness to those who do not yet believe that Jesus is Lord, it was important to bind believers under obligation to abstain from eating food offered to idols, from eating blood, and from sexual immorality. (For God's definition of sexual immorality, see Leviticus, Chapter 18.) Because these things were strictly forbidden in the Law of Moses and punishable by death, any Jew would find it difficult to accept the Gospel message of Jesus from someone doing these things while claiming to follow the Jewish Messiah and worship the God of Israel.

This means that living by the New Covenant standard of faith does not contradict the Old Covenant standard but rather gives us supernatural power to uphold the Law which is written upon our hearts by doing what is pleasing to God. (See Romans 3:31.) This is a demonstration that followers of Jesus are truly called out from this world and its ways. Proclaiming the Gospel with our mouths is easy, but it is how we conduct our lives as God's holy people that tells the watching world about the God we serve.

At the Jerusalem Council, the apostles and elders established these regulations, not to require obedience to the Old Covenant in any way but, to keep believers in the New Covenant aligned with God's will for their lives so that everyone who believes can receive all that has been promised through faith in Christ, both in this age and in the age to come. Unlike the religious leaders of the old system, the apostles and elders did not make it difficult for believers to enter into the Kingdom of Heaven. Praise God!

As a quick side note, at one point in his travels Paul had Timothy circumcised, which would seem to be a contradiction of the decision of the Jerusalem Council. Timothy's mother was Jewish which qualified him as an Israelite (Jewishness passes through the mother because paternity was impossible to prove in those days) but his father was Gentile, which was why he had not been circumcised previously. In order to not cause a big fuss among the unbelieving Jews and new converts to Christianity in the cities on their itinerary, Paul exercised willing deference so that Jesus Christ could be the primary focus of conversation, not circumcision. However, Paul utterly refused to force Titus, who had been born 100% Gentile, to be circumcised in order to be accepted into the faith. (See Acts 16:1-3; Galatians 2:3; Book of Titus.)

Conflict Resolution

Jesus also taught His disciples about the binding and loosing authority of the ekklesia in the context of conflict resolution. This included expulsion or admittance to the Church (forbidding or allowing) and addressing sin within the called out people of God.

> Matthew 18:15-18: **If your brother or sister sins, go and point out their fault, just between the two of you.** If they listen to you, you have won them over. But if they will not listen, **take one or two others along**, so that 'every matter may be established by the testimony of two or three witnesses. **If they still refuse to listen, tell it to the church [ekkelsia];** and if they refuse to listen even to the church [ekklesia], treat them as you would a pagan or a tax collector. Truly I tell you, **whatever you bind on earth will be bound in heaven, and whatever you loose on earth will be loosed in heaven**.

According to this teaching, sin in the community and conflicts between believers should respectfully escalate step-by-step. First, the offended parties meet privately to address the situation. Next, one or two other believers are included as witnesses. If the person still will not listen, the matter is brought to the authority of the church/ekklesia for a verdict. Finally, if the offender will not heed the decision of church leadership, they are to be expelled from the ekklesia and treated like an unbeliever and traitor.

The church at Corinth experienced this when a believer was caught continually having sexual relations with his father's wife. He was expelled from the church and turned over to Satan for the destruction of his flesh. (See 1 Corinthians 5:1-5, 9-13.) But let us consider how we treat unbelievers and enemies of God. We proclaim the Gospel of Jesus Christ and salvation by grace through faith for all sinners who repent. Therefore, when the man in Corinth was truly repentant for his sin, the Corinthian church reinstated, welcomed, and comforted him so that he would not be overly discouraged or eternally damned. (See 2 Corinthians 2:5-11.)

It is not a coincidence that in this same passage where Jesus taught about binding and loosing, or admittance and expulsion due to sin, He explained that offenses between believers are minor by comparison to the way that all of us have sinned against God. (See Matthew 18:21-35.) If the financial figures in the Parable of the Unforgiving Servant were converted to modern day equivalents, God paid our debt of 10,000 talents (multi-billion dollar debt.) Conflicts between believers amount to 100 denarii (several thousand dollars.) Releasing someone who hurts or offends us from such a small amount is a disproportionately low expectation if we truly understand what Jesus has done for us. Jesus could have come to avenge all of our wrongs against God but instead He came to give His life so that we could be forgiven and live free. In fact, this is the ministry we have been called to as God's called out ones – the ministry of reconciliation. God's desire is to reconcile people to Himself by not holding their sins against them through their faith in the blood of Jesus. (See 2 Corinthians 5:18-21.) As God's called out people and as governed by the Holy Spirit, God has given us the keys to the Kingdom of Heaven including authority in the earth to forgive sins.

> *John 20:22-23: And with that he breathed on them and said, "Receive the Holy Spirit. **If you forgive anyone's sins, their sins are forgiven; if you do not forgive them, they are not forgiven.***

When Jesus was on the cross being crucified, He pleaded, "Father, forgive them for they know not what they do." (See Luke 23:34.) Similarly, Stephen said almost the same thing when unbelievers were stoning him for telling them Jesus is the Messiah. (See Acts 7:60.) The Apostle Paul also extended mercy to everyone who abandoned him when he met with trials and intense persecution. (See 2 Timothy 4:16.)

Moreover, Paul rebuked believers sharply for not being able to peaceably resolve disputes between themselves and even more so for taking their disputes to the court system of this world. He emphasized that it is more important for us to learn to forgive one another, allow ourselves to be wronged, and live out the teachings of Jesus to turn the other cheek, go the extra mile, and give our cloak to the one who steals our tunic. (See 1 Corinthians 6:1-11; Matthew 5:39-41.)

However, when it came to false teachers who opposed the work of God with destructive heresies which caused confusion and dissention in the Church, Paul had no mercy. He named them by name and by the authority given to him by God for the ekklesia, expelled them from the people of God, turning them over to Satan so that they could learn not to blaspheme. (See 1 Timothy 1:20; 2Timothy 2:17-19, 4:14-15.)

Appointing Leaders in the Ekklesia

Jesus builds His Church on the truth that He is King. Jesus also appoints the leaders of His Church in order for them to carry out His commands in the earth and execute justice among His people.

The first 120 followers of Jesus knew the significance of God's sovereign selection for positions of leadership. Even without the Holy Spirit which had not been poured out yet, they knew that the decision was not theirs to make and so thy cast lots to hear from God. (See Acts 1:12-26.) Significantly, they would have known from the Hebrews Scriptures how the prophet Samuel had been instructed by God to appoint only the leaders whom God selected due to the fact that God looks at the heart of a person and not the outward appearances or apparent qualifications. (See 1 Samuel 9:15-17, 16:3,7,12.)

A little while later in the Church's earliest history as the Church grew in Jerusalem, arguments broke out between believers and disharmony set in due to inequitable distribution of food. The apostles knew that it would not be right for them to allow this issue to divert their focus from the Word of God and prayer and so they appointed Deacons. (See Acts 6:3-7.) The word for *deacon* is the same word used for a *waiter* and, practically speaking, they served the needs of God's people. Deacons were nominated by the people based on their exemplary lives of service to God. As the Gospel spread, the position of Deacon became a common function in Church life and the Apostle Paul gave various guidelines for ensuring the genuineness of any nominee's faith, lifestyle, and service. (See 1 Timothy 3:8-13; Titus 1:5-9.)

As churches were formed and became established in various cities, the apostles selected and appointed *elders* in each church. (See Acts 14:21-23.) After selecting the elders to be appointed, the apostles prayed and laid hands on the elders in order to share their governing authority over God's people with them for their city. Elders assisted the apostles by presiding over the Church in their local area, with particular care for financial and theological matters and protecting the local flock from false teachers. (See Acts 20:17-28.) The Apostle Paul also gave guidelines for the character qualities required for those serving in the function of elder. (See 1 Timothy 3:1-7, 5:17-25; Titus 1:5-9.)

All of this was in accordance with the model of the Old Testament since the days of Moses. At the advice of his father-in-law, Moses selected men of integrity who feared the Lord and hated a bribe to share the burden of governing the people and judging the local and/or smaller cases in matters of justice. Later, seventy of these men were appointed by God as the elders of Israel when God shared with the elders the same spirit that was on Moses so that they could govern and judge according to God's ways. (See Exodus 18:13-26; Numbers 11:10-29.)

In addition to deacons and elders, the Holy Spirit also revealed to listening believers the foreordained plans of God for individuals within their midst. As this happened, these people were set apart so that God could fulfill His purposes through them for His Church and His Kingdom.

> *Acts 13:2-3: While they were worshiping the Lord and fasting,* **the Holy Spirit said, "Set apart for me Barnabas and Saul for the work to which I have called them."** *So after they had fasted and prayed,* **they placed their hands on them and sent them off**.

It is noteworthy that the God's people did not determine God's call upon anyone's life but, rather, recognized and confirmed God's pre-existing purpose. Examples of this pattern include David, who was anointed to be the King of Israel many years before he was appointed King, (See 1 Samuel 16:13; 2 Samuel 2:11, 5:1-4;) Jeremiah, who was called by God as a prophet before forming Jeremiah was formed in his mother's womb, (Jeremiah 1:5;) and Paul, who was chosen as an apostle of God before the foundation of the earth, anointed as an apostle when he first came to faith in Jesus Christ, and appointed as an apostle when the Church at Antioch sent him on his first missionary journey. (See Galatians 1:15; Acts 9:15.) Once God's purpose was revealed by the Holy Spirit, believers fasted and prayed, laid hands on God's chosen ones and sent them on their way.

Laying on of Hands

The laying on of hands is another practice which is prevalent throughout the Scriptures as a method of transferring blessing, imparting spiritual gifts, and appointing the leaders of God's people. In the Old Testament, Jacob laid hands on the heads of Joseph's sons Ephraim and Manasseh to adopt them as his own children and to bless them, and then he prophesied about their lives and their descendants. (See Genesis 48:1-22.) Later, Moses laid his hands on Joshua to impart, or transfer, his anointing of wisdom for leading the people of Israel so that Joshua became his successor. (See Numbers 27:12-23; Deuteronomy 34:9.) When the tribe of Levi was selected by God for the work of ministering to Him and to the Tabernacle, all of Israel gathered together and laid hands on the Levites in order to demonstrate that the Levites served God on their behalf. (See Numbers 8:5-15.) When the High Priest blessed the people of Israel, he raised his hands with his palms towards the people to symbolize that he was laying his hands on all of them in order to bless them. (See Leviticus 9:22; Numbers 6:22-27.)

Now, in the New Covenant, the laying on of hands continues and is used to consecrate believers with Christ's perfect righteousness, to fill one another with the Holy Spirit, to impart spiritual gifts, to heal the sick, and to set believers apart for God's special tasks.

> *Acts 9:12, 17:* In a vision he has seen a man named Ananias come and **place his hands on him to restore his sight."** ... Then Ananias went to the house and entered it. **Placing his hands on Saul**, he said, "Brother Saul, the Lord--Jesus, who appeared to you on the road as you were coming here--has sent me **so that you may see again and be filled with the Holy Spirit.**"

> *Acts 19:6:* **When Paul placed his hands on them, the Holy Spirit came on them, and they spoke in tongues and prophesied.** *(See also Acts 8:17.)*

> *1Timothy 4:14:* Do not neglect your gift, which was **given you through prophecy when the body of elders laid their hands on you.** *(See also 2 Timothy 1:6.)*

> *Mark 16:17-18:* And these signs will accompany those who believe: In my name they will drive out demons; they will speak in new tongues; they will pick up snakes with their hands; and when they drink deadly poison, it will not hurt them at all; **they will place their hands on sick people, and they will get well.**

> *Acts 28:8:* His father was sick in bed, suffering from fever and dysentery. Paul went in to see him and, after prayer, **placed his hands on him and healed him.**

Through the laying on of hands as prompted by the Holy Spirit, God's chosen ones were appointed to their God-given missions, callings, and tasks. Some people worked within the Church, some were sent out by the Church, and as everyone did their part, God's purpose was fulfilled in the earth. This said, the Apostle Paul warned not to be hasty in laying hands on people to appoint them to positions of authority within the Church. If their lives are full of sin and they are given authority to govern others through the laying on of hands, then those who laid hands share some level of responsibility for the damage their sin causes within the Body. (See 1 Timothy 5:22.)

Being appointed by to a position of leadership within the Church is a serious responsibility of eternal weight. We cannot take it lightly or treat it like a position of leadership in this world. For example, before the crucifixion, Jesus' disciples were constantly competing to hold the top place of power and authority in His ministry. But after Jesus' resurrection, none of them ever competed for greatness again, and each one of them went on to serve God with all they had and eventually give their lives in the cause of spreading the word that Jesus is King.

> *Matthew 20:25-28:* Jesus called them together and said, "You know that the rulers of the Gentiles lord it over them, and their high officials exercise authority over them. **Not so with you.** Instead, **whoever wants to become great among you must be your servant, and whoever wants to be first must be your slave**-- just as the Son of Man did not come to be served, but to serve, and to give his life as a ransom for many." *(See also Matthew 23:8-11; Mark 10:35-45; Luke 9:46-48; James 3:16-17.)*

The Christian life is not a democracy, it is a monarchy. Jesus is King. May we be eager to serve our King and serve others as He leads us. If we are in leadership, may we walk in reverence and submission to God in all of our thoughts, words, and actions. May the Church come into fullness as the called out people of God in righteousness, mercy, and speaking the truth in love so that the world will see that Jesus is King.

CONFLICT RESOLUTION
Scripture Reading & Worksheet

www.manifestinternational.com

Read each of the following passages and then use the chart below for study and reflection.
- Matthew 18:15-19
- Matthew 5:21-26
- James 4:1-12
- Luke 12:13-15
- 1 John 3:12-18

List the three stages Jesus prescribed for conflict resolution when others have hurt you.		

What did Jesus command for times when you are the one at fault?

How do these passages challenge you to be more pro-active in your approach to conflict resolution?

What did James say is the source of most inter-personal conflicts?	How did Jesus respond to the conflict between brothers?

How do these passages challenge you to greater selflessness as the solution to your conflicts?

List three questions you still have about resolving conflicts in a godly manner.		

What is your conclusion or main take-away from these passages?

Fellowship of One Family*

The first 120 disciples of Christ in Jerusalem were filled with the same and singular passion – Jesus. They were so consumed with the love of their Savior and couldn't help but to love one another and share everything with one another. Nothing was important to them anymore except Jesus and knowing Him. Possessions that were once the pride of life were now offered for the common good of anyone among them who had need. No one considered themselves better than anyone else because Jesus had died for them all. They assembled to worship Jesus and they ate common meals together, enjoying one another's company, praying together, praising God, and sharing communion.

Even before the Holy Spirit was poured out, they were completely and totally devoted to obeying Christ's commands. Men and women alike were now all of one mind and considered equal as followers Jesus.

> Acts 1:14 KJV: These all continued **with one accord in prayer and supplication**, with the women, and Mary the mother of Jesus, and with his brethren.

The word for *one accord* in Greek is a combination of two words which mean to *rush along* and *in unison*. It is used to describe groups of people who agree unanimously about what is true and what needs to be done. It is reminiscent of a great harmony, like a symphony of many different instruments coming together to play a composed melody at the direction of a common conductor.

After Pentecost, because the Holy Spirit had been poured out, this natural devotion was raised to a supernatural dimension as 3,120 people were of *one accord*, sharing the same heart and mind. As the Holy Spirit circumcised their hearts in selflessness, they were compelled to share everything that they owned so that everyone had what they needed.

> Acts 2:42-47: They **devoted themselves to the apostles' teaching and to fellowship, to the breaking of bread and to prayer**. Everyone was filled with awe at the many wonders and signs performed by the apostles. **All the believers were together and had everything in common.** They sold property and possessions to give to anyone who had need. **Every day they continued to meet together in the temple courts. They broke bread in their homes and ate together with glad and sincere hearts, praising God** and enjoying the favor of all the people. And the Lord added to their number daily those who were being saved.

> Acts 4:32-35: **All the believers were one in heart and mind. No one claimed that any of their possessions was their own, but they shared everything they had.** With great power the apostles continued to testify to the resurrection of the Lord Jesus. And **God's grace was so powerfully at work in them all that there were no needy persons among them. For from time to time those who owned land or houses sold them, brought the money from the sales and put it at the apostles' feet, and it was distributed to anyone who had need.**

This type of community was a living demonstration of what God had always intended for society. When God created Adam & Eve and told them to fill the earth with their family, this is what He had in mind.

God's Design for Community

When God gave His Law to the people of Israel, He articulated His will for His people towards one another. God's Laws clearly outlined His views for restitution for stolen property, moved landmarks, fair treatment of slaves, dealing with a neighbor's stray animal, not pretending that you did not witness a crime, testifying truthfully, deceitful seduction, betrayal, family inheritance, and a whole host of other issues that the people daily faced in their dealings with one another. God's Laws for social responsibility, equity, fairness, and the administration of justice placed higher value on human life, dignity, and care for creation than any other society in history ever had. Because God is the One who created every person and everything, His statutes and precepts reveal His love for all He created and His desire for harmony and peace.

Moreover, the purpose of implementing God's Laws was to demonstrate His goodness towards His people and then, as His people lived in accordance with His Laws, their kindness towards one another would reveal God's love through them to the whole world.

> *Deuteronomy 4:6-8: Observe them carefully, for **this will show your wisdom and understanding to the nations**, who will hear about all these decrees and say, "**Surely this great nation is a wise and understanding people.**" What other nation is so great as to have their gods near them the way the LORD our God is near us whenever we pray to him? **And what other nation is so great as to have such righteous decrees and laws as this body of laws** I am setting before you today?*

> *Psalm 67:1-2: May God be gracious to us and bless us and make his face shine on us-- **so that your ways may be known on earth, your salvation among all nations**.*

Notably, God's statutes for His people towards one another are slightly different from the rules for His people towards non-Israelites. Through God's Law, Israelites were instructed to lend freely to their fellow Jews with an open hand, without charging interest, without a tight fist, and without a grudge in their hearts. (See Exodus 22:25; Leviticus 25:36.) God also made provision for the poor, the orphan, and the widow who could not provide for themselves, and demanded fair treatment of the foreigner residing among the Israelites. In fact, foreigners in Israel were never to be abused, mistreated, or oppressed but welcomed and included whenever possible.

> *Deuteronomy 23:19-20: **Do not charge a fellow Israelite interest**, whether on money or food or anything else that may earn interest. **You may charge a foreigner interest, but not a fellow Israelite**, so that the LORD your God may bless you in everything you put your hand to in the land you are entering to possess.*

> *Deuteronomy 15:4, 7-8, 10-11: However, **there need be no poor people among you**, for in the land the LORD your God is giving you to possess as your inheritance, he will richly bless you,... **If anyone is poor among your fellow Israelites** in any of the towns of the land the LORD your God is giving you, **do not be hardhearted or tightfisted toward them. Rather, be openhanded and freely lend them whatever they need... Give generously to them and do so without a grudging heart**; then because of this the LORD your God will bless you in all your work and in everything you put your hand to. There will always be poor people in the land. Therefore I command you to **be openhanded toward your fellow Israelites who are poor and needy in your land**.*

> *Leviticus 23:22: When you reap the harvest of your land, do not reap to the very **edges of your field or gather the gleanings of your harvest. Leave them for the poor and for the foreigner residing among you**. I am the LORD your God. (See also Exodus 23:9; Leviticus 19:9-10; Deuteronomy 24:18-20, 14:29.)*

All of this is to say that after the outpouring of the Holy Spirit on the day of Pentecost, Christians began to organically and genuinely align their lives with God's original design for community. They considered themselves to be brothers and sisters in the family of God and they depended on one another for the things they needed. This was particularly true because many of them gave up everything in order to follow Christ or had been disowned by their families for worshipping Jesus. Therefore, they shared everything that they had with each other so that every believer had what they needed. They placed high priority on taking care of fellow believers so that there would be no lack among them.

> *1 John 3:16-18: This is how we know what love is: Jesus Christ laid down his life for us.* ***And we ought to lay down our lives for our brothers and sisters. [fellow believers] If anyone has material possessions and sees a brother or sister in need but has no pity on them, how can the love of God be in that person?*** *Dear children, let us not love with words or speech but with actions and in truth.*

> *James 2:14-16: What good is it, my brothers and sisters, if someone claims to have faith but has no deeds? Can such faith save them?* ***Suppose a brother or a sister [fellow believer] is without clothes and daily food. If one of you says to them, "Go in peace; keep warm and well fed," but does nothing about their physical needs, what good is it?***

> *1 John 4:19-21:* ***We love because he first loved us. Whoever claims to love God yet hates a brother or sister [fellow believer] is a liar.*** *For whoever does not love their brother and sister, whom they have seen, cannot love God, whom they have not seen.* ***And he has given us this command: Anyone who loves God must also love their brother and sister. [fellow believer]***

> *Galatians 6:10: Therefore, as we have opportunity, let us do good to all people,* ***especially to those who belong to the family of believers.***

The word most often used in the New Testament to address the people of the Church, is *brethren* which is also translated *brothers and sisters*. This word indicates people who came out of the same womb and signifies people of the same bloodline, ancestor, or people group. We as believers come out of the same womb (the tomb of Christ) into the family of God through the blood of Jesus. This connects us to one another in a profoundly significant and eternal bond. We are family.

In fact, Jesus acknowledged the bond of spiritual family as deeper and more significant than the bond of natural family. As His ministry progressed, His own family thought He had lost His mind and did not believe Him. (See Mark 3:21; John 7:5.) Although He made provision for the care of His mother before His death, Jesus publicly elevated the role of His disciples as His family over that of biological family.

> *Mark 3:33-35:* ***"Who are my mother and my brothers?"*** *he asked. Then he looked at those seated in a circle around him and said, "Here are my mother and my brothers!* ***Whoever does God's will is my brother and sister and mother."***

The people God has selected to be His are our family for eternity. Like any good father, it is our Father's desire for us to get along with one another as His sons and daughters and to share with one another, help each other, and resolve conflicts with one another as brothers and sisters in the same family.

KOINONIA - FELLOWSHIP

Christian fellowship is an expression of our oneness and family bond. The word for fellowship in Greek is *koinonia* which means *association* or *community* describing joint participation or partnership. Each member is an essential piece of the whole. It can also mean *communion, intercourse,* and *intimacy* which clearly indicate that the magnitude of *koinonia* is not just casual getting together over pot-luck dinners and pleasant conversation. Rather, we are one body which is not whole if a single piece is missing.

> *Romans 12:4-5: For just as each of us has one body with many members, and these members do not all have the same function, so in Christ we, though many, **form one body, and each member belongs to all the others**.*
>
> *1Corinthians 12:4-6, 12, 27: There are different kinds of gifts, but **the same Spirit** distributes them. There are different kinds of service, but **the same Lord**. There are different kinds of working, but in all of them and in everyone it is **the same God** at work... **Just as a body, though one, has many parts, but all its many parts form one body, so it is with Christ**... Now **you are the body of Christ**, and **each one of you is a part of it**.*
>
> *Ephesians 4:4-6: **There is one body and one Spirit**, just as you were called to **one hope** when you were called; **one Lord, one faith, one baptism; one God and Father of all**, who is over all and through all and in all.*

In Christ we have become one. We all have the same heart – the Holy Spirit; the same King – Jesus; and the same Father – God. This *oneness* is so important that Jesus passionately prayed for us as believers function in unity with one another. This harmony among us is one of the ways by which those who do not know Christ as their Savior may be drawn in to know Him.

> *John 17:20-23: "My prayer is not for them alone. I pray also for those who will believe in me through their message, <u>**that all of them may be one**</u>, Father, just as you are in me and I am in you. May they also be in us **so that the world may believe that you have sent me**. I have given them the glory that you gave me, **that they may be one as we are one**-- I in them and you in me--**so that they may be brought to complete unity. Then the world will know that you sent me and have loved them even as you have loved me**.*

God's intent for the Church is for all of His people to be unified as ONE body so that we are a living, breathing, walking, talking demonstration of God's nature of giving, serving, and loving. Through our self-sacrificing participation and partnership with one another, we reveal that we are different than the self-serving world and its competitive ways.

This is not just a dream. This happened in the earliest days of the Church as the Gospel message spread to new territories and Christian communities were formed. Even today, the oneness of Christians is more profound than any other bond in the world. We do not just share intellectual beliefs and a common book. We have a bond with one another that is deeper than flesh and blood, more powerful than family heritage, and which far surpasses any natural form of partnership or association. In Christ, we are one.

Gathering Together

In the earliest days of the Church, worshippers of Jesus gathered together as a new faith, a new family, and a new people of God and God continually added to their numbers. The word for gathering together is *synago*. It is the same word used to describe gathering fish into a net, collecting sheaves of harvest, or assembling for an important meeting. Christian gatherings are designed to be a preview of the ultimate eternal harvest celebration where the children of God rejoice in His goodness.

Believers opened their hearts and the homes to one another and for worshipping Jesus. This is because in those days, there were no church buildings. In fact, there were no church buildings for the first three hundred years of Christianity and because of heavy persecution, believers often had to meet in secret.

When they gathered together, they would pray, fast, seek the will of the Lord, function in their spiritual gifts, and share communion. In their flow of service, any and every believer was welcome to share what the Holy Spirit was revealing to them.

> *1Corinthians 12:7,11: Now **to each one the manifestation of the Spirit is given for the common good**. ... All these are the work of one and the same Spirit, and **he distributes them to each one, just as he determines**.*

> *1Corinthians 14:26,31: What then shall we say, brothers and sisters? When you come together,* ***each of you has a hymn, or a word of instruction, a revelation, a tongue or an interpretation... For you can all prophesy in turn so that everyone may be instructed and encouraged.***

In the early years of Christianity, the Holy Spirit orchestrated the flow of Christian gatherings. Those with more knowledge of the Scriptures taught other believers and strengthened them in their knowledge of God. The Elders and Deacons in any given city were there to guard and guide the people in the ways of God and to serve the needs of the people as they arose in the course of life.

However, this changed drastically after Constantine became Emperor of Rome in 313 AD. Constantine professed to be a Christian because he believed that the God of the Christians gave him control of the Roman Empire. Overnight, Christianity went from being heavily persecuted (including throwing Christians to wild animals in the Colosseum for entertainment) to being the favored religion of the civilized world in that day. Home churches were forbidden and buildings which had been pagan temples became the meeting places for Christian meetings. Then, in keeping with the pagan temple customs, priests and leaders were appointed often through bribery or cronyism and were given titles like Father, Master, and Pope even though Jesus had specifically instructed His followers not to call anyone father or master except God alone, and not to let anyone call them father or master. The priests became the only ones with access to the holy books while the people had no Bibles of their own to read. The flow of service changed so that leaders gave dissertations and dictated to people what they needed to do while the people were expected to remain silent and submissive. Moreover, Constantine's zeal for political power mixed with his questionable profession of Christian faith diverted the focus of Christianity toward establishing a world empire for his benefit in the name of God rather than establishing the Kingdom of God in the hearts of the people. Christianity became paganized, a far cry from Jesus' life and teachings, and lacking any resemblance to the gatherings of the first disciples of Christ.

However even today, God continues to love each of us as His children individually and gift us in unique ways that contribute to the whole of what He is doing in the earth and in His Kingdom. When we gather together, it is still God's desire for us to be like a symphony conducted by Jesus with each instrument playing its part as empowered by the Holy Spirit.

Greatest is Love

All of us can function in the gifts God has given us in ways that contribute to the Body of Christ and encourage each other in our faith. This said, spiritual maturity is something much greater than flowing spiritual gifts. Both individually and corporately, maturity is love. (See 1Corinthiahs 13.)

The earliest Christians were *cut to the heart* when they understood the love of God for them. To them, everything else seemed trivial by comparison. It was this revelation of the love of Jesus that made loving one another and sharing everything with one another so effortless. Jesus only gave one command to His disciples: to love one another as He loves us.

> *John 15:12-14, 17:* ***My command is this: Love each other as I have loved you.*** *Greater love has no one than this: to* ***lay down one's life for one's friends.*** *You are my friends if you do what I command. ...* ***This is my command: Love each other.***

We cannot love one another unless we truly know the love of Jesus for ourselves. Loving and serving each other entails trusting God enough to lay aside our own agendas, preferences, ambitions, and needs in order to submit ourselves to God and to one another. This is how the world will see that we are a fellowship of the family of God.

www.manifestinternational.com

Prayer for Oneness
Scripture Reading

Read each of the following passages and then use the chart below for study and reflection.
- John 17

This was Jesus' prayer for His disciples before He went to the cross. What stands out to you?

Summarize 3 prayer requests Jesus made to the Father in these passages.		

List three significant words or phrases that stood out to you.		

What insight does this give you about God's desire for unity in the Body of Christ?

How does Jesus' example of prayer impact your prayer life for other believers or the Church?

List three questions you still have about unity in the Church (locally or globally.)		

What is your conclusion about this passage?

CORNERSTONE – UNIT 3.4

ONE ANOTHER
Scripture List*

Acts 4:32: All the believers were **one in heart and mind**. No one claimed that any of their possessions was their own, but they shared everything they had.

Mark 9:50: Salt is good, but if it loses its saltiness, how can you make it salty again? Have salt among yourselves, and **be at peace with each other**.

John 13:14: Now that I, your Lord and Teacher, have washed your feet, you also should **wash one another's feet.**

John 13:34-35: "A new command I give you: **Love one another**. As I have loved you, so you must love one another. By this everyone will know that you are my disciples, if you **love one another**."

John 15:12, 17: My command is this: **Love each other as I have loved you...** This is my command: **Love each other**.

Romans 1:12: that is, that you and I may be **mutually encouraged by each other's faith**.

Romans 12:5,10,16: In Christ we, though many, form one body, and **each member belongs to all the others**...10 **Be devoted to one another in love. Honor one another** above yourselves... 16 **Live in harmony with one another**. Do not be proud, but be willing to associate with people of low position. Do not be conceited.

Romans 13:8: Let no debt remain outstanding, except the continuing debt to **love one another**, for whoever loves others has fulfilled the law.

Romans 14:13: Therefore let us **stop passing judgment on one another**. Instead, make up your mind not to put any stumbling block or obstacle in the way of a brother or sister.

Romans 15:5,7: May the God who gives endurance and encouragement give you the **same attitude of mind toward each other that Christ Jesus had...** 7 **Accept one another**, then, just as Christ accepted you, in order to bring praise to God.

Romans 15:14: I myself am convinced, my brothers and sisters, that you yourselves are full of goodness, filled with knowledge and competent to **instruct one another**.

Romans 16:16a: **Greet one another with a holy kiss.** *(Also 1 Corinthians 16:20; 2Corinthians 13:12; 1Peter 5:14.)*

1 Corinthians 1:10: I appeal to you, brothers and sisters, in the name of our Lord Jesus Christ, that all of you **agree with one another in what you say** and that there be **no divisions among you**, but that you be **perfectly united in mind and thought**.

1 Corinthians 12:25: so that there should be no division in the body, but that its parts should have **equal concern for each other**.

2 Corinthians 13:11: Finally, brothers and sisters, rejoice! Strive for full restoration, **encourage one another, be of one mind, live in peace**. And the God of love and peace will be with you.

Galatians 5:13,15,26: You, my brothers and sisters, were called to be free. But do not use your freedom to indulge the flesh; rather, **serve one another humbly in love**... 15 If you bite and devour each other, watch out or you will be destroyed by each other... 26 Let us not become conceited, provoking and envying each other.

Galatians 6:2: **Carry each other's burdens**, and in this way you will fulfill the law of Christ.

Ephesians 4:2: Be completely humble and gentle; be patient, **bearing with one another in love.**

Ephesians 4:25,32: Therefore each of you must put off falsehood and **speak truthfully to your neighbor**, for we are all members of one body... 32 **Be kind and compassionate to one another, forgiving each other**, just as in Christ God forgave you.

Ephesians 5:21: **Submit to one another out of reverence for Christ.**

Philippians 2:3,5: Do nothing out of selfish ambition or vain conceit. Rather, in humility **value others above yourselves**... 5 In your **relationships with one another**, have the same mindset as Christ Jesus:

Colossians 3:9, 13,16: **Do not lie to each other**, since you have taken off your old self with its practices... 13 **Bear with each other and forgive one another** if any of you has a grievance against someone. Forgive as the Lord forgave you... 16 Let the message of Christ dwell among you richly as you teach and admonish one another with all wisdom through psalms, hymns, and songs from the Spirit, singing to God with gratitude in your hearts.

1Thessalonians 3:12: May the Lord make your **love increase and overflow for each other** and for everyone else, just as ours does for you.

1Thessalonians 4:9: Now about your **love for one another** we do not need to write to you, for you yourselves have been taught by God to love each other.

1Thessalonians 5:11,15: Therefore **encourage one another and build each other up**, just as in fact you are doing... 15: Make sure that nobody pays back wrong for wrong, but always strive to **do what is good for each other** and for everyone else.

2Thessalonians 1:3: We ought always to thank God for you, brothers and sisters, and rightly so, because your faith is growing more and more, and the **love all of you have for one another is increasing.**

Titus 3:3: At one time we too were foolish, disobedient, deceived and enslaved by all kinds of passions and pleasures. We lived in malice and envy, **being hated and hating one another.**

Hebrews 3:13: But **encourage one another daily**, as long as it is called "Today," so that none of you may be hardened by sin's deceitfulness.

Hebrews 10:24-25: And let us consider how we may **spur one another on toward love and good deeds**, not giving up **meeting together**, as some are in the habit of doing, but **encouraging one another**--and all the more as you see the Day approaching.

Hebrews 13:1: Keep **on loving one another as brothers and sisters.**

James 4:11: Brothers and sisters, **do not slander one another**. Anyone who speaks against a brother or sister or judges them speaks against the law and judges it. When you judge the law, you are not keeping it, but sitting in judgment on it.
James 5:9: **Don't grumble against one another**, brothers and sisters, or you will be judged. The Judge is standing at the door!

James 5:16: Therefore **confess your sins to each other and pray for each other so that you may be healed**. The prayer of a righteous person is powerful and effective.

1Peter 1:22: Now that you have purified yourselves by obeying the truth so that you **have sincere love for each other, love one another deeply, from the heart**.

1Pe 3:8: Finally, all of you, be like-minded, be sympathetic, love one another, be compassionate and humble.

1Peter 4:9: **Offer hospitality to one another** without grumbling.

1Peter 5:5: In the same way, you who are younger, submit yourselves to your elders. All of you, clothe yourselves with **humility toward one another**, because, "God opposes the proud but shows favor to the humble."

1John 1:7: But if we walk in the light, as he is in the light, we **have fellowship with one another**, and the blood of Jesus, his Son, purifies us from all sin.

1John 3:11,23: For this is the message you heard from the beginning: **We should love one another**... 23: And this is his command: to believe in the name of his Son, Jesus Christ, and **to love one another as he commanded us**.

1John 4:7,11,12: Dear friends, let us **love one another**, for love comes from God. Everyone who loves has been born of God and knows God...11 Dear friends, since God so loved us, we also ought to **love one another**... 12 No one has ever seen God; but if we **love one another**, God lives in us and his love is made complete in us.

2John 1:5: And now, dear lady, I am not writing you a new command but one we have had from the beginning. I ask that we **love one another**.

ONE ANOTHER WORKSHEET
Accompanies One Anothers Scripture List

John 13:34-35: A new command I give you: Love one another. As I have loved you, so you must love one another. By this everyone will know that you are my disciples, if you love one another.

1. Read through the **One Anothers Scripture List**. What is the Lord highlighting to you in these Scriptures?

2. What did Jesus mean when He said, "As I have loved you..."

3. In the past and present, how have your responses to others *not* demonstrated the love of Jesus?

4. Select one Scripture for you from the One Anothers Scripture List. Slowly read this Scripture out loud three times. What do you sense the Lord speaking to you through this Scripture?

5. In what ways is God asking you to walk and live in more love for others?

6. How will you continue to walk in faith rather than slipping back into old patterns?

7. Praise God for what He has done for you. Jesus is King!

Basic Training Exercise

CARING CORRECTLY

1 Thessalonians 5:14 NIV – And we urge you, brothers and sisters, warn those who are idle and disruptive, encourage the disheartened, help the weak, be patient with everyone.

DESCRIPTION

Loving others as Jesus loves us includes understanding how to recognize what state they are in on their journey with Him. Jesus warned us not to judge by outward appearances but to judge with righteousness.

For example, perhaps what appears to be idleness is actually someone who is intently waiting upon the Lord. Maybe what looks like disruption is actually a disheartened person in need of encouragement. Possibly what seems to be faithless is actually one who is weak and in need of help.

Only the Lord knows each of our hearts and His desire is for us to love one another well. He is willing to share His insight with us so we can be and do for others what they need at the right time in their lives.

As such, putting Caring Correctly into practice is about seeking the Lord for His input about what another person is actually in need of so we can love them the way Jesus wants us to.

CONSIDERATIONS

Has there been a time when you felt misunderstood by others or that they cared for you incorrectly? How could they have Cared Correctly for you?

Has someone Cared Correctly for you but you did not appreciate or recognize it at first? How so? When did you recognize that they had Cared Correctly for you?

Have you ever misunderstood or cared for someone incorrectly? How could you have handled the situation differently?

In what ways did Jesus Care Correctly? Did He give people what they demanded or what they needed? Who did He take His directions from?

Category: Christlike Care

Basic TRAINING
SPIRITUAL EXERCISES

PURPOSE:
To accurately discern the spiritual state of others so that we can care for them correctly.

To love others well by doing what is right for them rather than what they want.

SPIRITUAL FRUIT:
Love for others.

Improved kindness for others on their journey with Jesus.

Increased discernment of phases of spiritual life.

PRAYER

Father, thank you that you sent Jesus to demonstrate how to care for people the way you want me to. Help me to learn from you about what others need before jumping to conclusions or making wrong judgments. Teach me how to love the way you do. In Jesus' name, Amen.

PRACTICE

1. Ask the Lord to highlight someone to you that He would like you to Care Correctly for.

2. From your perspective, write down how you see their situation, behavior, attitude, etc.
   - What does it look like to you?
   - How are you inclined to handle the situation?
   - Are there feelings that come up for you when you think about this? Does it make you angry, sad, fearful, etc?
   - Does it remind you of incidents you've had with them in the past? With others? Is this the same or different?

3. Shift from your own perspective. Ask the Holy Spirit about this person and their situation.
   - Ask God to show you what is really going on with them.
   - Ask God to reveal the truth to you about the situation.
   - Ask God what they need from you at this time in their life.

4. Take note of the differences between your impressions from #2 and God's insights from #3.
   - How are they different? How are they similar?
   - What did God show you that you had not considered?
   - Was there any way that your emotions or past experiences were hindering your perspective of the situation? How so?

5. Ask God how He wants you to Care Correctly for this person. With His help, do what He tells you.

NOTES:
_____
_____

ADDITIONAL SCRIPTURES:
Romans 14:1
1 Thessalonians 2:11
Titus 3:10
1 Corinthians 3:4
2 Thessalonians 3:15
1 Corinthians 5:11
Hebrews 10:24
Ephesians 4:29
John 7:24

Unit Three – Key Questions
The Community of God

Use this worksheet to test your grasp of the material and exercises of Unit Three.

What is God's design for Christian community?	

What happens when we are baptized?	What is communion?

What is the authority of the Church?	How are believers supposed to resolve conflicts?

Why do believers need one another? What is God's view of diversity and unity?	How does God want us to love one another?

What is one thing you learned that you did not know before?	What questions do you still have about this subject?

Group Training Exercise

UNIT THREE: GROUP EXERCISES – TWO OPTIONS

BAPTISM BY IMMERSION

DESCRIPTION

Baptism is an outward demonstration of the change that took place in our heart when we believed Jesus Christ as our Lord and Savior. Jesus Christ commanded all of His disciples to baptize new disciples in the name of the Father, the Son, and the Holy Spirit. Baptism in Christ's day was done through full immersion under water. In fact, even Jesus was baptized in this way. This type of baptism is rooted in a practice ordained in God's Law for ritual cleansing, called a mikveh in Hebrew. Ritual cleansing like this was required of priests before they could serve God and was required of common people in order to remain clean before God.

For believers today, this type of baptism symbolizes our inclusion in Christ's death and resurrection. Our old self dies as it is submerged under the water and we emerge out of the water as a new creation in Christ. As we are literally submerged into the waters of baptism, we figuratively include ourselves in the death of Jesus and we put to death the sinful nature we inherited from Adam. Coming up out of the waters of baptism signifies our participation in Jesus' resurrection. Our old life is rolled away and we emerge as a new creation in Christ. Hallelujah!

If you or anyone in your group has not been water baptized, it can be done by your fellow disciples in any body of water, including a pond, the ocean, or a bathtub. It is a time for great rejoicing as a fellow believer commits themselves to Jesus and demonstrates their new life in the New Covenant with God.

SCRIPTURE PORTION

Matthew 28:19-20 NIV - Therefore go and make disciples of all nations, baptizing them in the name of the Father and of the Son and of the Holy Spirit, and teaching them to obey everything I have commanded you. And surely I am with you always, to the very end of the age."

GROUP PRACTICE

1. Prepare:
   - Ask the group if there is anyone who has not been baptized who wants to be.
   - Ask the group if there was anyone who was baptized or sprinkled as a child who wants to affirm their faith and/or rededicate their life to Christ.
   - Meet with the people who want to be baptized before the day of baptism in order to discuss with them the seriousness of this act of faith and their understanding of the commitment they are entering into.
   - Determine which body of water you will gather at to submerge these believers in baptism.

2. Before baptizing someone, have them affirm their faith in Jesus Christ. Ask them:
   - Do you believe that Jesus is Lord?
   - Do you believe that God raised Jesus from the dead?
   - Wait for their genuine response of faith through verbal spoken agreement or affirmation of these statements.

3. Pray for them and listen to anything the Holy Spirit may desire for you to say to them at this very special time in their life of faith.
   - Allow members of the group to offer words of prayer and/or encouragement for the person being baptized.

4. When you are both ready, say to them: "I baptize you in the name of the Father, the Son, and the Holy Spirit."
   - Submerge them under the water and help to raise them up out of the water.

5. Rejoice! Affirm them as a child of God and a new creation in Christ. Welcome them into God's family and God's Kingdom!

PURPOSE:
Outwardly demonstrate our inner and eternal covenant commitment to Jesus Christ.

Be cleansed from the old and emerge as a new creation.

GROUP SIZE:
Any size group.

SCRIPTURES
Mark 16:16
Matthew 28:19
1 Peter 3:21
Romans 6:3-4
Colossians 2:11-12
1 Corinthians 12:13
Acts 2:38
Acts 8:38
Acts 9:18
Acts 10:47
Acts 22:16

Category: Basics

Basic TRAINING
SPIRITUAL EXERCISES

Group Training Exercise

COMMUNION TOGETHER

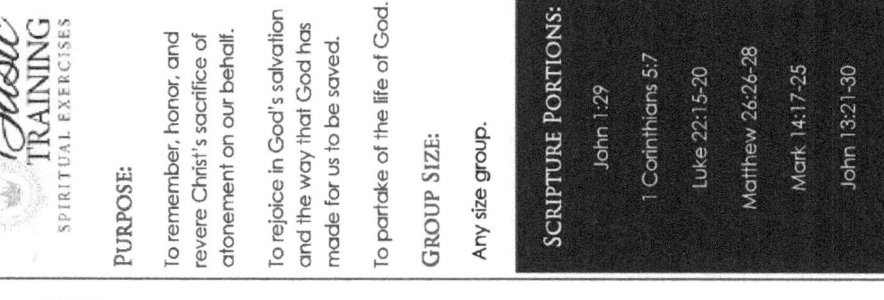

DESCRIPTION

Jesus Christ is our eternal Passover Lamb. Like the Israelites painted the blood of the lamb on their doorposts to be protected from the destroyer, Jesus shed His blood so that our sins are forgiven. Through His blood painted on the doorposts of our hearts, we can be protected from destruction of sin, the world, the flesh, and the evil one. Jesus' body was broken so that we can freely enter into the presence of God to worship. When we take communion, we remember this great deliverance and what Jesus Christ did for us and receive in ourselves the life of God.

The first disciples of Christ took communion (or "brake bread") regularly. Consecrated bread and wine were made readily available for believers to serve themselves or take communion together. As a holy nation and a royal priesthood, every believer is a priest of God and able to administer the body and blood of Christ with due reverence. (1 Peter 2:9) This said, communion and the benefits of Christ's sacrifice are only available to those who believe that Jesus is Lord and that God raised Him from the dead. This means that if you do not yet believe in Jesus Christ as your Lord and Savior, you should abstain from communion or better yet, believe Jesus and partake.

Practicing the partaking of Communion is about commemorating Christ's sacrifice, renewing our faith in what He has done for us, and to looking forward to His return.

As you take communion together as a group, take a moment to look around the room at the people of God. These are your people. We are one nation, one people, one family, one body, one Kingdom chosen by God to be His. Hallelujah!

SCRIPTURE PORTION

Luke 22:19-20 NIV - And he took bread, gave thanks and broke it, and gave it to them, saying, "This is my body given for you; do this in remembrance of me." In the same way, after the supper he took the cup, saying, "This cup is the new covenant in my blood, which is poured out for you.

PURPOSE:

To remember, honor, and revere Christ's sacrifice of atonement on our behalf.

To rejoice in God's salvation and the way that God has made for us to be saved.

To partake of the life of God.

GROUP SIZE:

Any size group.

SCRIPTURE PORTIONS:

John 1:29

1 Corinthians 5:7

Luke 22:15-20

Matthew 26:26-28

Mark 14:17-25

John 13:21-30

John 6:53-57

1 Corinthians 11:23-34

GROUP PRACTICE

1. Prepare the bread and wine.
   - Consecrate the bread and wine to the Lord by praying over them. For example, "I consecrate this bread and wine to the Lord for holy use and purpose."
   - Do not use this bread or wine for casual snacking.

2. Perceive the body and blood of Jesus.
   - Jesus said of the bread and wine, "this *is* my body" and, "this *is* my blood" even when He still had a natural body.
   - Read the Communion Scriptures about what the body and blood of Jesus have done for us.
   - Believe that these Scriptures apply to the body and blood you are about to partake of.

3. Examine yourself and your faith.
   - Do you believe that Jesus Christ shed His blood for the forgiveness of your sins?
   - Do you believe that you are totally forgiven?
   - Do you believe that you can receive all of the benefits of Christ body and blood through faith in Jesus?

4. Optional: Have people share one aspect of Christ's sacrifice that they are focusing on as they take Communion today.

5. Remember the Lord's death and proclaim His return.
   - Praise God that because of Jesus's sacrifice, you are protected from the destroyer until Jesus returns.

6. Partake.
   - As you eat the body and drink the blood of Jesus, be consciously strengthened with the life and power of God in your inmost being. The indestructible life of Christ and the same power that raised Christ from the dead is in you.

7. Praise God and rejoice in His salvation!

Category: Basics

ALL RIGHTS RESERVED © 2019 Wendy Bowen

www.manifestinternational.com

UNIT FOUR: MIRACLES

KEY SCRIPTURE VERSE FOR UNIT FOUR
God also testified to it by signs, wonders and various miracles, and by gifts of the Holy Spirit distributed according to his will. - Hebrews 2:4

CLASS 1: POWER FROM HEAVEN
1 Reading, 1 Exercise
When Jesus poured out the Holy Spirit, His anointing was transferred to us to give us power from above to work miracles in His name.

CLASS 2: AUTHORITY IN CHRIST
1 Reading, 1 Scripture Reading, 1 Exercise
By faith in Jesus, all believers have God-given authority to heal the sick, cast out demons, raise the dead, and do greater works in His name.

CLASS 3: WALKING LIKE JESUS
1 Reading, 1 Exercise
Jesus equips and commands us to walk as He walked, in constant communion with God and total submission to His direction. When we do this, our lives become miraculous!

CLASS 4: GIFTS OF THE HOLY SPIRIT
1 Reading, 1 Exercise
The Holy Spirit distributes various gifts as needed in situations we encounter. All believers can flow in any of these gifts as God guides and enables us so that everyone is strengthened in the Lord.

KEY QUESTIONS

GROUP EXERCISES

Power From Heaven*

Before Jesus ascended into heaven, He met with His disciples to commission them for Kingdom work. In order for His disciples to do the works that Jesus did, they needed power from above.

> *Act 1:8-11: But **you will receive power when the Holy Spirit comes on you**; and you will be my witnesses in Jerusalem, and in all Judea and Samaria, and to the ends of the earth." **After he said this, he was taken up before their very eyes, and a cloud hid him from their sight**. They were looking intently up into the sky as he was going, when suddenly two men dressed in white stood beside them. "Men of Galilee," they said, "why do you stand here looking into the sky? This same Jesus, who has been taken from you into heaven, will come back in the same way you have seen him go into heaven."*

The words used to describe the Holy Spirit *coming upon* believers is the word for *overtake* or *overwhelm*. As an analogy, it is the same word used to describe being overrun or overpowered by an enemy. The word for *pouring out* the Holy Spirit is the word used for *gushing* as in the analogy of a fire hose bursting forth. When the disciples were gathered together in the upper room on the day of Pentecost, they heard the sound of a mighty rushing/gushing wind as the Holy Spirit was poured out upon them.

> *Acts 2:2-4: Suddenly a **sound like the blowing of a violent wind came from heaven and filled the whole house where they were sitting**. They saw what seemed to be tongues of fire that separated and came to rest on each of them. All of them were filled with the Holy Spirit and **began to speak in other tongues as the Spirit enabled them**.*

Once the Holy Spirit was poured out, the believers in Jerusalem were supernaturally empowered by God. Jesus had told them that they would do greater works than He did and now they had power from heaven to do the works of God.

> *John 14:12: Very truly I tell you, **whoever believes in me will do the works I have been doing, and they will do even greater things** than these, because I am going to the Father.*

This whole scene was reminiscent of events which had occurred in the Old Testament. The Prophet Elijah had been taken up into heaven in a whirlwind while his successor Elisha watched. (See 2 Kings 2:11-12.) Elijah had been the world's most powerful prophet of the one true God. He did mighty works which proved his anointing from God. (See 1 Kings 18.) However, after this, Elijah found himself in a cave thinking that he was the only one who truly believed God. When Elijah left the cave, he was instructed by God to do three things, the first of which was to anoint Elisha as his successor, which Elijah did. (See 1 Kings 19.) When the time came for Elijah's dramatic departure from this world, Elisha requested a double portion of Elijah's spirit (his anointing from God) in order to be his successor and carry out his work. When Elijah was taken up into heaven his cloak, also called his mantle, fell down from above and Elisha took it as his own. Those who saw this transaction take place even noted, "Elijah's spirit now rests upon Elisha!" (See 2 Kings 2:15.) Elisha proceeded to do twice as many mighty works as Elijah in addition to fulfilling the two other portions of God's post-cave assignment to Elijah.

ELIJAH – 7 MIRACLES (See 1Kings 17-18, 2Kings 1-2.)	ELISHA – 14 MIRACLES (See 2Kings 2-6, 13.)
Commanded the weather	Parted the Jordan River
Fed by birds	Purified bad water with a bowl of salt
Food supply during famine	Cursed mocking boys
Raised a widow's son from the dead	Water pooled without rain
Fire from heaven	Oil for a widow to pay her debts
Fire from heaven three more times	Raised a woman's son from the dead
Parted the waters of the Jordan River	Purified poisonous food with flour
	Food multiplication: 20 loaves feed 100
	Healed an incurable leper
	Discerned servant's lie and smote him
	Made a sunken ax head float in water
	Opened servant's eyes to see angels
	Blinded the enemy army
	Dead man raised to life on Elisha's bones

The story of Elijah and Elisha is a prophetic example of what happened when Jesus ascended to heaven and poured the Holy Spirit into believers. Christ's disciples were now empowered to carry out His purpose and to work miracles the way that He did. Like Elijah, Jesus was the Anointed One of the one true God and did great and mighty works and miracles in the earth. Then, He found Himself in a cave called the grave as the only one who truly believed God, since everyone else had deserted Him. As Jesus stepped out of the grave, He knew God's purpose for Him included anointing His successors. For the next 40 days, He commissioned His disciples and told them about their assignment to be His witnesses to the ends of the earth. Then, He ascended to heaven in the clouds. Then, Jesus sent down the Holy Spirit, which fell upon believers like Jesus' robe or mantle from God. The Spirit of Jesus would rest upon His disciples so that they could do His works, and even greater works, with power from heaven.

When the Holy Spirit Comes Upon You

There are a few other noteworthy Old Testament examples of the Spirit of the Lord coming upon people. First, in the days of Moses, Moses was the only one who was able to approach God to receive wisdom from Him in order to lead the people of Israel. The workload of administering justice for the people became overwhelming. Therefore, the Lord told Moses to gather seventy elders of Israel together so that He could share the Spirit of the Lord, which was on Moses, with the elders. This way, they would be able to help in bearing Moses' burden because they were empowered by the same Spirit that Moses had so that they could do the works that Moses did. When the Spirit of the Lord came upon the elders of Israel, they prophesied. Moses was so delighted at this event that he uttered words that came to pass at Pentecost, "I wish that all of the Lord's people were prophets and that the Lord would put His Spirit on them!" (See Numbers 11:16-30.)

Other Old Testament examples include Othiniel, Gideon, Jephthah, and Samson from the Book of Judges each experienced the Spirit of the Lord coming upon them, rushing upon them, clothing them, or stirring them so that they were strengthened with power to do great exploits for God. They were particularly empowered for going to war against enemies in oftentimes seemingly impossible situations. (See Judges 3:10, 6:34, 11:29, 13:25, 14:6, 19, 15:14.) The Spirit of the Lord also came upon Saul, Israel's first anointed king. When this happened, Saul prophesied and even onlookers wondered aloud, "Can anyone be a prophet? Even Saul?" (See 1 Samuel 10:1-12.) In another instance, the Spirit of the Lord came upon Saul in righteous anger over the way that enemies were treating the Israelites, and he led Israel to victory in battle. (See 1 Samuel 11:6.) Lastly, the Spirit of the Lord came powerfully upon David, the next king of Israel. This anointing made David a brave warrior and a man of war with good judgment, able to slay giants and defeat all of Israel's enemies by God's power which was with him. (See 1 Samuel 16:10, 18.) Moreover, this list does not include the experiences that the Prophets of the Old Testament had with the Spirit of the Lord, which we do not have time to get into in detail right now.

Most significantly, Jesus demonstrated this working dynamic of receiving power from Holy Spirit as power from above. After Jesus was baptized by John the Baptist, the Holy Spirit descended upon Him and rested upon Him like a dove. (See Matthew 3:16; Mark 1:10; Luke 3:22; John 1:32-33.) Following this, Jesus began His ministry with power from heaven. In His first public speech, He announced that *the Spirit of the Lord was upon Him*, anointing Him to proclaim the Kingdom of God, to heal the sick, to cast out demons, to raise the dead, and to destroy the works of the devil who is the ultimate enemy of all mankind.

> *Luke 3:21-22: When all the people were being baptized, Jesus was baptized too. And as he was praying, heaven was opened and **the Holy Spirit descended on him in bodily form like a dove**. And a voice came from heaven: "You are my Son, whom I love; with you I am well pleased."*

> *Luke 4:18-19: "**The Spirit of the Lord is on me**, because he has anointed me to **proclaim good news to the poor**. He has sent me to proclaim **freedom for the prisoners** and recovery of **sight for the blind**, to **set the oppressed free**, to proclaim the year **of the Lord's favor**." (Quoting Isaiah 61:1-2.)*

> *Acts 10:38: how **God anointed Jesus** of Nazareth **with the Holy Spirit and power**, and how he went around **doing good** and **healing all who were under the power of the devil**, because God was with him.*

Because Jesus was born by the power of the Holy Spirit, He had the perfect nature of God within Him. This empowered Him from within for perfect conduct according to God's standard and, accordingly, He maintained right-standing with God at all times. This said, when the Holy Spirit descended upon Jesus, He received dynamite power from heaven to do the works of God. The power of God was working both within Jesus for perfect character and resting upon Jesus to enable His works against the kingdom of darkness and all the enemies of mankind.

You Will Receive Power

The word for *power* in Greek is *dynamis* from which we derive our word for *dynamite* and it certainly expresses explosive power. The word dynamis is technically defined as "great power or strength, power for performing miracles, and the power resting upon armies." However, the word dynamis can also be mean "virtue or moral power and excellence of soul." These two meanings express two different dynamics of the Holy Spirit that Jesus clearly demonstrated in action.

Along these lines, after the Holy Spirit was poured out on the day of Pentecost, throughout the Book of Acts, believers were *full of the Holy Spirit* or *filled with the Holy Spirit*. In our language, these words appear to be the same. However, in the Greek they are different, and their difference expresses the exact dynamic that Jesus demonstrated. The word for full in Greek is *pleres* which means to be complete or lacking nothing as in an empty vessel which is full of something. The word for filled in Greek is *pimplemi* which means furnished, accomplished, or fulfilled.

Being full of the Holy Spirit denotes the development and maturity of character of Christ in a believer. Fullness *(pleres)* is evidenced through the fruit of the Spirit including love, joy, peace, patience, kindness, goodness, faithfulness, gentleness, self-control and self-sacrificing devotion to God. (See Galatians 5:22-23.) Believers need inward power from above to behave this way because it is so completely the opposite of standard, selfish human nature. Being full of the Holy Spirit is also what gives believers supernatural strength to endure with integrity and faithfulness through life's trials and opposition to the faith.

> *Acts 6:3-5: Brothers and sisters, choose seven men from among you who are known to be **full of the Spirit** and wisdom. We will turn this responsibility over to them and will give our attention to prayer and the ministry of the word." This proposal pleased the whole group. They chose Stephen, a man **full of faith and of the Holy Spirit**; also Philip, Procorus, Nicanor, Timon, Parmenas, and Nicolas from Antioch, a convert to Judaism.*

> *Acts 7:55: But Stephen, **full of the Holy Spirit**, looked up to heaven and saw the glory of God, and Jesus standing at the right hand of God. [while being stoned to death]*

> *Acts 11:24a: He [Barnabas] was a good man, **full of the Holy Spirit** and faith*

Being filled with the Holy Spirit indicates an immediate instance or surge for the moment or for a special task. Filling *(pimplemi)* of the Holy Spirit is evidenced by supernatural ability from God to prophesy, dream dreams, speak in other languages, proclaim the Gospel with boldness, heal the sick, cast out demons, and raise the dead. These things require power from heaven because the miraculous stands in contrast to God's created order and no one can do these things without spiritual power.

> *Acts 2:4: All of them were **filled with the Holy Spirit** and began to speak in other tongues as the Spirit enabled them.*

> *Acts 4:8: Then Peter, **filled with the Holy Spirit**, said to them: "Rulers and elders of the people!*

> *Acts 4:31: After they prayed, the place where they were meeting was shaken. And they were all **filled with the Holy Spirit** and spoke the word of God boldly.*

> *Acts 9:17: Then Ananias went to the house and entered it. Placing his hands on Saul, he said, "Brother Saul, the Lord--Jesus, who appeared to you on the road as you were coming here--has sent me so that you may see again and be **filled with the Holy Spirit**."*

> *Acts 13:8-11: But Elymas the sorcerer (for that is what his name means) opposed them and tried to turn the proconsul from the faith. Then Saul, who was also called Paul, **filled [pimplemi] with the Holy Spirit**, looked straight at Elymas and said, "You are a child of the devil and an enemy of everything that is right! You are full [pleres] of all kinds of deceit and trickery. Will you never stop perverting the right ways of the Lord? Now the hand of the Lord is against you. You are going to be blind for a time, not even able to see the light of the sun." Immediately mist and darkness came over him, and he groped about, seeking someone to lead him by the hand.*

Today, it is no different for us. As we follow Jesus, we become full of the Holy Spirit as the Lord permeates more and more of our lives and character. Then, as we set out to do the works of God, we are filled with the Holy Spirit to give us power from above.

Read this verse again, but this time, read it as your own anointing and assignment from God.

> *Luke 4:18-19: "**The Spirit of the Lord is on ME**, because he has **anointed ME** to **proclaim good news to the poor**. He has sent **ME** to proclaim **freedom for the prisoners** and **recovery of sight for the blind**, to **set the oppressed free**, to proclaim the **year of the Lord's favor**."* (emphasis added)

Basic Training Exercise

SPIRIT UPON ME

Luke 4:18-19 NIV - The Spirit of the Lord is on **me**, because he has anointed **me** to proclaim good news to the poor. He has sent **me** to proclaim freedom for the prisoners and recovery of sight for the blind, to set the oppressed free, to proclaim the year of the Lord's favor.

DESCRIPTION

In order to do the works that Jesus did, we need the Holy Spirit to come upon us. There are numerous examples from the Old Testament of the Spirit of the Lord coming upon normal people to give them supernatural power to fulfill God's work.

Now that the Holy Spirit has been poured out from heaven, the Spirit of the Lord comes to dwell inside of us when we believe Jesus. This is the internal anointing. When the Holy Spirit comes upon us at certain times in powerful ways to aid us in the works of God's Kingdom, it is the external anointing. Both the internal and external anointing are the Spirit of the Lord but they function in different ways for God's purposes.

It is by the Spirit coming upon us believers that they proclaimed the Gospel, prophesied, spoke in other tongues, healed the sick, cast out demons, and raised the dead. The Spirit of the Lord comes upon us today for the same purposes and more. This said, God's power is not to be used for the fulfillment of our own personal aims or for the manipulation of events. It is for the work of God and glorifying the name of Jesus.

Practicing Spirit upon Me is about engaging with the external anointing of God by inviting the Holy Spirit to come upon us as we fulfill God's purposes in the earth.

PRAYER

Father, I believe that you have anointed me to work the works of Jesus with your power from heaven. Allow me to experience your Spirit coming upon me so that I may move in your power and purposes. In Jesus' name, Amen.

Category: Miracles

Basic TRAINING
SPIRITUAL EXERCISES

PURPOSE:
To understand and experience the Spirit of the Lord coming upon us.

To work the works of Jesus by His guidance and power.

SPIRITUAL FRUIT:
Power of the Holy Spirit.

Increased faith and power for miracles.

Deeper experience of God's work for us and through us.

CONSIDERATIONS

In your life with the Holy Spirit, have you experienced more of God's internal power or His external power?

In what ways have you experienced the power of God coming upon you? What was this like for you?

In what ways do you think approaching the Holy Spirit **only** for internal power could be beneficial? Lacking?

In what ways do you think approaching the Holy Spirit **only** for external power could be beneficial? Lacking?

What do you think is the right approach to fulfilling God's purposes in cooperation with both the internal and external power? How will this affect your approach to the Holy Spirit?

PRACTICE

1. Read through the list of Additional Scriptures.
   - Take note that the power of God did not come upon anyone to fulfill their own selfish desires but to fulfill God's purposes.

2. Ask God to reveal to you a situation in your life in which He desires to pour His Spirit upon you to help you.
   - For example, living by faith in His salvation, deliverance, healing, miracles, or any other situation in your life.
   - Ask the Lord to give you one or two Scriptures for this area. (Note: Using only one or two will focus your faith.)

3. In your times of prayer, invite the Holy Spirit to come upon you. Say, "Holy Spirit, clothe me with power from heaven."
   - Briefly wait for anything the Lord may do or say before you begin to enter into prayer.
   - As you pray, alternate between speaking your Scriptures, singing your Scriptures, and speaking/singing in tongues until you sense the presence or power of God.

4. Once you sense the Spirit of the Lord upon you, listen to the Holy Spirit and do whatever you sense He tells you to do.
   - Praise God for what He does! To Him be all glory!

NOTES: _____

ADDITIONAL SCRIPTURES:
Acts 1:8
Acts 2:1-13
Acts 4:8, 31
Acts 9:17
Acts 10:38
Luke 11:13

Old Testament Examples:
Judges 3:10, 6:34, 11:29, 13:25, 14:6, 19, 15:14
1 Samuel 10:1,6,9; 11:6, 16:13
Numbers 11:16-30

Category: Miracles

POWER & AUTHORITY*

God gave Jesus all power and authority over all creation in order to carry out His Kingdom purpose. We previously learned that the word for power in Greek is *dynamis*, like dynamite, meaning strength or ability, as in being stronger than an opponent. On the other hand, authority is rank and the right to do something, as in being the boss. The word for authority is *exousia* and is defined as "the power of choice or the liberty to do as one pleases, including the power of rule or government, or jurisdiction." Jesus has all dynamis and exousia over all creation and now He now shares that with us as we go out to do His Kingdom work.

> *Matthew 28:18-20:* Then Jesus came to them and said, **"All authority in heaven and on earth has been given to me. Therefore go and make disciples of all nations**, baptizing them in the name of the Father and of the Son and of the Holy Spirit, and **teaching them to obey everything I have commanded you**. And surely I am with you always, to the very end of the age."

> *Ephesians 1:18-23:* - I pray that the eyes of your heart may be enlightened in order that you may know the hope to which he has called you, the riches of his glorious inheritance in his holy people, and **his incomparably great power [dynamis] for us who believe. That power [dynamis] is the same as the mighty strength he exerted when he raised Christ from the dead** and seated him at his right hand in the heavenly realms, **far above all rule and authority [exousia],** power [dynamis] and dominion, and every name that is invoked, not only in the present age but also in the one to come. And God **placed all things under his feet and appointed him to be head over everything for the church**, **which is his body**, the fullness of him who fills everything in every way.

Authority was God's original design for mankind. God gave Adam and Eve all authority in the earth in their state of purity and innocence and they had God-given command over all creation including the animals, fish, birds, and plants. All they had to do was speak the word, and all of creation had to obey. For example, Adam could say to the birds, "come here," or to the clouds, "move from here to there," and they had to obey because they were subject to Adam. Furthermore, before the wrong-tree incident, man outranked the devil. All Adam had to say to the serpent was, "NO." But unfortunately, he didn't.

As God's Son, authority was Jesus' birthright. He could do anything that He pleased, and all creation had to obey. Unlike Adam, Jesus maintained His rank over the devil even when the evil one tested Him for forty days in the wilderness by saying, in essence, "NO." Jesus' divine nature always led Him in purity so that He used His God-given authority correctly according to God's will. Jesus also had authority from God to forgive sin, something only God can do and which inherently releases people from the devil's subjection. As such, the signs and wonders of God that followed Jesus proved His authority from God.

> *Mark 1:27:* The people were all so amazed that they asked each other, "What is this? **A new teaching—and with authority! He even gives orders to impure spirits and they obey him."** (See also Luke 4:36.)

> *Luke 5:23-24:* Which is easier: to say, 'Your sins are forgiven,' or to say, 'Get up and walk'? **But I want you to know that the Son of Man has authority on earth to forgive sins."** So he

said to the paralyzed man, "I tell you, get up, take your mat and go home." (See also Matthew 9:1-8, Mark 2:5-11.)

Matthew 8:27: The men were amazed and asked, "What kind of man is this? **Even the winds and the waves obey him!"***(See also Mark 4:41.)*

Jesus' message was, "Repent, for the Kingdom of Heaven is at hand!" He did not come to condemn, to judge, or to oppress but to forgive, show mercy, and set free. Everywhere Jesus went, He proclaimed or taught about the Kingdom of God and then demonstrated God's love and power by healing the sick, casting out demons, cleansing lepers, raising the dead, multiplying food, and commanding the weather. It was not just power that poured out through Jesus – it was the love of God offering salvation, deliverance, healing, and sustenance for all who would believe. Here is a chart of some of Jesus' miracles.

The Blind Receive Sight	
2 Blind Men	Matthew 9
Blind Man	Mark 8
Man Born Blind	John 9
Blind Man	Matthew 20, Mark 10, Luke 18
The Lame Walk	
Man Lame 38 years	John 5
Paralyzed Man	Matthew 9, Mark 2, Luke 5
Lepers are Cleansed	
Leper	Matthew 8, Mark 1, Luke 5
Ten Lepers	Luke 17
The Deaf Hear	
Deaf and Mute Man	Mark 7
Deaf and Mute Boy	Mark 9
The Dead are Raised	
Girl in Death Bed	Matthew 9, Mark 5, Luke 8
Man in Coffin at Funeral	Luke 7
Man in Grave/Four Days Dead	John 11
The Sick Are Healed	
Woman Bleeding 12 Years	Matthew 9, Mark 5, Luke 8
Woman with Fever	Matthew 8, Mark 1, Luke 4
Man Near Death	Matthew 8, Luke 7
Boy Very Sick/Near Death	John 4
Man with Swelling/Dropsy	Luke 14
Deformed Hand Restored	Matthew 12, Mark 3, Luke 6
Cut Off Ear Restored	Luke 22
Demons are Cast Out	
Boy with Violent Seizures	Matthew 17, Mark 9, Luke 9
Girl with Tormenting Evil Spirit	Matthew 15, Mark 7
Man with Evil/Unclean Spirit	Mark 1, Luke 4
Mute Man	Matthew 12, Luke 11
Woman Crippled 18 Years	Luke 13
Man Driven to Insanity	Matthew 8, Mark 5, Luke 8
Mute Man	Matthew 9

Jesus was not limited to these miracles or to these illnesses. In fact, these examples are just the highlights that the writers of the Gospels chose to write about for our edification. However, these writers also made it definitively clear that Jesus healed ALL diseases for those who came to Him in faith.

> *Matthew 4:23-24 - Jesus went throughout Galilee, teaching in their synagogues, proclaiming the good news of the kingdom, **and healing every disease and sickness among the people**. News about Him spread all over Syria, and people brought to Him **all who were ill with various diseases, those suffering severe pain, the demon-possessed, those having seizures, and the paralyzed; and He healed them**.*

> *See also Matthew 9:35, 12:15, 14:25-26, 15:30-31; Mark 1:32-39, 3:10-11, 6:54-56; Luke 4:40-41, 6:17-19, 7:21, 9:11; John 6:2, 20:30, 21:25; Acts 10:38.*

All of this is to say that Jesus' miracles testified to Jesus' absolute power and authority over all creation and revealed a loving God's perfect and pleasing will on earth as it is in heaven. Accordingly, when Jesus' disciples asked Him how we should pray, He responded with a simple answer:

> *Matthew 6:9-13: "This, then, is how you should pray: " 'Our Father in heaven, hallowed be your name, **your kingdom come, your will be done, on earth as it is in heaven. Give us today our daily bread**. And **forgive us our debts**, as we also have **forgiven our debtors**. And lead us not into temptation, but **deliver us from the evil one**.'*

Jesus used His authority to bring heaven to earth. Now, He sends us for the very same purpose, and He has given us power through the Gospel to do it. What, then, is the Gospel?

The Gospel is the Power

The Gospel is the power of God. God is not the power, Jesus is not the power, and the anointing of the Holy Spirit is not the power – the Gospel is the power. Again, power is strength or ability.

> *Romans 1:16: For I am not ashamed of the gospel, **because it [the Gospel] is the power of God that brings salvation to everyone who believes**: first to the Jew, then to the Gentile.*

> *1 Corinthians 15:2-4: **By this gospel you are saved**, if you hold firmly to the word I preached to you. Otherwise, you have believed in vain. For what I received **I passed on to you as of first importance**: that **Christ died for our sins** according to the Scriptures, that **he was buried**, that he was **raised on the third day** according to the Scriptures,*

> *1 Corinthians 1:22-24: Jews demand signs and Greeks look for wisdom, but **we preach Christ crucified**: a stumbling block to Jews and foolishness to Gentiles, but to those whom God has called, both Jews and Greeks, **Christ the power of God** and the wisdom of God.*

Through His life, death, and resurrection, Jesus paid for all of our sins and, therefore, the effects and consequences of sin have absolutely no legal right to our lives. Think of it this way: if we owed money to a creditor, then they would have the legal right to pursue us for the debt owed to them. This could include sending bills, calling relentlessly, seizing some of our assets, etc. However, if the debt was paid in full, then the creditor would have no more right to pursue us. Similarly, all of mankind is in debt because of sin and, until this debt is paid, curses, sickness, oppression, and death have the right to pursue us. However, since Jesus paid our sin-debt in full the charges against us have been cancelled and instead of sin's consequences, we have the right to blessing, health, and life – on earth as it is in heaven.

> *Colossians 2:13-14: When **you were dead in your sins** and in the uncircumcision of your flesh, God made you alive with Christ. He forgave us all our sins, **having canceled the charge of our legal indebtedness**, which stood against us and condemned us; he has **taken it away, nailing it to the cross**.*

*Colossians 1:21-23: Once you were alienated from God and were enemies in your minds because of your evil behavior. But now he has reconciled you by Christ's physical body through death to **present you holy in his sight, without blemish and free from accusation**-- if you continue in your faith, established and firm, and **do not move from the hope held out in the gospel**. This is the gospel that you heard and that has been proclaimed to every creature under heaven, and of which I, Paul, have become a servant.*

The curse of God's Law is the presiding standard of retribution for our sin and stumbling and, without Christ, it has the right to enforce its consequences in our lives. However, when we believe Jesus, we are no longer subject to the curse of the Law. No matter how much we stumble, Jesus took it all upon Himself. This profound exchange is the Gospel. Jesus Christ, who never sinned, had all of our sins imputed to Him, charged against Him, and placed on His account. (See Galatians 3:13.) Through faith, we, who are incapable of righteousness, have Jesus' righteousness imputed to us, credited to our account, and given to us as a free gift. He became sin. We become the righteousness of God. (See 2 Corinthians 5:21.) Accordingly, anything which is outside of God's perfect and pleasing will for us as it is in heaven has no legal grounds to be in our lives.

Curse of the Law Deuteronomy 28: (See also Leviticus 26.)	The Power of the Gospel (See many many other Scriptures...)
Lack: verses: 15-19, 23-24, 26, 38-42, 48, 63 **Sickness:** verses: 21-22, 27-28, 34-35, 58-62 **Defeat:** verses: 25-26, 29-33, 43-44, 48-57 **Unholiness:** verses: 15, 25 , 37, 45-47, 53-58 **Enmity with God:** verses: 34, 36, 48, 61, 65-67 **Sinfulness:** verses: 15, 45-47, 53-58 **Wandering/Exile from God:** verses: 29,32, 36-37, 41, 63-68	*Romans 8:32: He who **did not spare** his own Son, but **gave him up** for us all--how will he not also, along with him, **graciously give us all things**?* *1Peter 2:24: "He himself bore our sins" in his body on the cross, so that we might die to sins and live for righteousness; "**by his wounds you have been healed**."* *Colossians 2:15: And having disarmed the powers and authorities, he made a public spectacle of them, **triumphing over them by the cross**.* *Hebrews 10:14: For by one sacrifice he has **made perfect forever those who are being made holy**.* *1Peter 2:25: For "you were like sheep going astray," **but now you have returned to the Shepherd and Overseer of your souls**.* *Ephesians 1:7: In him we have redemption through his blood, **the forgiveness of sins**, in accordance with the riches of God's grace* *Ephesians 2:13: But now in Christ Jesus you who once were far away **have been brought near by the blood of Christ**.*

Think of it this way: Hypothetically, if we are all deathly allergic to bee stings then when we are stung by a bee, we know that we are going to die. That bee sting has *power* over us because, as the bee venom permeates our being and kills us, it proves to be stronger than we are. However, if we possess the anti-venom to bee stings, then all bee stings are rendered powerless and have no effect. Similarly, sin is like a bee sting, and the Law of God is like the bee venom enforcing consequences of the sting which pervade our being until we perish. (See Romans 6:23.) Christ's resurrection proves that Jesus is stronger than sin and death so, therefore, the Gospel is like the anti-venom that renders sin powerless, nullifies its effects. We apply the anti-venom by faith and it grants us immunity from stings that lead to death for all eternity.

*1Corinthians 15:55-57: "Where, O death, is your victory? Where, O death, is your sting?" The **sting of death is sin**, and the **power of sin is the law**. But thanks be to God! He **gives us the victory through our Lord Jesus Christ**.*

*Hebrews 2:14-15: Since the children have flesh and blood, he too shared in their humanity so **that by his death he might break the power of him who holds the power of death--that is, the devil**-- and free those who all their lives were held in slavery by their fear of death.*

In short, Jesus overpowered all of our enemies through His life, death, and resurrection and the Gospel renders all sin, the curse, the devil, and even death *powerless* against everyone who believes Christ. Therefore, the Gospel of Jesus Christ is the answer to every affliction and oppression facing everyone that we know. This said, the power of the Gospel is only accessed through faith. For this reason, when Jesus' first followers asked Him what God required of them, His answer was simple: **believe**.

*John 6:28-29: Then they asked him, "**What must we do to do the works God requires?**" Jesus answered, "**The work of God is this: to believe in the one he has sent**."*

It is only through faith in Christ that we receive all of the benefits of His salvation and do the works that He did. He sends us out to proclaim the Gospel, which is the power of God to work miracles, signs, and wonders, so that we receive and reveal to others God's will on earth as it is in heaven.

Authority in Christ

Jesus' authority over all creation was His birthright as the Son of God and He used it to serve those whose lives had been damaged by the effects of sin. (See Philippians 2:6-7.) While He was on the earth, He shared this authority with His disciples when He sent them out to proclaim the Kingdom of Heaven and to do the works that He had been doing, namely, miracles. Notably, He cautioned His followers to remain focused on what was truly significant – not their authority in Jesus' name but that they knew Him and were known by Him.

*Matthew 10:1, 7-8: Jesus called his twelve disciples to him and **gave them authority to drive out impure spirits and to heal every disease and sickness**... As you go, **proclaim this message: 'The kingdom of heaven has come near.' Heal the sick, raise the dead, cleanse those who have leprosy, drive out demons**. Freely you have received; freely give. (See also Mark 6:7-13; Luke 9:1-6, 10:1-23.)*

*Luke 10:19-20: **I have given you authority** to trample on snakes and scorpions and **to overcome all the power of the enemy; nothing will harm you**. However, do not rejoice that **the spirits submit to you**, but **rejoice that your names are written in heaven**.*

After His resurrection, Jesus commissioned His disciples into their Kingdom assignment. Because we who believe were included with Christ in His resurrection, His authority has become our born-again birthright as sons and daughters of God. (See 1 Peter 1:3; John 1:12) Post-resurrection, our authority in Christ is not just an assignment, it is part of who we have become.

When Jesus ascended to heaven, it was confirmed that Jesus Christ is supreme over everything created because He is seated at the right hand of God in the throne room of heaven. (See Colossians 1:15-20.) We who believe were with Jesus when He ascended to heaven, and therefore, we are seated in Him in the throne room of God, and we have the same God-given *authority* that He has.

*Philippians 2:9-11: Therefore **God exalted him to the highest place and gave him the name that is above every name, that at the name of Jesus every knee should bow, in heaven and on earth and under the earth**, and every tongue acknowledge that Jesus Christ is Lord, to the glory of God the Father.*

*Ephesians 2:6: And God raised us up with Christ and **seated us with him in the heavenly realms in Christ Jesus**,*

In Christ and according to God's will, we now have authority over creation, we outrank the devil and all of his cohorts, and we have the right to declare that sins have been forgiven in the name of Jesus. God placed everything under subjection to Jesus so that through faith in Him, we can execute God's will in the earth and do the works that Jesus did the way that He did them. Through this we reveal Christ's victory over sin, death, and the devil and we make it known that Jesus has absolute authority over all.

> *Ephesians 3:10-11: His intent was that now, **through the church, the manifold wisdom of God should be made known to the rulers and authorities in the heavenly realms**, according to his eternal purpose **that he accomplished in Christ Jesus our Lord**.*

> *John 20:21-23: Again Jesus said, "Peace be with you! **As the Father has sent me, I am sending you.**" And with that he breathed on them and said, "Receive the Holy Spirit. **If you forgive anyone's sins, their sins are forgiven; if you do not forgive them, they are not forgiven.**"*

POWER & AUTHORITY TO SAVE

In the Scriptures, a person's name often indicates their personality or purpose. The name Jesus means *God saves*, and this is certainly descriptive of God's purpose for Him. When Jesus described His mission on the earth, He described it like this:

> *John 3:17: For God did not send his Son into the world to condemn the world, but **to save the world through him**.*

> *John 12:47: If anyone hears my words but does not keep them, I do not judge that person. For **I did not come to judge the world, but to save the world**.*

> *Luke 19:10: For the Son of Man came **to seek and to save the lost**."*

We previously examined how Elijah's anointing and mission became Elisha's anointing and mission and how Elijah's cloak and a double portion of his spirit equipped Elisha with everything that he needed to fulfill his task. Now that the Holy Spirit has been poured out, Christ's anointing and purpose has become the anointing and purpose of each one of us as His disciples. His intent is for His followers to do His works with the same heart of love of God towards all people. Miracles are not for the purpose of being spiritually powerful to make ourselves look good or gain a following. The power of God for miracles is for the purpose of salvation, deliverance, healing, and sustenance.

> *1Timothy 2:3-4: God our Savior, **who wants all people to be saved** and to come to a knowledge of the truth.*

> *1Timothy 4:10: **That is why we labor and strive**, because we have put our hope in the living God, **who is the Savior of all people**, and especially of those who believe.*

God's desire is to save. Jesus came to save. Power from heaven being given to us to work miracles is God's expression of love and confirming the name of His only Son Jesus so that the whole world can be saved through faith in Him.

www.manifestinternational.com

ALL AUTHORITY TO GO
Scripture Reading & Worksheet

Read each of the following passages and then use the chart below for study and reflection.
- Matthew 10
- Luke 9:1-6
- Luke 10:1-24
- Mark 16:15-20

How did Jesus command His disciples to proclaim the message of His Kingdom?

List three significant words or phrases that stood out to you.		

What insight does this give you about God's power for sharing the Gospel?

What insight does this give you about persecution for moving in spiritual power and authority?

How do these passages change your views about sharing Jesus with other people?

List three questions you still have about God following believers with signs and wonders.		

What is your conclusion or main take-away from these passages?

Basic Training Exercise

CAST OUT DEMONS

Matthew 10:1, 7-8 NIV - Jesus called his twelve disciples to him and gave them authority to drive out impure spirits and to heal every disease and sickness... As you go, proclaim this message: 'The kingdom of heaven has come near.' Heal the sick, raise the dead, cleanse those who have leprosy, drive out demons. Freely you have received; freely give.

DESCRIPTION

Jesus gave authority to us as His disciples to cast out demons, also known as unclean spirits. Demons keep people in bondage to states of mind or behaviors from which they desire to be free. Demonic oppression can be the cause of torments, addictions, compulsions, and chronic or irrational behaviors which plague people with trouble.

The aim in Christ is freedom from all oppression for everyone. Unbelievers may be possessed, oppressed, or afflicted by any sort of demon. Christ followers cannot be possessed by demons but can experience oppression due to harassment from unclean spirits. When a believer commands demons to leave in the name of Jesus, deliverance from these torturous afflictions can happen in an instant. This said, once the unclean spirits have been cast out, the formerly oppressed person must also modify their behavior to live by faith in Christ's freedom so that the demons do not return.

Therefore, to practice Casting Out Demons is about discerning the unclean or demonic spirits so that we can expose and expel them in the name of Jesus, bringing liberty to the captives with the power of God!

PRAYER

Father, thank you that you have granted me authority to cast out demons. Help me to discern spirits afflicting and oppressing me and others and the power to cast them out by faith, In Jesus' name, Amen.

Category: Miracles

ALL RIGHTS RESERVED © 2018 Wendy Bowen

www.ministriesinternational.com

Basic TRAINING
SPIRITUAL EXERCISES

PURPOSE:

To grow in exercising our God-given authority over the powers of the devil.

To set ourselves and others free from demonic oppression through the name of Jesus.

To fill ourselves and others with the Holy Spirit rather than unclean spirits.

SPIRITUAL FRUIT:

Greater functioning in God's authority for us as His children.

Deeper experience of God's ways and work on our behalf.

Freedom from oppression.

Repentance from ungodliness.

Renewed purity in the Holy Spirit.

PRACTICE

1. Identify potential areas of demonic oppression. For example, behaviors that are irrational, uncharacteristic of the person's normal state, uncontrollable, or addictive.
   - For example, some common oppressions include:

Anger	Rejection	Infirmity
Fear	Self-loathing	Pornography
Anxiety	Religion	New Age spirits
Jezebel	Depression	Bitterness
	Witchcraft	Abandonment
Regret	Offense	Divination	Hopelessness
		Leviathan	Manipulation

2. Ask the Holy Spirit to reveal to you any demonic or unclean spirits which are the cause of oppression or affliction.
   - Write down what you hear the Holy Spirit saying.
   - If you do not have one word for it, write down a brief description of what the unclean spirit causes. For example, "a spirit that causes me to hate myself."

3. Believe in your heart that it is God's will for those captive to demonic spirits to be set free.
   - Believe that as Christ's disciple, you have authority to cast out demons in His name.

4. Expel the demons. Take authority and command the spirit. (Speak the way you would command a dog to sit.)
   - Say something like, "In the name and authority of the name of Jesus, I command the spirit of [name of unclean spirit] to leave right now and never return."
   - If you do not have a specific name for the spirit, address it as an unclean spirit or spirits.

5. Refill with the Holy Spirit and live out your liberty.
   - Ask the Lord to fill the formerly oppressed person with the Holy Spirit in place of the unclean spirits.
   - Encourage them to change any behaviors which may have become habitual due to the demonic oppression.

NOTES: _____

ADDITIONAL SCRIPTURES:

Mark 1:23-27
Matthew 8:16, 28-34
Acts 10:38
Acts 16:16-24
Luke 10:19-20
Luke 11:24-26
Acts 19:11-20
1 Timothy 4:1
Ephesians 6:12

Walking Like Jesus*

Jesus did not come only to die for us but also to live for us in order to reveal the perfect will of God in action. Jesus' life is the exact image of God in the earth and whatever Jesus did was exactly what God desired to be done in each situation. (See Hebrews 1:3; John 14:9.)

God's design in giving us the Holy Spirit is for us to walk by the Spirit like Jesus did rather than our own desires and ideas. This is how He guides us into the works He has ordained for us to do and this is what transforms us into Christ's likeness in our inward nature as the children of God. When we truly allow ourselves to be led by the Spirit of the Lord, our lives will become more and more miraculous.

> *Romans 8:5-6: Those who live according to the flesh have their minds set on **what the flesh desires**; but those who live in accordance with the Spirit have their minds set on **what the Spirit desires**. The **mind governed by the flesh is death**, but the **mind governed by the Spirit is life and peace**.*

> *Romans 8:12-14: Therefore, brothers and sisters, we have an obligation--but it is not to the flesh, to live according to it. For if you live according to the flesh, you will die; but **if by the Spirit you put to death the misdeeds of the body**, you will live. For **those who are led by the Spirit of God are the children of God**.*

The only way that we will fulfill the good works which God has prepared for us is to live like Jesus and be led by the Spirit of the Lord the way that Jesus was. Living by the guidance of God through the Holy Spirit is not about doing whatever the most godly thing seems to be in any given situation. Instead, we must set our hearts to seek God's guidance above all else and allow Him to correct and guide us along with way, trusting that He will. This requires faith that He is who He says He is and trust that He is a gentle Shepherd, not a harsh master. (Consider Matthew 25:14-30.) The more we listen, the more He will guide us.

> *Mark 4:24-25 NLT: Then he added, "Pay close attention to what you hear. **The closer you listen, the more understanding you will be given--and you will receive even more. To those who listen to my teaching, more understanding will be given**. But for those who are not listening, even what little understanding they have will be taken away from them." (See also Matthew 25:29; Luke 8:18.)*

Dead Works and Good Works

If we continue living our lives according to our fleshly desires or if we continue to try to fulfill the will of God in our own strength or concept of what God's will is, then we are producing *dead works*. A dead work is a work that does not lead to life. Neither our flesh nor our religious concepts of obedience or piety have any ability to produce the righteousness of God leading to everlasting life. We are saved entirely by faith.

> *Galatians 3:2-3: I would like to learn just one thing from you: **Did you receive the Spirit by the works of the law, or by believing** what you heard? Are you so foolish? After **beginning by means of the Spirit, are you now trying to finish by means of the flesh**?*

This said, faith alone without works is also dead.

*James 2:17-18: In the same way, **faith by itself, if it is not accompanied by action, is dead.** But someone will say, "You have faith; I have deeds." Show me your faith without deeds, and I will show you my faith by my deeds.*

Christ redeemed us so that we may be saved by God's grace through faith in Him and so we may do good works for His Kingdom and according to His purposes.

*Ephesians 2:8-10: For it is by grace you have been saved, through faith--and this is not from yourselves, it is the gift of God-- **not by works, so that no one can boast.** For we are God's handiwork, **created in Christ Jesus to do good works, which God prepared in advance for us to do.***

Now, because the Holy Spirit is within us, we do not have to wonder as the saying goes, "What would Jesus do?" By standards of logic and common sense, Jesus was completely unpredictable, and God's ways often seem like foolishness to our natural mind. (See 1 Corinthians 1:18.) Unfortunately, this is how a lot of us are trying to follow Jesus. We read about Him, imagine the way that we think He is or how we think He would handle a situation, and then we do it according to our own imagined or intellectual concept of Jesus and God's will. We do what we think we should be doing rather than actually seeking Him and waiting for Him to guide us.

Rather, when we allow ourselves to be guided by the Holy Spirit, we know for ourselves what Jesus **is doing** right NOW because Jesus is in us and He is doing it through us right NOW. This said, excelling at living our lives by the indwelling Holy Spirit does not happen overnight, and it cannot be rushed, forced, or faked. In fact, it seems that the more we try to rush, force, and fake it, the worse things go for us. We cannot lean on our own understanding – and even our own understanding of God. We have to become like little children in order to be led by Him and to walk in His miracles.

*Proverbs 3:5-6: **Trust in the LORD** with all your heart and **lean not on your own understanding**; in all your ways **submit to him**, and he will make your paths straight.*

*Matthew 18:3: And he said: "Truly I tell you, **unless you change and become like little children**, you will never enter the kingdom of heaven.*

To be clear, I am not suggesting that God desires us to be stupid people or discard the capacities which He has given us. Rather, I am saying that, as we make decisions, we should choose to follow the guidance of the Holy Spirit, even if it does not seem to measure up with our common sense or a logical way of approaching things. Our common sense and religious ideas will produce nothing but death. But the Holy Spirit will teach us what we need to know to follow God's path for our lives and fulfill the works He has for us to do. Actually, living by the Holy Spirit gives us the highest intelligence available and He promises to teach us all things!

*1Corinthians 1:25: For the foolishness of God is **wiser than human wisdom**, and the weakness of God is **stronger than human strength.***

*1John 2:20, 27: But you have an **anointing from the Holy One [the Holy Spirit]**, and all of you **know the truth.** ... As for you, the anointing [the Holy Spirit] you received from him remains in you, **and you do not need anyone to teach you.** But as **his anointing [the Holy Spirit] teaches you about all things** and as that anointing is real, not counterfeit--just as it has taught you, **remain in him.***

CHRIST IN YOU

The Biblical writer who best expressed this abiding relationship of us in Christ and Christ in us through the Holy Spirit was John. John emphasized Jesus' teaching about His relationship with God the Father and our relationship with Christ through the Holy Spirit. These are a mirror image of one another.

Jesus walked on earth in a flesh like ours as a demonstration for us of what it looks like to live by the guidance of God's Spirit. When we do what Jesus did by abiding in Him the way He abided in the Father, we will say what He is saying and do what He is doing. It is only through this abiding relationship that we are empowered to carry out God's purposes in the earth.

Let's take a look at the parallels between Jesus' relationship with His Father and our relationship with Christ now that He has ascended to heaven and poured the Holy Spirit into our hearts.

Jesus could do nothing by Himself, only what He saw the Father doing – *mirrors* – We can do nothing apart from Him and our flesh profits nothing:

> *John 5:19-20: Jesus gave them this answer: "Very truly I tell you, the **Son can do nothing by himself; he can do only what he sees his Father doing**, because whatever the Father does the Son also does. For **the Father loves the Son and shows him all he does**. Yes, and he will show him even greater works than these, so that you will be amazed.*

> *John 6:63: **The Spirit gives life; the flesh counts for nothing.** The words I have spoken to you--they are full of the Spirit and life.*

> *John 15:5: "I am the vine; you are the branches. If you remain in me and I in you, you will bear much fruit; **apart from me you can do nothing**.*

God did not leave Jesus alone – *mirrors* – Jesus does not leave us alone as orphans:

> *John 8:29: The one who sent me **is with me**; he has **not left me alone**, for I always do what pleases him."*

> *John 14:16-18: And I will ask the Father, and he will give you another advocate to help you and **be with you forever**-- **the Spirit of truth**. The world cannot accept him, because it neither sees him nor knows him. But you know him, for **he lives with you and will be in you**. **I will not leave you as orphans**; I will come to you.*

God was in Jesus and Jesus was in God – *mirrors* – Christ is in us and we are in Christ:

> *John 10:38: But if I do them, even though you do not believe me, believe the works, that you may know and understand that **the Father is in me, and I in the Father**."*

> *John 14:10-11,17,20,23: Don't you believe that **I am in the Father, and that the Father is in me**? The words I say to you I do not speak on my own authority. Rather, **it is the Father, living in me, who is doing his work**. Believe me when I say that **I am in the Father and the Father is in me**; or at least believe on the evidence of the works themselves. ... **the Spirit of truth**. The world cannot accept him, because it neither sees him nor knows him. But you know him, **for he lives with you and will be in you**. ... On that day you will realize that **I am in my Father, and you are in me, and I am in you**. ... Jesus replied, "Anyone who loves me will obey my teaching. My Father will love them, and **we will come to them and make our home with them**.*

> *John 15:4-7: **Remain in me, as I also remain in you**. No branch can bear fruit by itself; it must remain in the vine. Neither can you bear fruit unless you remain in me. "I am the vine; you are the branches. **If you remain in me and I in you**, you will bear much fruit; apart from me you can do nothing. If you do not remain in me, you are like a branch that is thrown away and withers; such branches are picked up, thrown into the fire and burned. **If you remain in me and my words remain in you**, ask whatever you wish, and it will be done for you.*

Jesus had life in Him – *mirrors* – We have life in us:

> *John 1:4:* **In him was life**, *and that life was the light of all mankind.*

> *John 5:26: For as the Father has life in himself, so he has granted* **the Son also to have life in himself.**

> *John 6:40,47-48,54,57: For my Father's will is that everyone who looks to the Son and* **believes in him shall have eternal life**, *and I will raise them up at the last day." ... Very truly I tell you, the one who* **believes has eternal life. I am the bread of life.** *... Whoever eats my flesh and drinks my blood* **has eternal life**, *and I will raise them up at the last day. ... Just as the living Father sent me and* **I live because of the Father**, *so the one who feeds on me* **will live because of me.**

> *John 11:25 : Jesus said to her, "***I am*** the resurrection and*** the life.*** The one who*** believes in me will live***, even though they die;*

> *John 14:6,19: Jesus answered, "I am the way and the truth and the life. No one comes to the Father except through me… Before long, the world will not see me anymore, but you will see me.* **Because I live, you also will live.**

God taught Jesus, showed Jesus what to do and what to say, and Jesus obeyed God's commands – *mirrors* – Jesus teaches us all that He knows, shows us what to do and what to say, and we keep His commands

> *John 8:28-29: So Jesus said, "When you have lifted up the Son of Man, then you will know that I am he and that* **I do nothing on my own but speak just what the Father has taught me**. *The one who sent me is with me; he has not left me alone, for* **I always do what pleases him**."

> *John 12:49-50: For* **I did not speak on my own, but the Father who sent me commanded me to say all that I have spoken**. *I know that his command leads to eternal life. So* **whatever I say is just what the Father has told me to say**."

> *John 14:15,21,23,26,31: "***If you love me, keep my commands.*** ... Whoever has my commands and keeps them is the one who loves me.*** The one who loves me will be loved by my Father, and I too will love them and show myself to them." ... Jesus replied, "***Anyone who loves me will obey my teaching***. My Father will love them, and we will come to them and make our home with them. ... But the Advocate,*** the Holy Spirit***, whom the Father will send in my name,*** will teach you all things and will remind you of everything I have said to you***. ... but he comes so that the world may learn that*** I love the Father and do exactly what my Father has commanded me***. "Come now; let us leave.*

> *John 15:3,10,15:* **You are already clean** *because of the word I have spoken to you. If you* **keep my commands**, *you will remain in my love, just as* **I have kept my Father's commands** *and remain in his love. ... I no longer call you servants, because a servant does not know his master's business. Instead, I have called you friends,* **for everything that I learned from my Father I have made known to you.**

> *John 16:13,15: But when he, the* **Spirit of truth**, *comes,* **he will guide you into all the truth.** *He will not speak on his own;* **he will speak only what he hears, and he will tell you** *what is yet to come. ... All that belongs to the Father is mine. That is why I said* **the Spirit will receive from me what he will make known to you.**"

> *1Jo 2:20,27: But you have an anointing from the Holy One, [the Holy Spirit] and* **all of you know the truth**. *... As for you, the anointing you received from him remains in you, and you*

*do not need anyone to teach you. But as **his anointing teaches you about all things** and as that anointing is real, not counterfeit--just as it has taught you, remain in him.*

Jesus' teaching was not His own but God's – mirrors – Our teaching is not our own but Christ's:

*John 7:16: Jesus answered, "**My teaching is not my own. It comes from the one who sent me.** ...*

*John 14:24,26: Anyone who does not love me will not obey my teaching. **These words you hear are not my own; they belong to the Father who sent me.** ... But the Advocate, **the Holy Spirit**, whom the Father will send in my name, **will teach you all things and will remind you of everything I have said to you.***

*John 15:15: I no longer call you servants, because a servant does not know his master's business. Instead, I have called you friends, **for everything that I learned from my Father I have made known to you.***

*Mat 28:19-20: **Therefore go and make disciples of all nations**, baptizing them in the name of the Father and of the Son and of the Holy Spirit, and **teaching them to obey everything I have commanded you**. And surely I am with you always, to the very end of the age."*

Jesus is the Son of God – mirrors – We are the children of God:

*John 3:16: For God so loved the world that **he gave his one and only Son**, that whoever believes in him shall not perish but have eternal life.*

*John 10:36: what about the one whom the Father set apart as his very own and sent into the world? Why then do you accuse me of blasphemy because I said, **'I am God's Son'**?*

*John 1:12: Yet **to all who did receive him**, to those **who believed** in his name, he gave the right to **become children of God**--*

Jesus is the light of the world – mirrors – We are the light of the world:

*John 1:4: In him was life, and that life was **the light of all mankind**.*

*John 9:5: While I am in the world, **I am the light of the world**."*

*John 8:12: When Jesus spoke again to the people, he said, "**I am the light of the world**. Whoever **follows me** will never walk in darkness, but will **have the light of life**."*

*John 12:36,46: Believe in the light while you have the light, so that you may **become children of light**." When he had finished speaking, Jesus left and hid himself from them. ... **I have come into the world as a light**, so that no one who believes in me should stay in darkness.*

*Mat 5:14: "**You are the light of the world**. A town built on a hill cannot be hidden.*

Jesus did not sin – mirrors – We will not sin:

*1Jo 3:5-6,9: But you know that he appeared so that he might take away our sins. **And in him is no sin. No one who lives in him keeps on sinning.** No one who continues to sin has either seen him or known him. ... **No one who is born of God will continue to sin**, because God's seed remains in them; **they cannot go on sinning**, because they have been born of God.*

1Jo 5:18: We know that **anyone born of God does not continue to sin**; *the One who was born of God keeps them safe, and the evil one cannot harm them.*

God loves Jesus – mirrors – Jesus loves us:

John 5:20: For **the Father loves the Son** *and shows him all he does. Yes, and he will show him even greater works than these, so that you will be amazed.*

John 14:21: Whoever has my commands and keeps them is the one who loves me. **The one who loves me will be loved by my Father, and I too will love them** *and show myself to them."*

John 15:9: **As the Father has loved me, so have I loved you.** *Now remain in my love.*

God sent Jesus into the world – mirrors – Jesus sends us into the world to be like Him and do His works.

John 6:38: For **I have come down from heaven** *not to do my will but to do the will of him who sent me.*

John 12:45: **The one who looks at me is seeing the one who sent me.**

John 14:9: Jesus answered: "Don't you know me, Philip, even after I have been among you such a long time? **Anyone who has seen me has seen the Father.** *How can you say, 'Show us the Father'?*

John 13:20: Very truly I tell you, **whoever accepts anyone I send accepts me**; *and* **whoever accepts me accepts the one who sent me.**"

Mat 28:19-20: Therefore **go and make disciples of all nations**, *baptizing them in the name of the Father and of the Son and of the Holy Spirit, and* **teaching them to obey everything I have commanded you.** *And surely* **I am with you** *always, to the very end of the age."*

*Mar 16:15-18: He said to them, "***Go into all the world and preach the gospel to all creation.** *Whoever believes and is baptized will be saved, but whoever does not believe will be condemned. And* **these signs will accompany those who believe**: *In my name they will drive out demons; they will speak in new tongues; they will pick up snakes with their hands; and when they drink deadly poison, it will not hurt them at all; they will place their hands on sick people, and they will get well."*

John 14:12: Very truly I tell you, **whoever believes in me will do the works I have been doing, and they will do even greater things than these**, *because I am going to the Father.*

Only through the Holy Spirit can we be guided by God into the good works which He has prepared for us. When we are led by the Holy Spirit in us directing us, empowering us, and strengthening us, will we become like Jesus and we will not produce dead works but good works of eternal life. We will walk like Jesus walked, talk like He talked, do the things He did, and endure through the trials of life in order to receive our eternal rewards.

Basic Training Exercise

OBEDIENCE TO THE MASTER

Romans 6:1-17 NIV - Don't you know that when you offer yourselves to someone as obedient slaves, you are slaves of the one you obey—whether you are slaves to sin, which leads to death, or to obedience, which leads to righteousness? But thanks be to God that, though you used to be slaves to sin, you have come to obey from your heart the pattern of teaching that has now claimed your allegiance.

Basic TRAINING
SPIRITUAL EXERCISES

PURPOSE:

To listen to God's voice.

To discern the will of the Lord for us for today.

To present ourselves to God to do His will.

DESCRIPTION

The Apostle Paul knew that He had been bought with a price. God purchased us for Himself with the precious blood of Jesus. This redemption sets us free from wrong "masters" so that we can obey God.

It is true that Jesus calls us His friends but He is also our King. The Kingdom is a monarchy, not a democracy. Our King has the right to give us orders, instructions, and daily tasks. Unfortunately, we often live according to our own agenda, desires, ambitions, the pattern of this world, or the expectations of others rather than turning ourselves over to obey God exclusively.

We are God's servants. A servant eagerly awaits their master's orders and executes them without argument or contradiction. The master sets the agenda each day for their own purposes and has the right to shift the focus of the servant anytime they need to.

To practice Obedience to the Master is about receiving daily "orders" from the Lord about the things that He has for us **today** so that we can obey Him even if it means we have to alter our own plans.

CONSIDERATIONS

Has there been a time when you knew that God was telling you to do something other than what you had planned? What was this like for you? What did you do?

What difficulties do you encounter when thinking of yourself as a servant/slave? Why are you offended?

Are you willing to allow God to change your plans today? This week? This year? For your life?

PRAYER

Jesus, you are my King. Forgive me for the times I have treated You too casually by not listening to or obeying Your instructions. I come before You now as a servant to my Master to receive Your directions and to do Your will. Speak to me now so I can obey Your voice. In Jesus' name. Amen.

PRACTICE

1. Each morning, set a time and find a quiet and private place where you can spend time with God.
   - If you need to wake up earlier to make this time, do so.
   - Bring your Bible and a notebook to take note of anything significant the Lord may share with you.

2. Be still for a moment. Then, offer yourself to God.
   - Offer the day ahead to God, saying, "Jesus, I offer this day to you as a sacrifice. I desire to do Your will today."
   - Wait for anything He might say to you before you begin.

3. Begin to ask the Lord for His guidance for the day. Give Jesus enough time to respond to you. Take notes of your King's responses as needed. Use the following questions as a guide for your conversation.
   - King Jesus, what do you have for me today?
   - Is there anything You want me to do?
   - Is there anywhere You want me to go?
   - Is there anyone You want me to reach out to or serve?
   - Is there any issue in me that You want to address?
   - Is there anyone You want me to forgive or bless?
   - Is there anything You want me to acquire or give away?
   - Is there anything on my calendar today that is **not** Your will? How do You want me to handle that?
   - Is there any fruit of the Spirit that You desire for me to execute my tasks with today? (love, joy, peace, etc.)

4. Thank the Lord for His guidance. Ask Him to help you to do the things He has revealed to you **today**, without making excuses – especially the things you might not desire to do.

SPIRITUAL FRUIT:

Greater alignment with God's will.

Increased awareness of God in our daily life and routine.

Increased worship through offering of ourselves.

Improved clarity of God's desires for us.

ADDITIONAL SCRIPTURES:

John 10:27

Psalm 123:2

1 Corinthians 6:20

1 Corinthians 7:23

Isaiah 30:21

Hebrews 3:7,15

Jeremiah 31:33

Romans 12:1

Philippians 2:6-8

NOTES: _____

Category: Listening to God

CORNERSTONE – UNIT 4.4

Gifts & Gathering
Scripture Reading

Read the Book of 1 Corinthians, Chapters 12, 13, 14 and then use the chart below for study and reflection.

Summarize the Apostle Paul's message in these passages.	

3 Highlights or Significant Points:	Questions you still have about this:
1.	
2.	
3.	

Imagine yourself in a gathering like Paul describes, experiencing the scene and the story.		
Who are you?	What do you see?	What do you hear?
What do you smell?	What do you sense?	How do you feel?

What insight does this give you into God's design for Christian gatherings?

Notes & Lessons Learned:

Basic Training Exercise

HOLY SPIRIT: PROPHECY

1 Co 14:3 NIV *The one who prophesies speaks to people for their strengthening, encouraging and comfort.... But if an unbeliever or an inquirer comes in while everyone is prophesying, they are convicted of sin and are brought under judgment by all, as the secrets of their hearts are laid bare. So they will fall down and worship God exclaiming, "God is really among you!"*

GIFTS OF THE HOLY SPIRIT

The Gifts of the Holy Spirit in 1 Corinthians 12 are gifts which are freely distributed by God when believers gather together. Jesus demonstrated that spiritual maturity includes operating in any and all of these gifts as God wills. *Note:* These gifts are different than those in Romans 12 and Ephesians 4.

DESCRIPTION

The Holy Spirit gift of Prophecy is distributed by the Holy Spirit when believers are gathered together. By definition, prophecy is "a discourse emanating from divine inspiration and declaring the purposes of God, whether by reproving and admonishing the wicked, or comforting the afflicted, revealing hidden things, or foretelling future events.*" As such, the Holy Spirit gift of Prophecy is for edification, exhortation, comfort, and may also be used to expose or bring conviction of sin.

Any believer can function in this gift at any time as God grants them revelation. This said, the Scripture is clear that all hearers of prophecy must test/judge the word of prophecy for themselves before receiving it as from the Lord or taking action on the word. As a general guideline, words from the Lord will impart hope and restoration while words of condemnation or manipulation are not from God.

Practicing the Holy Spirit Gift of Prophecy is about listening to God when we are with people for anything He may desire to say to them and then speaking it forth on His behalf.

Basic TRAINING
SPIRITUAL EXERCISES

PURPOSE:

To speak forth God's words of encouragement, and alignment with His will.

To convey the heart of God towards others.

To discern accurately the situations in the lives of others so we can help them according to God's will.

SPIRITUAL FRUIT:

Speaking the truth in love to others.

Building up the Church.

Compassion coupled with words of exhortation to right action.

Considerate warnings and rebukes to those who need correction.

Comfort for the afflicted.

*Definition from Thayer's

ADDITIONAL SCRIPTURES:

1 Corinthians 14:1-5, 29-33, 39

Acts 11:28

Acts 13:1-2

Acts 21:8-14

Acts 21:9

1 Thessalonians 5:19-22

1 John 4:1

PRAYER

Father, thank you that you desire to speak through me by your Spirit so that others may be brought into the fullness of your love and blessings. Help me to speak your words to others so that they can know you more. In Jesus' name, Amen.

PRACTICE

1. When you are with someone, take some time to ask the Lord if there is anything He desires to say to them.
   - While you are with the person, listen to them and listen to the Holy Spirit at the same time.

2. Pay careful attention to what the Holy Spirit reveals to you as you focus on the person you are with. Pay attention for things such as:
   - Scripture verses or passages that come to your mind.
   - Simple phrases which seem to come into your mind (which may hold significance to them even if not to you.)
   - Pictures or visions you see with the eyes of your heart (which you must then describe to them.)
   - Revelation of the call of God on their life or some aspect of how God has gifted them.
   - Discernment of the time or season of life with God that they are in and God's purpose in it.
   - Instructions from God for what they are to do next.
   - Insight into an area of their life which God desires to heal.
   - Invitations to deeper trust in God and His ways.
   - Warnings of danger ahead.
   - Calls to repentance or rebuke for ungodliness or unbelief.
   - A scene or prophetic act the Lord wants you to do to demonstrate His message to them.

3. Share the insights you receive from the Lord with the person you are with or do what the Lord tells you to do.
   - Encourage them to test the word and take it to the Lord in prayer for application.
   - Give God all the glory for speaking through you!

NOTES:

UNIT FOUR – KEY QUESTIONS
Miracles

Use this worksheet to test your grasp of the material and exercises of Unit Four.

How do we access God's power for miracles?	
Is the Holy Spirit within us or upon us?	**What is the difference between being full or filled with the Holy Spirit?**
What is the difference between power and authority?	**What is God's power and authority for?**
How do we do what Jesus would do?	**What is the purpose of the Gifts of the Holy Spirit?**
What is one thing you learned that you did not know before?	**What questions do you still have about this subject?**

UNIT FOUR: GROUP EXERCISES

Use the Cast Out Demons Exercise to minister to one another. **AND/OR**:

Group Training Exercise

HOLY SPIRIT: PROPHECY

DESCRIPTION

The Holy Spirit gift of Prophecy is distributed by the Holy Spirit when believers are gathered together for their edification, exhortation, comfort. To prophesy simply means to speak by divine inspiration as God's representative.

As followers of Christ, any one of us can be enabled by the Holy Spirit to speak the words of God. This could be in the form of a simple phrase, a picture that we see with the eyes of our heart, a sense that we know something that we have no other way of knowing, or an impression that comes to mind about or for those we prophesy to. As we prophesy, we cooperate with God in order to accurately communicate what He is saying to the recipient. We must be careful not to add to God's words or leave anything out.

When we receive prophetic words from others, we listen with our spirit in order to discern the words of God. As a general guideline, the Holy Spirit speaks truth, encourages faith, testifies to eternal hope, imparts God's unconditional love, and conveys God's work on our behalf for our good. On the other hand, words of guilt, shame, fear, punishment, accusation, curse, or manipulation to have personal desires fulfilled are not from the Holy Spirit. We can receive words from the Holy Spirit as the words of God Himself to us and we should reject words that are not from the Holy Spirit, rendering them powerless in our lives by the blood of Jesus.

Practicing the Holy Spirit Gift of Prophecy is about listening to God with one another so that everyone is strengthened in the Lord.

SCRIPTURE PORTION

1 Corinthians 14:26b, 29-31 NIV - When you come together, each of you has a hymn, or a word of instruction, a revelation, a tongue or an interpretation. Everything must be done so that the church may be built up. ... Two or three prophets should speak, and the others should weigh carefully what is said. And if a revelation comes to someone who is sitting down, the first speaker should stop. For you can all prophesy in turn so that everyone may be instructed and encouraged.

Category: Spiritual Gifts

Basic TRAINING — SPIRITUAL EXERCISES

PURPOSE:

Listen to God speak to you by His Spirit as a group.

Speak forth what God is revealing to your group or its members.

Encourage one another with words from God.

GROUP SIZE:

Any size group.

SCRIPTURE PORTIONS

1 Corinthians 12:7-11

1 Corinthians 14

1 John 4:1

Amos 3:7

1 Thessalonians 5:21

Acts 2:17

Joel 2:28

GROUP PRACTICE

1. Start your time as a group with worshipping the Lord and praying in the Spirit for at least 20 to 30 minutes
   - Invite the Holy Spirit to speak to you as a group or to any individuals within the group that the Lord may highlight. Wait upon the Lord with your spiritual ears open to Him.
   - Open the floor for prophetic words.

2. When anyone in the group believes that they have a revelation or a word from the Lord, they can share it. Speak one at a time so everyone can hear. Examples include:
   - Scripture verses or passages that come to mind.
   - Simple phrases which seem to come into your mind (whether they make sense to you or not.)
   - Pictures or visions you see with the eyes of your heart (which you must then describe to the group.)
   - Discernment God's purpose for the group.
   - Instructions from God for what the group is to do next.
   - Warnings of danger ahead.
   - A scene or prophetic act the Lord wants you to do to demonstrate His message.

3. After the person has shared their insight from the Lord, pause for a moment to weigh what has been said.
   - In your Spirit, do you sense a "Yes" or a "No" to this?
   - Does this agree with what God has been speaking to you?
   - Does this apply Scripture and revelation of God's ways?

4. Continue to wait upon the Lord and share with one another what He is speaking to you.
   - Sometimes what one speaker says prompts confidence in others to share their insights. Try not to leave words unsaid.
   - Try to discern if there is a theme to what the Lord is saying.

5. Praise God for His insights and for speaking to and through you!

ALL RIGHTS RESERVED © 2019 Wendy Bowen
www.manifestinternational.com

UNIT FIVE: SUFFERING & PERSECUTION

KEY SCRIPTURE VERSE FOR UNIT FIVE
Therefore, since Christ suffered in his body, arm yourselves also with the same attitude, because whoever suffers in the body is done with sin. As a result, they do not live the rest of their earthly lives for evil human desires, but rather for the will of God. - 1 Peter 4:1-2

CLASS 1: GODLY SUFFERING
1 Reading, 1 Exercise
Believers will encounter hardships and trials as we follow Jesus. We share in some aspects of Christ's sufferings but not all suffering is for righteousness sake.

CLASS 2: TRIALS, TESTINGS, & TRIBULATION
1 Reading, 1 Exercise
Various types of trials stretch our faith and prove how firmly established our hearts are in the Lord.

CLASS 3: SOVEREIGNTY & THORNS
1 Reading, 1 Exercise
There are certain types of suffering that Christians do not have to accept as part of God's sovereign plan for them and others that cannot be avoided.

CLASS 4: PERSECUTION TO THE END
1 Scripture Reading, 1 Exercise
Scripture guarantees that we will all be persecuted for truly following Jesus. Believers must be prepared to stand in faith until the return of Christ.

KEY QUESTIONS

GROUP EXERCISES

GODLY SUFFERING - FOR RIGHTEOUSNESS

Every trial we face as followers of Christ is about one thing – it is a test of whether we really believe that God loves us and that His plans for us are good. Every time things happen in our lives which could cause us to doubt God's love for us in Christ, it is a new opportunity to believe afresh that Jesus truly is who He says He is, that His sacrifice was sufficient for all that we face, and that He will faithfully fulfill everything that He has promised. Undoubtedly, all of us will endure all sorts of suffering in our lives. However, when we hear the heart of God asking us through these trials and the pain *Do you believe that I am good?*, *Do you believe that I love you?*, *Do you believe that I am enough?*, *Do you believe what I have promised you?*, and *Do you believe that I have finished it?*, let us keep our eyes on Jesus and our minds on heaven and resoundingly answer back to Him, *Yes!*

We serve a King who came willingly to lay down His life as a sacrifice to God so that we could be with Him for eternity. Now, He tells us to go and do likewise by offering ourselves to God unreservedly.

> *Romans 12:1: Therefore, I urge you, brothers and sisters, in view of God's mercy,* **to offer your bodies as a living sacrifice**, *holy and pleasing to God--***this is your true and proper worship***. (Consider also 2Timothy 2:10.)*

This said, I am not writing this to encourage anybody to recklessly throw themselves in the face of danger, and I certainly do not want to inspire any martyr complexes. Rather, it is important for all of us as Christ followers to be prepared and strengthened to follow Him to the fullest, no matter the cost.

DIFFERENT PURPOSE

Before we go even one step further, let us clarify one major difference between Jesus' suffering and ours.

Jesus is the only One appointed by God who could ever suffer and die for our sins and accomplish God's plan of salvation. You and I cannot suffer and die to pay for the sins of ourselves or others and our wounds, blood, or death have no sacrificial atoning value. God appointed Jesus exclusively for this task, and He completed it. He knew the will of God from the foundation of the earth.

> *Hebrews 10:14: For* **by one sacrifice** *he has made perfect forever those who are being made holy. (Consider also Hebrews 9:27-28.)*

> *Revelation 13:8: All inhabitants of the earth will worship the beast--all whose names have not been written in the Lamb's book of life,* **the Lamb who was slain from the creation of the world.**

Moreover, our commission is slightly different than Christ's. Jesus came the first time to provide the way of salvation through faith in Him. Now, as His followers, He sends us out to tell everyone about God's salvation through Jesus Christ. Even though our task is slightly different than His, our purpose is similar enough to His that we can expect to face the same type of opposition He faced. Fortunately, the way He endured through trials gave us an example of righteousness and love in the face of the most horrific antagonism.

> *John 15:18-21: If the world hates you,* **keep in mind that it hated me first.** *If you belonged to the world, it would love you as its own. As it is, you do not belong to the world, but I have chosen you out of the world. That is why the world hates you. Remember what I told you:*

> *'A servant is not greater than his master.'* If they persecuted me, **they will persecute you also**. If they obeyed my teaching, they will obey yours also. **They will treat you this way because of my name**, for they do not know the one who sent me.
>
> *1Peter 4:1:* Therefore, **since Christ suffered** in his body, **arm yourselves also with the same attitude**, because whoever suffers in the body is done with sin.
>
> *1Peter 2:21:* To this you were called, because Christ suffered for you, **leaving you an example, that you should follow in his steps**.

Ok, now that we've clarified this, we can keep going.

Suffering for Doing Right

Jesus was without sin, He always spoke the truth, and His life was a demonstration of perfect love. Therefore, He was not crucified for being a bad person, for deceit or trickery, or because He deserved it. He came to carry out God's fore-ordained purpose for Him, and He laid down His life in perfect submission to God and without rebellion against the God-appointed religious leaders or the governing powers in the world. Accordingly, He did not suffer for doing wrong but for doing right.

In contrast, we will be far more likely to do wrong things than Jesus. When we do wrong, we may suffer the consequences of our own wrong choices. However, suffering for doing wrong, making bad choices, or rebelling against authority is not the same as suffering for doing right.

> *Galatians 6:7-8:* Do not be deceived: **God cannot be mocked. A man reaps what he sows. Whoever sows to please their flesh, from the flesh will reap destruction**; whoever sows to please the Spirit, from the Spirit will reap eternal life.
>
> *1Peter 2:19-20:* For it is commendable if someone bears up under **the pain of unjust suffering because they are conscious of God**. But how is it to your credit if you **receive a beating for doing wrong and endure it**? But if you suffer for doing good and you endure it, **this is commendable before God**. (Also, 1Peter 3:17.)
>
> *1Peter 4:15, 19:* **If you suffer, it should not be as a murderer or thief or any other kind of criminal, or even as a meddler.** ... So then, those who suffer according to God's will should commit themselves to their faithful Creator and **continue to do good**

Furthermore, unless the governing authorities demand that we renounce our faith in Christ in order to submit to them or to their laws, we cannot use our faith as an excuse for breaking the law. For example, even though He is the King who appoints all kings and the Son of the God who dwelt in the Temple, Jesus paid taxes to Caesar and He paid the Temple tax. (See Matthew 22:21, 17:24-27; Mark 12:17; Luke 20:25.) Jesus did not have to do these things but He did them willingly in order to not offend the governing authorities or incite any form of doctrinal rebellion. He did not come to start a political or religious insurgence but to usher in the Kingdom of God. The same is true for us.

> *Romans 13:1:* Let everyone **be subject to the governing authorities**, for there is no authority except that which God has established. The **authorities that exist have been established by God**.
>
> *1Peter 2:13-14:* **Submit yourselves for the Lord's sake to every human authority**: whether to the emperor, as the supreme authority, or to governors, who are sent by him to punish those who do wrong and to commend those who do right.

Moreover, Jesus' suffering was not due to following some perverse religious teaching or subjecting Himself to pain in order to win God's favor. Jesus suffered out of selfless love for God and for us.

All of this is to say that, when we encounter various forms of suffering in our lives, not all suffering is suffering for righteousness. If we are truly sharing in Christ's sufferings, it will be due to our obedience to God. This said, as we offer ourselves to God for His Kingdom and purposes, He will inevitably lead us into sharing in the sufferings of Jesus, which is suffering for righteousness.

> *1Peter 4:13: But rejoice inasmuch as you **participate in the sufferings of Christ**, so that you may be overjoyed when his glory is revealed.*

Christ's Example for Us in Trials

Jesus responded righteously to every trial He faced. He did so because He lived by the abiding direction of the Holy Spirit which always led Him in the will of God. Now that the Holy Spirit dwells in us, He guides us through our trials so we can learn to respond like Jesus. Here, in chronological order, are some examples of the trials Jesus faced and how He victoriously endured through them with God as our example.

Murder at Birth: From the time Jesus was born, the governing authorities of this world and God's people wanted Him dead. (See Matthew 2.) When they heard that a King was born in Israel, they sought to exterminate Him so they could retain control and power for themselves. God warned Jesus' parents in a dream and they escaped to Egypt for a time.

For us, as we are "birthed" into faith in Jesus and/or begin to follow Him in greater ways, we will often face natural or spiritual attacks. At the outset of our newfound faith or at the commencement of new "seasons" in our life and with Him, it can seem like the forces of this world conspire against what God has commissioned us to do. There may be times when God leads us to flee from things which can hinder or destroy God's work in our lives or to remain hidden for a time for our own protection.

Submission & Waiting for God's Timing: At age twelve, Jesus was ready to begin ministry. He had perfect character because God's nature was in Him and He already had wisdom which confounded the religious authorities. (See Luke 2:41-52.) However, it was not yet time for Jesus to begin His ministry and instead, He went home with His parents and submitted Himself to them. For the next eighteen years, Jesus waited patiently for the time God ordained for Him to begin His ministry without rebellion against the religious authorities or their teachings.

For us, there will be times when we have to wait for God and His timing. Things He has spoken to our hearts are not for us to fulfill in our own strength or strategies and we have to learn to wait upon the Lord for His promises to us to be fulfilled in His way and in His timing. As such, waiting upon the Lord is one of the most important expressions of our devotion to God and our submission to His will over our own desires. It proves through our actions that we are functioning by the nature of Jesus who submitted Himself and not by the nature of the evil one who exalted himself. Moreover, it is during these times when we must remain in submission to the authorities which God has appointed to rule over us. If God has truly called us to greatness then as we submit ourselves to Him, He will exalt us in due time.

> *1Peter 5:5-6: In the same way, you who are younger, **submit yourselves to your elders**. All of you, clothe yourselves with humility toward one another, because, "God opposes the proud but shows favor to the humble." **Humble yourselves, therefore, under God's mighty hand, that he may lift you up in due time**.*

Temptation to Sin: Before Jesus began His ministry, He was led by the Holy Spirit into the wilderness to be tempted by the devil for 40 days. (See Matthew 4:1-11; Mark 1:12-13; Luke 4:1-13.) The word for *tempt* can also be translated test and, during this time, the devil tested Jesus with every possible provocation to sin and ungodliness. But Jesus never sinned becuase He was empowered by the nature of God within Him and He declared the Scriptures as a weapon of truth against the lies of the enemy.

Now, we have the Holy Spirit dwelling inside of us the same way Jesus did. Therefore, we have the same dynamis power in us to resist temptation and strengthen in character, virtue, and purity.

> *1 John 3:9:* **No one who is born of God will continue to sin, because God's seed remains in them**; they cannot go on sinning, because they have been born of God. (Also 1 John 5:18.)

Religious Error: Throughout His ministry, Jesus was hated by the religious leaders who constantly attempted to trap Him into error or deception. Even with their extensive knowledge of the Scriptures, they did not recognize Jesus as God and so they challenged Him and tested Him. Jesus simply but strongly rebuked the religious leaders for their error. They were rendered incapable of answering His questions.

> *John 3:10:* **You are Israel's teacher**," said Jesus, "and **do you not understand these things?**

> *John 5:39-40:* **You study the Scriptures diligently** because you think that in them you have eternal life. **These are the very Scriptures that testify about me**, yet you refuse to come to me to have life.

> *Matthew 22:46:* **No one [of the Pharisees] could say a word in reply**, and from that day on **no one dared to ask him any more questions**.

Jesus also rebuked the religious leaders because they considered their man-made rules and traditions to be equal with or sometimes even superior to God's Law.

> *Mark 7:6-9:* He replied, "Isaiah was right when he prophesied about you hypocrites; as it is written: " 'These people honor me with their lips, but their hearts are far from me. **They worship me in vain; their teachings are merely human rules.' You have let go of the commands of God and are holding on to human traditions**." And he continued, "You have a fine way of **setting aside the commands of God in order to observe your own traditions!**"

Now, Jesus sends us out to be like Him and not be entangled by the traditions and religious observances that have entered into the Church if they are outside of the commands of Jesus and the Word of God. He promises us that when we stand before religious people, the Holy Spirit will give us wisdom that they will not be able to contest.

> *Mark 13:9-11:* You must be on your guard. **You will be handed over to the local councils and flogged in the synagogues.** On account of me you will stand before governors and kings as witnesses to them. And the gospel must first be preached to all nations. Whenever you are arrested and brought to trial, **do not worry beforehand about what to say. Just say whatever is given you at the time, for it is not you speaking, but the Holy Spirit.**

Other's Demands, Unbelief, and Offense: The religious leaders often demanded a sign from Jesus to prove His authority from God. He refused to indulge their demands. He knew that, even though He had performed many miraculous signs, no sign would be enough to convince them.

> *Matthew 12:39:* He answered, "A wicked and adulterous generation asks for a sign! **But none will be given** it except the sign of the prophet Jonah. (See also Mark 8:12; Luke 11:29.)

> *Luke 16:31:* He said to him, 'If they do not listen to Moses and the Prophets, **they will not be convinced even if someone rises from the dead.**'

> *Luke 20:8:* Jesus said, "**Neither will I tell you by what authority** I am doing these things."

Jesus also faced skeptics in His hometown and could not do many miracles there because of their unbelief. (See Matthew 13:53-58; Mark 6:1-6; Luke 4:14-30.) Plus, during His ministry years, Jesus was surrounded by ordinary people who wanted to believe Him, but somehow they could not quite get fully onboard in their faith that He is the Messiah. Jesus' most common expression to followers like these was, "O, you of little faith," which gently chided them for their unbelief and addition to other comments He made about their hard hearts or the fact that they were slow to believe. On a few occasions, with a sigh of exasperation, Jesus asked, "Do you still not believe?"

There were also those who proclaimed their undying loyalty and devotion to Jesus. In response, Jesus brought into view the ultimate price. (Consider Luke 9:57-58; 18:18-30; John 6:32-70.) When He taught things like this, which were difficult for His followers to comprehend, many people said that He had lost His mind, accused Him of being evil, or deserted Him. Jesus let the Scriptures and the works of God defend Him. He did not defend Himself or demand their loyalty or submission. Instead, He let them go their own way and blessed those who were not offended by Him.

> *John 6:60-61, 66-67: On hearing it, many of his disciples said, "This is a hard teaching. Who can accept it?" Aware that his disciples were grumbling about this, Jesus said to them, **"Does this offend you**? ... From this time **many of his disciples turned back and no longer followed him**. "You do not want to leave too, do you?" Jesus asked the Twelve.*

> *John 10:37-38: **Do not believe me unless I do the works of my Father**. But if I do them, even though you do not believe me, **believe the works**, that you may know and understand that the Father is in me, and I in the Father." (See also John 5:36, 10:25, 14:11.)*

> *Luke 7:22-23: So he replied to the messengers, "Go back and report to John **what you have seen and heard**: The blind receive sight, the lame walk, those who have leprosy are cleansed, the deaf hear, the dead are raised, and the good news is proclaimed to the poor. **Blessed is anyone who does not stumble on account of me**." (See also Matthew 11:6.)*

When Peter rebuked Jesus for talking about how He must suffer, be rejected and die, Jesus said, "Get behind me, Satan," rebuking the evil one who was speaking through Peter's mouth. Then, Jesus proceeded to walk towards His destiny as Savior of the world.

Now, Jesus sends us out to be like Him. We have nothing to prove to anyone and have no need to defend ourselves or to defend God for the way He is guiding our lives. And when those around us don't believe in full faith with us as we walk with Jesus, we can continue walking firmly and faithfully in obedience to the Lord while gently chiding them for their small view of God's greatness, or rebuking them for speaking for the enemy.

Counting the Cost: Jesus counted the cost before leaving the comforts of Heaven to fulfill His task from God. Then when the time approached for Jesus' greatest trial, He petitioned God in intense prayer in the Garden of Gethsemane, asking if there was any other way for God's wrath to be satisfied. In Gethsemane, Jesus again counted the cost of laying down His life. Then, He submitted Himself willingly and offered all of Himself out of total devotion and love for God.

> *Matthew 26:38-39, 46: Then he said to them, "**My soul is overwhelmed with sorrow to the point of death**. Stay here and keep watch with me." Going a little farther, he fell with his face to the ground and prayed, "**My Father, if it is possible, may this cup be taken from me. Yet not as I will, but as you will**." ... **Rise! Let us go!** Here comes my betrayer!"*

Now, Jesus sends us out to offer our lives to God no matter what it costs us to follow Him. He made it clear in no uncertain terms that following Him costs everything and that His followers should *count the cost* before declaring our allegiance. To follow Jesus with all our heart and all we have, we must put to death our carnal nature and willful desires for what we want and how we want God to do things in order to submit ourselves to the will of God and see it fulfilled.

> *Luke 14:26-27, 33: If anyone comes to me and does not **hate father and mother, wife and children, brothers and sisters--yes, even their own life**--such a person cannot be my disciple. And whoever does not **carry their cross and follow me** cannot be my disciple. ...*

*In the same way, those of you who do not **give up everything you have** cannot be my disciples. (Consider also Philippians 3:7-11.)*

Betrayed, Falsely Accused, Unjustly Condemned: In His greatest trial, Jesus was betrayed by a close friend, turned over to the religious authorities, offered up to the governing world powers, given a mock trial which scarcely complied with any form of order or legal standards, and was sentenced to death at the hands of the very people that He came to save. The time had come for Jesus to fulfill the Scriptures written about His suffering and death so He did not rebuke or resist, nor would He allow any of His followers to do so.

*John 18:11, 36: Jesus commanded Peter, "**Put your sword away!** Shall I not drink the cup the Father has given me?" ... Jesus said, "My kingdom is not of this world. **If it were, my servants would fight** to prevent my arrest by the Jewish leaders. But now my kingdom is from another place." (Also Matthew 26:52.)*

Jesus was led like a lamb to the slaughter and did not open His mouth because He trusted God without reservation. (See Isaiah 53:7.) When Jesus stood before the religious leaders, before Pilate, before Herod, and before the people of Israel and the masses of the world, He never defended Himself.

*Matthew 27:12: When he was accused by the **chief priests and the elders, he gave no answer**.*

*Mark 15:5: But **Jesus still made no reply**, and **Pilate** was amazed.*

*Luke 23:8-9: When **Herod** saw Jesus, he was greatly pleased, because for a long time he had been wanting to see him. From what he had heard about him, he hoped to see him perform a sign of some sort. He plied him with many questions, but **Jesus gave him no answer**.*

Jesus warned us to understand that these types of things will happen to us as well, even from those we love the most. He told us in advance so that we, like Him, can stand firm in our faith.

*Luke 21:16-19: **You will be betrayed** even by parents, brothers and sisters, relatives and friends, **and they will put some of you to death. Everyone will hate you because of me**. But not a hair of your head will perish. **Stand firm, and you will win life**.*

*John 16:1-2: All this **I have told you so that you will not fall away**. They will put you out of the synagogue; in fact, the time is coming when anyone who kills you will think they are offering a service to God.*

Apparent Loss/Defeat and Shame: From an onlooker's perspective, it seemed that Jesus was a total failure. He willingly allowed darkness to have its glory for a moment as He endured the most brutal beating, scourging, and crucifixion the world has ever known. He took upon Himself all of the wrath, punishment, curse, sickness, and evil oppression of the world trusting that God would fulfill His purpose.

*Luke 22:52-53: Then Jesus said to the chief priests, the officers of the temple guard, and the elders, who had come for him, "**Am I leading a rebellion,** that you have come with swords and clubs? Every day I was with you in the temple courts, and you did not lay a hand on me. **But this is your hour--when darkness reigns**."*

*Philippians 2:6-8: Who, **being in very nature God**, did not consider equality with God something to be used to his own advantage; rather, **he made himself nothing** by taking the very nature of a servant, being made in human likeness. And being found in appearance as a man, **he humbled himself by becoming obedient to death-- even death on a cross!***

Even though Jesus counted the cost of giving His life, He *scorned the shame*. This means that Jesus knew the cost and thought it was a small price to pay in order to complete the work of God.

> *Hebrews 12:2b:* **For the joy set before him he endured the cross, scorning its shame**, *and sat down at the right hand of the throne of God.*

Now, Jesus sends us out to face trials with faith and willingness because we consider our sufferings a light thing compared to the great value and worth of knowing Him. We can turn the other cheek, allow ourselves to appear to be failures in the eyes of this world, and die to ourselves because we trust that God is at work on our behalf and for our good. (See Romans 8:28.)

> *Philippians 3:10: I want to know Christ--yes, to know the power of his resurrection and* **participation in his sufferings, becoming like him in his death**

Not Holding a Grudge: During all of this humiliation, physical pain, and spiritual anguish, Jesus maintained His heart of mercy and compassion – even for those who were crucifying Him. He forgave His enemies without animosity or contention. He wanted all of them to be saved and to have a chance to know God.

> *Luke 23:34a: Jesus said,* "**Father, forgive them, for they do not know what they are doing**."

Now, Jesus sends us out and gives us strength from within by the Holy Spirit to walk in love and mercy for others, including those who treat us shamefully and persecute us.

> *Matthew 5:44-45: But I tell you,* **love your enemies and pray for those who persecute you**, *that you may be children of your Father in heaven. He causes his sun to rise on the evil and the good, and sends rain on the righteous and the unrighteous.*

LEARNING OBEDIENCE

Jesus, the Son of Man, took on flesh and blood like ours and showed us how to endure through trials with perfect faith and right conduct. Through His suffering, Jesus learned the challenges we face as we try to obey God in the trials of this life. Therefore, He is able to be compassionate and understanding when we face trials and temptations in our lives. Praise God!

> *Hebrews 5:7-8: During the days of Jesus' life on earth, he offered up prayers and petitions with fervent cries and tears to the one who could save him from death, and he was heard because of his reverent submission.* **Son though he was, he learned obedience from what he suffered**

> *Hebrews 4:15: For we do not have a high priest who is unable to empathize with our weaknesses,* **but we have one who has been tempted in every way, just as we are--yet he did not sin**.

Most importantly, Jesus did not doubt God's love for Him. He did not doubt His Father's ability to do all that He had promised and planned. Jesus knew God was worthy of His submission, His hope, His faith, His love, His sacrifice, and His life.

Therefore, as we follow Jesus, not by outward imitation but by the inward leading of the Holy Spirit, we can anticipate that the Holy Spirit will guide us to respond rightly no matter what trial we may face. Assuredly, trials of righteousness will come to test our resolve, our devotion, our willingness, and our faith.

And so again I say, through every trial and through all the pain, when we hear the heart of God asking, *Do you believe that I am good?*, *Do you believe that I love you?*, *Do you believe that I am enough?*, *Do you believe what I have promised you?*, and *Do you believe that I have finished it?*, let us keep our eyes on Jesus and our minds on heaven and resoundingly answer back to Him, *Yes!*

Basic Training Exercise

SON OF DAVID – SON OF MAN

Basic TRAINING
SPIRITUAL EXERCISES

Matthew 21:7-9 NIV - They brought the donkey and the colt and placed their cloaks on them for Jesus to sit on. A very large crowd spread their cloaks on the road, while others cut branches from the trees and spread them on the road. The crowds that went ahead of him and those that followed shouted, "Hosanna to the Son of David!" "Blessed is he who comes in the name of the Lord!" "Hosanna in the highest heaven!"

DESCRIPTION

King David was a man of war who conquered Israel's enemies triumphantly. God promised David that one of his sons/descendants would be the eternal King who would conquer all enemies of God's people.

In the days of Jesus, the Jews had great anticipation of this Son of David. They wanted a King who would come as a man of war – like David had been. Indeed, Jesus will come to conquer all His enemies at the end of the age. However, Jesus came the first time as a Suffering Servant and most often referred to Himself as the Son of Man. He shared the weakness of flesh and blood and suffered shamefully in order to conquer the greatest enemy of the human soul – sin.

In our lives today, we often look to Jesus to come and conquer our earthly problems like a triumphant man of war. At times, He does this. However other times, Jesus leads us to follow Him in suffering and taking up our cross rather than what seems to be earthly victory. This can be painful, disappointing, bewildering, humiliating, or unexpected for us as it may seem contrary to our view of God's promises for our lives. This said, as we share in Christ's sufferings and obedience to His teachings, we are on the path to experiencing God's resurrection power.

Practicing this Son of David exercise is about knowing when God is inviting us into Christ's likeness as a Suffering Servant rather than a conquering King so that we grow in our understanding of God's ways, His will, and His power to resurrect.

Category: Self-Denial

PURPOSE:

To recognize God's approach and wisdom in our situations.

To detach from our own expectations of how God should handle our problems.

To increase our willingness to share in the sufferings of Jesus.

SPIRITUAL FRUIT:

Sharing in sufferings of Christ.

Increased humility.

Developing discernment of God's dealings and purposes.

Increased freedom to obey God in our circumstances.

Greater surrender to God.

Reduced striving for outcomes.

PRAYER

Father, thank you for sending Jesus to be the perfect example of serving you as the Suffering Servant and the conquering King. Increase my understanding of how you want me like Him in the situations in my life and help me to walk in your ways. In Jesus' name, Amen.

CONSIDERATIONS

In what ways has Jesus revealed His great power to you?

In what ways has Jesus asked you to take up your cross?

In what ways has following Jesus been different or more difficult than you were originally expecting? How has this confused or disappointed you?

Do you think suffering is a sign of God's punishment? How so?

How did Jesus demonstrate humility by choosing the path of suffering rather than exercising His authority as King of all the earth? Do you think it was hard for Him? How?

PRACTICE

1. Write out a list of some of the situations or trials you are facing in your life right now.
   - Include every kind of trial you can think of like finances, relationships, spiritual blocks, health, persecution, etc.

2. One by one, ask God to speak to you about His perspective on each situation. Use the following questions as a guide:
   - God, do you want me to let you fight this one for me or is there something you are asking me to do about it?
   - God, are you asking me to turn the other cheek, go the extra mile, submit myself, keep my mouth shut, etc? How?
   - God, am I tolerating suffering like sickness, demonic oppression, evil influences, etc. that is not your will for me? What do you want me to do about this?
   - God, how do you want me to change my approach to this so that its recurring pattern/cycle in my life is broken?

3. Thank God for His wisdom for your situations. Put what He has revealed to you into practice in your life right away.

NOTES: _____

Category: Self-Denial

ADDITIONAL SCRIPTURES:

Isaiah 53

Matthew 5:10

James 1:2-3, 12

1 Peter 3:8-17; 4:1

Acts 14:22

Luke 9:23

Philippians 2:5-11

John 6:15

2 Corinthians 5:16

Matthew 22:43-45

Trials, Testing, & Tribulation*

In the Garden of Eden, the serpent was described as more crafty or subtle than any other of God's creatures. Even today, this subtlety makes the evil one an expert deceiver, distracter, and destroyer if we are not spiritually aware enough to discern his schemes.

> *Genesis 3:1:* Now **the serpent was more crafty** than any of the wild animals the LORD God had made. He said to the woman, "**Did God really say**, 'You must not eat ...'?"

> *2Corinthians 2:11:* In order that **Satan might not outwit us**. For we are **not unaware of his schemes**.

Regardless of how the enemy is attacking us or attempting to divert or deceive us, Jesus conquered it at the cross. Everything we need for victory, godliness, and the fulfillment of God's plans for us was provided through the work of Jesus. We receive it as a free gift, by grace through faith in what Jesus accomplish for us. Our job is to discern the schemes of the enemy in order to respond correctly to trials as they come.

> *2Peter 1:3-4:* His divine power **has given us everything we need for a godly life** through our knowledge of him who called us by his own glory and goodness. Through these he has given us his very great and precious promises, so that through them you may **participate in the divine nature**, having **escaped the corruption in the world caused by evil desires**.

We previously covered Jesus' parable of the four soils about how our hearts receive and respond to the word of God. Trials serve to amplify our response and thus, reveal the true condition of our hearts. This said, truth be told, there are only two ways to respond to the trials we face: with our flesh which is our inherited sinful Adamic nature or, by the power of the Holy Spirit, with Christlikeness which is our new nature in Him. Selfishness, self-defense, and focus on temporal values is our flesh. Trusting God, continuing to love, and prioritizing the eternal is Christlikeness by the Holy Spirit.

For a Christian, the token mark of being spiritually mature is to be like Jesus even to the extent of loving our enemies, praying for our accusers, and forgiving those who are murdering us. While our trials may be small by comparison, whatever we face, it is our right responses which prove us to be God's children. (Consider Matthew 5:43-48; Luke 23:34.) Now, Jesus calls us to be like Him and love one another as He loves us. True love is costly even when our lives are not on the line. Love costs us time and dignity; our own desires and way of doing things; our right to be right and our right to be mad and seek revenge. Love is not a feeling, it's a state of being which flows into action. (See 1 Corinthians 13:4-8; Romans 12:9-21.)

Knowing this as followers of Jesus, we set out to be like Him and bring the love of God to the whole world. Then, it happens. Someone whom we are loving with all this love that we have received from Jesus turns around and mocks us, rejects us, accuses us of being evil, or may work against us or our work for God. How do we respond? Do we respond like ourselves in self-defense, with a counter-mock, with retorted insults, or with equalizing rejection? Or do we respond like Christ, with mercy and love, compassion, kindness, forgiveness, and self-sacrifice?

Trials & Chastisement

Trials we face are not punishment from God because Jesus took all of our punishment upon Himself. (See Isaiah 53:3; James 1:13.) God is not the trial. He is training us through the trial. This is His chastisement and it can be unpleasant because when we want to justify or avenge ourselves, God instead tells us to deny ourselves, turn the other cheek, and trust Him, often in t the midst of much waiting, patience, and endurance. Through this specialized boot camp for character and faith, God brings us to spiritual maturity, making us like Jesus in responding to situations with right conduct and right beliefs.

> *Hebrews 12:7-8, 11:* **Endure hardship as discipline; God is treating you as his children.** *For what children are not disciplined by their father?... No discipline seems pleasant at the time, but painful. Later on, however, it* **produces a harvest of righteousness and peace** *for those who have been trained by it.*

Every trial and test of character and faith is an opportunity to be trained by God. Nevertheless, every trial feels like a spiritual, emotional, and often humiliating punch in the face. We should not be shocked but rather rejoice when trials come because God's righteous training through real life scenarios teaches us to love others and to carry out His purposes in spite of whatever is launched against us.

> *1Peter 4:12-13:* Dear friends, **do not be surprised at the fiery ordeal that has come on you to test you**, *as though something strange were happening to you.* **But rejoice** *inasmuch* **as you participate in the sufferings of Christ***, so that you may be overjoyed when his glory is revealed.*

Think of it like a loving heavenly Father training His children about how to defend themselves from a big schoolyard bully. The devil, the world and its ways, and our own fleshly desires intimidate and terrorize us while we live in this playground called the world. But our loving heavenly Father whispers to us through the Holy Spirit about how to handle all of these bullies the way that His beloved Son Jesus did.

The definition of *sin* is missing the mark and is an archery term used to describe an archer who did not hit the target perfectly. Major and minor offenses are still missing the mark. We all have yearnings from within for things other than what we have. These cravings of our flesh can range from totally ungodly, to things which may seem minor to us but are still out of alignment with God's will. Our flesh lures us by temptation and excuses or justifications for enabling us to indulge our lusts.

> *James 1:14-16:* but **each person is tempted** when they are dragged away **by their own evil desire** *and enticed. Then, after* **desire has conceived***, it* **gives birth to sin***; and sin, when it is full-grown, gives birth to death.* **Don't be deceived***, my dear brothers and sisters.*

When trials hit our life, they evoke a reaction within us. Will we miss the mark by giving into the desires of our flesh or obey the Holy Spirit? The Holy Spirit whispers to us in purity, truth, and holiness. God's grace is so sufficient that all things are permitted meaning that we are totally and absolutely free in Christ. This means that the enticement and allure of sin being forbidden has been nullified. This said, not all things are beneficial, good for us, or worth doing because they do not reflect the nature of Christ within us and are unloving towards others. (See 1Corinthians 6:12, 10:23.) The same divine nature which strengthened Jesus in the wilderness against all of Satan's temptations and testings is now within us to strengthen us so that we can respond the way that He did and pass the test.

> *James 4:7: Submit yourselves, then, to God.* **Resist the devil, and he will flee from you.**

TYPES OF TESTING

There are two primary types of testing which we will encounter as Christ followers. The first is a *negative test* in which the thing being tested is expected to fail and may even be tested in increasing levels of severity until it fails. The second is a *positive test* for genuineness in which the thing being tested is expected to be proven true. In the New Testament Greek, the words for this are *peirazo* and *dokimazo*, respectively.

God does not test us negatively. (See James 1:13.) Things which test us negatively [peirazo] include temptations, hardships, sicknesses, seemingly unfulfilled promises of God, deception, distraction, and accusation. While we are being negatively tested, it will seem that lies against God multiply in our mind and as this continues, we grow weary with discouragement, principally through thoughts of guilt, shame, and hopelessness, especially if we seem to be waiting a long time for God's promises to come to pass. Through all of this, our faith and character are tested.

For example, when Jesus was in the wilderness being tested by Satan, He was negatively tested [peirazo] by the evil one in every possible way. Another example of negative testing is when Jesus warned Peter that Satan had asked to *sift him like wheat*.

> *Luke 22:31: Simon, Simon [Peter,]* **Satan has asked to sift all of you as wheat**.

This expression is defined as "an inward agitation to try one's faith to the verge of overthrow." The enemy's aim in negatively testing us is to lure us into failure in our character and our beliefs through all means available in increasing levels of pressure until failure is accomplished. Often it seems like this happens in increasing measures of difficulty and oppression or in many different areas of our lives at one time, pushing us beyond what we can endure on our own. Indeed, the enemy is trying to push us to the point of failure.

This said, when these negative tests and temptations happen in our lives we can respond rightly by following the direction of the Holy Spirit. In the same way that Jesus and Holy Spirit filled Peter responded to trials, when we live by the Holy Spirit's direction, our faith and character will be proven genuine.

> *1Corinthians 10:12-13: So, if you think you are standing firm, be careful that you don't fall! No* **temptation [peirasmos]** *has overtaken you except what is common to mankind. And God is faithful; he will not let you be* **tempted [peirazo] beyond what you can bear**. *But* **when you are tempted [peirasmos], he will also provide a way out so that you can endure.**

On the other hand, there is positive testing [dokimazo] which proves that our faith is genuine. This is the type of testing done by a jeweler who examines a diamond to ensure that it is not a fake. For example, when someone is nominated to be a deacon, the church must prove their character by testing [dokimazo] them. (See 1 Timothy 3:10.) More significantly, before we partake of communion, ingesting the very blood and body of Jesus, we are encouraged to positively test [dokimazo] or examine ourselves to see if we are truly believing all that He has accomplished for us. (See 1Corinthians 11:28-30.) In fact, some believers were experiencing weakness, sickness, and even death because they were failing the positive test of faith by not believing all that Christ accomplished for us through His body and blood.

This means that, perhaps, some of the trials that we experience are because we are not fully perceiving and believing what Jesus accomplished for us through His life, death, and resurrection. Therefore, we should positively test ourselves. Is our faith the genuine article?

Unlike Jesus, when we are negatively tested [peirazo], sometimes we fail. There are times when we give into temptation or we stumble into sin or error. It is exactly at these times when we may repent and return to Jesus by trusting that His sacrifice is sufficient to cover all our stumbling. Even if we have been negatively tested to the point of personal catastrophe, God's grace is still unquestionably extended to us.

Then, we have the opportunity to positively test [dokimazo] ourselves and ask ourselves again if we really believe that Jesus finished it and that we are accepted by God because of Jesus in spite of our stumbling. We receive God's grace afresh and can carry on in our walk with Him.

In fact, this is the whole purpose of every trial. Whether positive testing or negative testing and whether a test of character or steadfastness, the genuineness of our faith is proven. Enduring through trials draw us to spiritual maturity so that in every area of our lives we are mature and complete in Christ and walking in God's will for us.

> *1Peter 1:6-7: In all this you greatly rejoice,* **though now for a little while you may have had to suffer grief in all kinds of trials.** *These have come* **so that the proven genuineness of your faith--of greater worth than gold,** *which perishes even though refined by fire--***may result in praise, glory and honor when Jesus Christ is revealed**.

> *James 1:2-4: Consider it pure joy, my brothers and sisters, **whenever you face trials of many kinds**, because you know that the **testing of your faith** produces perseverance. Let perseverance finish its work **so that you may be mature and complete, not lacking anything**.*

TESTING GOD

As a side note, as we encounter various kinds of trials and tests, we can negatively or positively test God.

When Jesus was being negatively tested by the evil one in the wilderness, He quoted from the Book of Deuteronomy, "You must not put the Lord your God to the test," from an incident in Israel's history. (See Luke 4:12; Deuteronomy 6:16.) In the historical account, shortly after the Israelites had walked through the waters of the Red Sea, they came to a place where there was no water and they started complaining. The conflict escalated until they professed that God must not be with them anymore or must have brought them out of Egypt in order to kill them in the wilderness. After the Lord showed Moses how to cause drinking water to miraculously gush out of a rock, Moses named the place Massah which means *testing* because they had tested God by saying, "Is God with us or not?" (See Exodus 17:1-7.) Even when they had seen God work great miracles on their behalf, they tested Him by their unbelief.

> *Psalm 78:18-19, 21-22, 32, 41, 56: They **willfully put God to the test** by demanding the food they craved. They **spoke against God**; they said, "**Can God really** spread a table in the wilderness?" ... When the LORD heard them, he was furious; his fire broke out against Jacob, and his wrath rose against Israel, for **they did not believe in God or trust in his deliverance**. ... In spite of all this, they kept on sinning; **in spite of his wonders, they did not believe**. ... **Again and again they put God to the test**; they vexed the Holy One of Israel. ... But they **put God to the test and rebelled against the Most High**; they did not keep his statutes.*

From this, we see that we put God to the test in a negative way when we do not believe Him or trust Him for our salvation, deliverance, healing, and sustenance. We negatively test God through our unbelief in His ability to fulfill His promises, when we doubt His goodness, or think that He has evil intentions for us even if this is what our circumstances seem to indicate.

However, the Apostle Paul encourages us to be so renewed in our minds away from the intellect, wisdom, and pattern of this world that we positively put God to the test.

> *Romans 12:1-2 - Therefore, I urge you, brothers and sisters, in view of God's mercy, to **offer your bodies as a living sacrifice**, holy and pleasing to God—this is your true and proper worship. Do not conform to the pattern of this world, but be transformed by the renewing of your mind. **Then you will be able to test [dokimazo] and approve what God's will is–His good, pleasing and perfect will.***

This said, our minds are renewed not through head knowledge of God but through putting our faith into action by positively testing God and His will. Jesus gave His disciples only one prayer to pray and this prayer includes the phrase, "Your Kingdom come, Your will be done, on earth as it is in heaven." (See Matthew 6:10.) Now, like a jeweler inspecting a diamond to confirm that it is real, we are encouraged to test the genuineness of God's perfect and pleasing will—on earth as it is in heaven. Therefore, each of us should constantly be putting God to the test in a positive way by genuinely trusting Jesus, particularly as we face trials and tests of life.

TRIBULATION

Jesus warned us that trials will come. In no uncertain terms, He prepared His followers for trials, particularly in the times to come before His return. He did this so that our faith does not fail and so we can endure to the end, no matter the cost.

> *John 16:33 ESV: I have said these things to you, that in me you may have peace. **In the world you will have tribulation**. But take heart; I have overcome the world."*

> *Luke 21:12-19: But before all this,* **they will seize you and persecute you.** *They will hand you over to synagogues and put you in prison, and* **you will be brought before kings and governors,** *and all on account of my name. And so you will bear testimony to me. But* **make up your mind not to worry beforehand how you will defend yourselves.** *For I will give you words and wisdom that none of your adversaries will be able to resist or contradict. You will be betrayed even by parents, brothers and sisters, relatives and friends, and* **they will put some of you to death. Everyone will hate you because of me. But not a hair of your head will perish. Stand firm, and you will win life.** *(See Luke 21 and Matthew 24.)*

The word used for *tribulation* means "pressing or pressure, trouble, oppression, distress, the afflictions of those hard pressed by siege and the calamities of war and the straights of want." We follow a crucified King. When we live our lives for the Kingdom of God by following Jesus and doing the things that He did, we wage war against the kingdom of the evil one. It is a clash of kingdoms that the world takes note of and that is opposed by all the forces of darkness. The epic battle to come between the powers of this world and the powers of darkness raging against the Kingdom of God will put every believer to the ultimate trial and test.

> *Daniel 7:25: He [the man of lawlessness] will* **speak against the Most High and oppress his holy people** *and* **try to change the set times and the laws. The holy people will be delivered into his hands for a time, times and half a time.**

> *Revelation 13:7-10: It [the beast] was* **given power to wage war against God's holy people and to conquer them.** *And it was given authority over every tribe, people, language and nation. All inhabitants of the earth will worship the beast--all whose names have not been written in the Lamb's book of life, the Lamb who was slain from the creation of the world. Whoever has ears, let them hear.* **"If anyone is to go into captivity, into captivity they will go. If anyone is to be killed with the sword, with the sword they will be killed."** *This calls for patient endurance and faithfulness on the part of God's people. (Similar to Jeremiah 15:2.)*

No kind of trial, test, trouble, or hardship can separate us from God's love and eternal purpose for us if we will remain firm in our faith. Even if we are imprisoned, beaten, or martyred, we have not been abandoned over to death like sheep led to the slaughter. NO! We are more than conquerors through the victory Christ has won for us!

> *Romans 8:35-39:* **Who shall separate us from the love of Christ? Shall trouble or hardship or persecution or famine or nakedness or danger or sword?** *As it is written: "For your sake we face death all day long; we are considered as sheep to be slaughtered." (Quoting Psalm 44:11, 22.)* **No, in all these things we are more than conquerors through him who loved us.** *For I am convinced that neither death nor life, neither angels nor demons, neither the present nor the future, nor any powers, neither height nor depth,* **nor anything else in all creation, will be able to separate us from the love of God that is in Christ Jesus our Lord.**

Jesus is with us in every trial to give us wisdom, strength, and courage to respond rightly, the way that He would respond if He were in our exact set of circumstances. God assured Jesus of eternal victory and Jesus believed Him. Now, because Jesus has already overcome the world, the flesh, and the devil, we are assured of our victory when our faith is in Him. Will our faith prove genuine?

> *Luke 18:7-8: And will not God bring about justice for his chosen ones, who cry out to him day and night? Will he keep putting them off? I tell you, he will see that they get justice, and quickly. However,* **when the Son of Man comes, will he find faith on the earth?**

Basic Training Exercise

ENEMY TACTICS

2 Corinthians 2:11 NIV – in order that Satan might not outwit us. For we are not unaware of his schemes.

Basic TRAINING
SPIRITUAL EXERCISES

DESCRIPTION

In the Garden of Eden, the serpent was described as more subtle than any other of God's creatures. Even today, this subtlety makes the evil one an expert deceiver, distracter, and destroyer if we are not aware enough to discern his schemes. Sometimes, it is an event in our lives that triggers an enemy infiltration of our thoughts. Other times, it is a persistent and gradual wearing down and decline of our faith or endurance.

Regardless of how the enemy is attacking us or attempting to divert or deceive us, Jesus conquered it at the cross. Everything we need for victory, godliness, and the fulfillment of God's plans for us was provided through the work of Jesus. We receive it as a free gift, by grace through faith in what Jesus accomplish for us.

In fact, when we do identify the real root of what the enemy is attacking in our lives, we realize that what the enemy is working against us is exactly what God is working in our favor. For example, if the enemy attack is discouragement, God is working courage in us.

To put Enemy Tactics into practice is about allowing the Lord to reveal the subtle ways that the evil one is laying temptations before us or has worked His way into our thoughts so that we can renew our faith, hope, trust, and freedom in Jesus and the work He finished for us through His death and resurrection.

PRAYER

Father, thank you that you sent your Son, Jesus, to destroy the works of the enemy including everything that attempts to separate me from you or discourage and distract me from your plans and purposes. Help me now to discern the tactics of the enemy in my life so that he has no place in me. In Jesus' name, Amen.

PURPOSE:

To discern the tactics of the enemy.

To remain faithful to Christ and God's purpose for us.

To live established in the truth and hope of the Gospel.

SPIRITUAL FRUIT:

Increased discernment of the attacks of the enemy.

Renewed identity in Christ and the finished work of the cross.

Restored faith and hope.

Repentance from focus on self.

Purging of evil, pride, and discouragement.

CONSIDERATIONS

Consider these enemy tactics, listed in no particular order:

- **Doubt/Unbelief**: particularly in God's goodness or grace
- **Discouragement**: looking to the size of the problem rather than the ability of God
- **Diversion**: turning from God's instructions or greater purpose
- **Failure**: looking at apparent failure, not trusting God for redemption and victory
- **Frustration**: losing patience, not trusting God's timing
- **Flesh**: temptation to do things in our own strength
- **Performance**: thinking God's plan can be thwarted by us
- **Condemnation**: guilty feelings over sins from past or present
- **Success**: accepting exaltation of man out of God's order
- **Shortcuts**: trying to skip stages of God's plan development
- **Weakness**: losing strength due to extended battles/service

PRACTICE

1. Ask the Holy Spirit to highlight one of the enemy tactics above that is relevant to your life right now.

2. Ask the Lord to show you how the enemy has subtly infiltrated your thoughts using this tactic. Talk to Him about:
   - When did the enemy start attacking you in this way? Was there an event which triggered this or was it gradual?
   - Ask the Lord to reveal to you the real root of the issue in your present situation. (i.e. pride, fear, a past wound, etc.)

3. Ask the Lord to show you how He conquered this enemy tactic through His death and resurrection.
   - What else do Scripture and the Holy Spirit say about this?

4. Ask the Lord how He wants you to humble yourself before Him and resist the devil so that he flees from you.
   - How is He guiding you into faith and rest in Him?
   - Is there something He is asking you to do in your situation?

5. Do whatever He says.

NOTES: _____

ADDITIONAL SCRIPTURES:

Enemy Schemes

Genesis 3:1

Daniel 7:25

Genesis 16

2 Chronicles 26:16

1 Samuel 15

Focus/Faith

Luke 4:1-13

Colossians 2:13-14

Hebrews 12:1-2

1 John 1:7

Romans 8:1

Colossians 1:9-14

John 6:15

Galatians 6:9

2 Corinthians 4:16

James 4:7

Category: Discernment

SUFFERING, THORNS, & MYSTERIES*

Jesus paid on the cross for our salvation, deliverance, healing, and sustenance and it is God's desire for us to experience the fullness of the blessing and benefits of what Jesus died to give us. This said, God has an enemy who launches attacks against our lives. This enemy is the father of lies and is constantly trying to convince us that God is not good, that Jesus is not Lord, and that we have done something to deserve less than the full experience of God's benefits and blessings as His children or that we have to do something to earn it.

While there are times when Jesus calls upon us to take up our cross, turn the other cheek, and follow Him in learning obedience through the things we suffer, there are other times when it is the enemy who is attempting to deceive us into accepting types of suffering which God has not ordained for us and which Jesus paid in full on the cross for us to be free from.

For starters, we are not perfected or sanctified through sickness or suffering. We are sanctified by the blood of Jesus, His Word, His name, and by the Holy Spirit. (See Hebrews 10:10,14; John 15:3, 17:17; 1Corinthians 6:11; Titus 3:5.) Moreover, sharing in the sufferings of Christ does not include sickness. Jesus was never sick. The words used to describe sharing the *sufferings* of Christ are defined as *an external suffering, hardship, or pain* **of the same kind**, or *to suffer evils, particularly persecutions,* **in like manner**. Jesus suffered by giving up the splendors and privileges of heaven in order to be born into a flesh like ours and live completely dependent on God's provision. He suffered when He willingly offered Himself to uncompromisingly obey the will of God, even though it included rejection by His own people and by the world, having insults hurled at Him without retaliating, being led like a lamb to slaughter without defending Himself, and being whipped, scourged, beaten, mocked, betrayed, and ultimately crucified to death while praying for his crucifiers to be forgiven. (See Isaiah 53:3, 7; John 1:11; 1 Peter 2:23-24.) Through all of this, Jesus relentlessly trusted in God's goodness and power to bring His promises to pass and unwaveringly prioritized eternal matters over the things of this world. Even as a beloved Son, Jesus learned obedience through the things He suffered – not through accepting sickness or oppression. (See Hebrews 5:8.)

I am not saying that sickness is not suffering—it is. Since the fall of Adam, there have been many and various forms of suffering in this world, including sickness. However, when we read Scriptures about glorying or being patient in tribulation, rejoicing in suffering, or receiving the Lord's comfort in our trials, we should know that sickness and disease are not what is being addressed. (See Romans 5:3, 12:12; Colossians 1:24; 2 Corinthians 1:4.) Jesus did not comfort the sick in their sickness, ask them to be patient, or perpetuate their sickness in any way—He healed the sick. Therefore, healing and health are what Jesus demonstrated to be God's will for us and what He has made available to us when we place our faith in Him. While it is true that we are exhorted to rejoice always in all things, we should not embrace or glory in our sickness as the Lord's will for us when Jesus died on a cross to pay for our healing.

Here are some other common lies of the enemy on this subject.

A Thorn in the Flesh

The enemy often succeeds in convincing believers that we will not be healed because our illness is a *thorn in the flesh*, like the Apostle Paul had. This is what the Apostle Paul said about his thorn in the flesh:

> *2 Corinthians 12:7b-9a: Therefore, in order to keep me from becoming conceited,* **I was given a thorn in my flesh, a messenger of Satan, to torment me.** *Three times I pleaded with the Lord to take it away from me. But He said to me, "My grace is sufficient for you, for My power is made perfect in weakness."*

The Apostle Paul was a Jewish man and, before becoming a follower of Jesus, he was schooled in the Scriptures with the finest education in the world in his day and was known to have excelled in his studies because of his extreme zealousness for God and His Word. (See Galatians 1:14.) In light of this, in several of Paul's letters, he used figures of speech from the Scriptures that were commonly known among his people. For example, in Paul's letter to Timothy, he said that the Lord had *saved him from the lion's mouth.* (See 2 Timothy 4:17.) In this, Paul was not referring to a literal lion. In Jewish history, there was a man who was literally delivered from the lion's mouth by God—Daniel. (See Daniel 6; Hebrews 11:33.) Hence, Paul was using an expression common to the Jewish people as a means of saying that even though no human had come to his defense, the Lord had spared him from enemies seeking to destroy him.

It was in this same manner that Paul used the expression *thorn in the flesh.* Paul did not mean that he had a literal thorn in his flesh but was using a figure of speech from the Scriptures. In the history of Israel, the Lord instructed the Israelites to destroy and drive out all the inhabitants who were occupying the Promised Land. He warned them that the inhabitants from the other nations would become like *thorns in the flesh* if the Israelites failed to drive them out completely because the wrong beliefs and practices of the nations would steer the Israelites away from worshiping Him as the only true God.

> *Numbers 33:52, 55:* **Drive out all the inhabitants of the land before you.** *Destroy all their carved images and their cast idols, and demolish all their high places. ... But if you do not drive out the inhabitants of the land,* **those you allow to remain will become barbs in your eyes and thorns in your sides.** *They will give you trouble in the land where you will live.*

> *Joshua 23:13: Then you may be sure that the LORD your God will no longer* **drive out these nations before you.** *Instead,* **they will become snares and traps for you, whips on your backs and thorns in your eyes**, *until you perish from this good land, which the LORD your God has given you.*

> *Judges 2:3 ESV: So now I say, I will not drive them out before you, but* **they shall become thorns in your sides**, *and their gods shall be a snare to you.*

> *Ezekiel 28:24: No longer will the people of Israel have* **malicious neighbors who are painful briers and sharp thorns.** *Then they will know that I am the Sovereign LORD.*

When Paul wrote about his *thorn in the flesh,* it was in a letter to the believers in Corinth in response to the fact that false apostles were attacking Paul and mocking his apostolic authority. The entire chapter leading up to his use of the expression thorn in the flesh pertains to persecution from these false apostles.

> *2Corinthians 11:23-28 - Are they servants of Christ? (I am out of my mind to talk like this.) I am more. I have* **worked much harder, been in prison more frequently,** *been* **flogged** *more severely, and been* **exposed to death** *again and again. Five times I received from the Jews the* **forty lashes** *minus one. Three times I was* **beaten with rods,** *once I was* **pelted with stones,** *three times I was* **shipwrecked,** *I spent a night and a day in the open sea, I have been constantly on the move. I have been* **in danger from rivers, in danger from bandits, in danger from my fellow Jews, in danger from Gentiles; in danger in the city, in danger in the country, in danger at sea; and in danger from false believers.** *I have labored and toiled and have often gone* **without sleep;** *I have known* **hunger and thirst and have often gone without food;** *I have been* **cold and naked.** *Besides everything else, I face daily* **the pressure of my concern for all the churches.**

Paul was literally, brutally, repeatedly, and physically assaulted by people in this world who refused to believe Jesus and by worldly believers who rejected his God-given authority. His boasting in these persecutions immediately precedes and follows his use of the expression *thorn in the flesh*. Accordingly, it seems fairly clear to me that persecution is what Paul was referring to as his *thorn in the flesh*. For someone to claim that Paul's thorn is some kind of illness or disease seems like a drastic leap out of the context of his letter to the Corinthians and the whole of Scripture. Also, since many claim that Paul's *thorn in the flesh* was a problem with his eyes or point to the bodily illness that first brought Paul to the Galatians, it is worth noting that Paul arrived in Galatia after being stoned by the crowd at Lystra so inhumanely that they thought he was dead. (See Galatians 4:13; Acts 14:19.) It would not be surprising if his body and his eyes were in a weakened or infirm state after such treatment.

But let's not stop there. We may still be left with the question of why God would allow *thorns in the flesh* in the first place, especially for His chosen people and the most influential apostle the world has ever known. Fortunately, God is so good that He states His purposes clearly. The nations that the Israelites were unable to drive out were left there by God in order to test the Israelites in their faithfulness to Him as the one true God and to teach them His methods for fighting battles.

> *Judges 3:1-4:* These are the nations **the LORD left to test all those Israelites** who had not experienced any of the wars in Canaan (**he did this only to teach warfare** to the descendants of the Israelites who had not had previous battle experience): the five rulers of the Philistines, all the Canaanites, the Sidonians, and the Hivites living in the Lebanon mountains from Mount Baal Hermon to Lebo Hamath. **They were left to test the Israelites to see whether they would obey the LORD's commands**, which he had given their ancestors through Moses.

God uses trials and persecution from unbelievers and false prophets to train us in the way of righteousness. (See Deuteronomy 13:1-11; Matthew 13:28-30; 2 Thessalonians 2:11; Hebrews 5:8.) We must never forget that we follow a crucified King who calls upon us to take up our own cross and follow after Him in these types of sufferings. (See Luke 9:23.) God is not going to take away the cross that Jesus told us to carry. When we look at Paul's thorn in this way, it makes perfect sense that God refused to take the thorn away and that Paul learned to delight in it. Suffering for the name of Jesus and for the Kingdom of God due to persecution is cause for great rejoicing. (See Matthew 5:10-13.) Paul's thorn was not sickness. This leaves us with no excuse for settling for receiving less than the healing Jesus died to give us.

God's Sovereignty or God Allowed It

Another tactic of the enemy against believers is to convince them that God's sovereign control over all things means that their sickness is from God. This is a lie.

We live in a fallen world and disease is a part of it. Since the fall of Adam, we earn or deserve sickness through disobedience. When God redeemed Israel and gave His Law, He revealed that the way to stay in health and live a long life is through obedience to Him. When we violate God's Law, we deserve a penalty which can include sickness—the wages of sin is death. (See Romans 6:23.) If we had not sinned, we would not have warranted punishment. Righteousness is our protection and the only way we can remain on the path of life and health.

So far, the "God allowed it" argument seems to be right and you could even add, "we deserve it." However, the way to pay the penalty for disobedience is through a blood sacrifice of high enough value to reconcile us to God and restore us to righteousness and its benefits, including health. Of course, this is exactly what Jesus came to do for us. His blood perpetually pays the penalty for everything we have ever done or could ever do to earn or deserve God's punishment. (See 1 John 1:7.) As long as our faith is in Jesus' perfect righteousness on our behalf, we can receive our healing as a free gift. Moreover, Jesus gave us authority over every disease, unclean spirit, and over the enemy so that we can forbid sickness in our lives. (See Luke 9:1, 10:19; Matthew 18:18.)

Therefore, not only does God **not** allow sickness—He has paid the price for us to not be sick. Sickness violates the covenant we have with God through faith in Jesus who redeemed us from the effects of the fall of man and transferred us to the Kingdom of Heaven where sickness is forbidden. It is our own wrong understanding of what Jesus has done for us, our unbelief in the benefits that God extends freely to us in the New Covenant, our unwarranted fear of an enemy who has been thoroughly defeated, or our determination to do things our own way rather than being led by the Holy Spirit that gives sickness a place in our lives. God does not allow sickness—we allow it through unbelief.

God is Teaching

Another common erroneous belief is to say of sickness that, "God is teaching me through this." This is a lie.

Not only does God **not** chastise us through sickness—He laid all sickness upon Jesus so that we can be healed. Jesus took all of our chastisement and all of our sickness upon Himself so that, through faith in Him, we have been healed by His wounds. (See Isaiah 53:4-5.)

Because of our faith in Jesus, God treats us as His beloved children and does not use sickness to chastise us. As if it is not enough to say that a loving Father would never inflict sickness on their own son or daughter, Jesus is our example of life as a child of God and as a beloved Son, Jesus was never sick.

God does not teach us about His goodness by being evil. God does not teach us about His faithfulness by being fickle. God does not teach us about His love and mercy by attacking our bodies with disease and torment. Moreover, God has given us a teacher and it is not sickness—it is the Holy Spirit. The Holy Spirit is constantly teaching us, leading us in truth, guiding us in paths of righteousness for the Lord's glory, and reminding us of everything that Jesus taught. (See John 14:26.) We have to allow the Holy Spirit to renew our mind, will, and emotions so that we come fully into alignment with God's good will toward us in Jesus.

In the name of "God teaching us," we will allow ourselves to be diverted by learning techniques, methods, and teachings which are birthed out of trusting in the knowledge of good and evil (including diets, supplements, medications, etc.) rather than righteousness as a free gift from God and healing by His wounds. In our desperate quest to be well, we may acquire lots of knowledge about God and still be sick because we never learn to believe that it is God's will for us to be well. (See 2 Timothy 3:5, 7; Colossians 2:23.) But as we submit ourselves to God and resist the evil one, he will flee from us and so will sickness.

It's a Mystery

When the enemy pushes people past their ability to comprehend and believe God, they will often say, "God works in mysterious ways," or "It's a mystery" to let themselves off the hook of persisting in faith.

God does not work in mysterious ways—He works according to His Word. While we don't know everything about God and can still be filled with childlike wonder about Him, we cannot use God's "mysteriousness" as an excuse for not receiving something from Him that Jesus died to give us.

God has revealed the biggest mystery of all redemptive history to us so that we can steward the mystery to the rest of the world. The mystery is this: Jesus died so we can have right standing with God and have the Spirit of the Lord dwelling inside of us. (See Romans 16:25-26; 1 Corinthians 2:7, 4:1; Ephesians 3:4-5; Colossians 1:26-27, 2:2; 1 Timothy 3:16.) The mystery was hidden in ages past, but now it is out in the open! Moreover, God has not locked up His Kingdom and blessings in secrecy and guesswork. We are God's children, and He desires to open all the storehouses of heaven to us. In fact, Jesus calls us His friends because He tells us everything that the Father has told Him and is willing to open up all of the secrets of the Kingdom of Heaven to us. (See John 15:15; Matthew 13:11.)

This is why we are encouraged to keep on asking, seeking, and knocking so that we can continue to receive, find, and have more and more of God's goodness opened to us. (See Matthew 7:7-8.) When we do this, we discover that the mystery of God has been revealed and the things that God has revealed have been revealed so that we may do them. (See Deuteronomy 29:29)

Basic Training Exercise

HELP MY UNBELIEF

Mark 9:21-24 NIV - Jesus asked the boy's father, "How long has he been like this?" "From childhood," he answered. "It has often thrown him into fire or water to kill him. But if you can do anything take pity on us and help us." "If you can'?" said Jesus. "Everything is possible for one who believes." Immediately the boy's father exclaimed, "I do believe; help me overcome my unbelief!"

DESCRIPTION

Unbelief prevents us from experiencing all of the blessings God has for us, including miracles. It occurs when we consider that our current circumstance is too difficult for God to handle or that our present problem has somehow not been addressed through the sacrifice and resurrection of Jesus. This does not mean we have no faith but that our faith has been stretched past our ability to believe.

This said, the free gift of salvation, deliverance, healing, and sustenance is ours to receive by faith. This means that when we have real faith in God, even if it is only the size of a mustard seed, everything is possible to us. We stop fearing anything or even thinking things like, "If you can...," to God because we start to truly entrust ourselves into His hands as our loving Heavenly Father no matter how grim our circumstances may appear to be.

Therefore, to practice Help My Unbelief is about recognizing that even though we have some faith, there are ways in which we are not fully trusting God. Recognizing these areas helps us turn them over the Lord, repent, and build our faith to receive from Him.

PRAYER

Father, I believe, help my unbelief! Show me the ways that I am not trusting you fully or am believing wrong things. Increase my faith in more areas of my life so that I can bring you greater glory. Show me how to exercise my faith by trusting you more in all things. In Jesus' name, Amen.

Category: Miracles

Basic TRAINING
SPIRITUAL EXERCISES

PURPOSE:
To resist and conquer various forms of unbelief.

To grow in faith and application of trusting God in our lives.

To experience more miracles because of greater faith.

SPIRITUAL FRUIT:
Strengthened faith and faithfulness.

Deeper experience of God's ways and work.

Repentance from self-reliance over trust in God.

Repentance from wrong beliefs.

Purified motives and approach to life.

CONSIDERATIONS

Consider these forms of unbelief, listed in no particular order:

- **Disbelief:** The inability or refusal to believe something. Says things like, "I do not believe that Jesus heals today."
- **Doubt/Unbelief:** Thinking something is too unbelievable to be real or having faith stretched past our ability to believe.
- **Misbelief:** Faith in something that is wrong. Says things like, "Time heals all wounds." Time does not heal, Jesus heals.
- **Self-Righteousness:** Faith in our own record before God rather than in Jesus' perfect record. Believes, "I deserve it," rather than in Jesus' perfect record.
- **Psychologizing:** Inspecting our past for reasons why we are unable to receive God's blessings. Says things like, "my father didn't love me so I doubt God does." This is the wrong basis for faith altogether. Jesus did not come as a psychologist, He came as a Savior.

PRACTICE

1. Ask the Holy Spirit to highlight one of the unbeliefs above that is relevant to your life right now.

2. Ask the Lord to show you how this unbelief has infiltrated your thoughts. Talk to Him about:
   - When did this unbelief begin? Was there an event which triggered this? Was it from a disappointment?
   - Ask the Lord to reveal to you the real root of the issue. For example, pride, fear, intellectualism, theology, etc.

3. Repent. Ask the Lord to forgive your unbelief.
   - Ask the Lord to forgive your unbelief. Receive forgiveness.
   - Ask the Lord to help you change your approach.

4. Ask the Lord how He wants to help you overcome this unbelief through greater faith and trust in Him.
   - How will He transform your faith and renew your mind?
   - Is there something He is asking you to do to build your faith?

5. Do whatever He says.

NOTES: _____

ADDITIONAL SCRIPTURES:	
Unbelief	
Matthew 13:58	
2 Kings 17:15-15	
Psalm 78	
Isaiah 65:2	
Faith	
Matthew 19:26	
Philippians 4:13	
Hebrews 11:1, 6	
Romans 10:17	
Mark 11:22-25	
1 Corinthians 2:5	
Romans 4:16	

Category: Miracles

CORNERSTONE – UNIT 5.4

PERSECUTION TO THE END & SIGNS OF THE TIMES
Scripture Reading

Read each of the following passages and then use the chart below for study and reflection.
- The Book of Matthew, Chapter 24
- The Book of Daniel, Chapter 7
- The Book of Revelation, Chapters 13 & 18
- 2 Thessalonians 2:1-12

General Summary of These Passages:	
Main Themes & Common Message:	**Key Verses:**
God's Commands to His People:	**Questions you still have about this:**
How does this change your impressions of the times we live in and the times to come?	
How is God asking you to respond to these passages in your life today?	

Basic Training Exercise

COUNT THE COST

Luke 14:27-33 ESV - Whoever does not bear his own cross and come after me cannot be my disciple. For which of you, desiring to build a tower, does not first sit down and count the cost, whether he has enough to complete it? Otherwise, when he has laid a foundation and is not able to finish, all who see it begin to mock him, saying, 'This man began to build and was not able to finish.' Or what king, going out to encounter another king in war, will not sit down first and deliberate whether he is able with ten thousand to meet him who comes against him with twenty thousand? And if not, while the other is yet a great way off, he sends a delegation and asks for terms of peace. So therefore, any one of you who does not renounce all that he has cannot be my disciple.

DESCRIPTION

Jesus made the terms of following Him explicitly clear. When we agree to be a disciple of Jesus, we enter in knowing that it will cost us everything, like a king who knows that he does not have enough strength, soldiers, or resources to win the battle or the war.

We serve a God who gave up everything and died on a cross for us. The evidence of our understanding of what our God did for us is found in the cost we are willing to pay as we obediently follow Jesus.

Jesus imperatively said His disciples must take up our cross and renounce all that we have in order to follow Him. The cross is an instrument of death and as such, disciples must be willing to suffer humiliation, loss, and even pay the ultimate price if God so wills. Not that we pursue sacrifice of our own design but that we position our hearts in readiness to sacrifice whatever might be required of us on our path with God. There is no such thing as a 50% disciple, a good-times only disciple, or a have it my way disciple. We must be hot or cold, all in or not in at all.

Practicing Count the Cost is about examining our willingness to follow Jesus, even when it hurts and even if it costs us everything.

Category: Self-Denial

Basic TRAINING
SPIRITUAL EXERCISES

PURPOSE:

- To understand the terms and requirements of following Jesus.
- To realistically assess our commitment to following Jesus.
- To increase our willingness to give all for Jesus.

SPIRITUAL FRUIT:

Absolute surrender to God and following Jesus.

Increased humility.

Increased readiness to suffer and sacrifice for Jesus and His Kingdom.

PRAYER

Father, thank you for paying the ultimate price for me. Help me to understand the worth of your sacrifice and increase my willingness to give my all for you. In Jesus' name, Amen.

CONSIDERATIONS

Consider the following aspects Jesus alluded to as the potential cost of following Him. Listed in no particular order:

- Hated by family, mother, father for name of Jesus.
- Homelessness: foxes have holes but not Son of Man.
- Losing/giving up all possessions to follow Jesus.
- Persecuted/ridiculed by family, friends, etc.
- Hated by world. Hated by all people.
- Death to self: arrogance, pride, selfishness, "my way," etc.
- Death to flesh: passions, sensual desires, preferences, etc.
- Ultimate price: death, loss of life for the name of Jesus.

TALK WITH GOD

In what ways have you followed God because He gives you what you want or has the power to bless you?

If Jesus never blessed you again, (material blessing, healing, guidance, etc.) would you still want to follow Him?

If you knew that God's purpose was for you to be martyred for Jesus, how would that change your walk of faith?

In what ways have you experienced persecution from family, friends, or others for following Jesus? What is your response?

In what ways have you been called upon to suffer or sacrifice for following Jesus? Did you do it? Joyfully?

In what ways has Jesus asked you to take up your cross and die to yourself or your flesh? How did it change you?

What do you think motivated Jesus to take up His cross? How did He do it? What example does that set for you?

After counting the cost, do you still want to be a disciple of Jesus? Why?

NOTES:
_____
_____
_____

Category: Self-Denial

ADDITIONAL SCRIPTURES:

Matthew 5:10

Luke 9:58

Matthew 24:9

Luke 4:26

John 15:18-25

James 1:2-3, 12

Acts 14:22

Mark 8:36

Luke 9:23

Philippians 2:5-11

Matthew 6:24

1 John 2:15-17

Revelation 3:16

UNIT FIVE – KEY QUESTIONS
Suffering & Persecution

Use this worksheet to test your grasp of the material and exercises of Unit Five.

What is the role of Christian suffering?

What is suffering for righteousness sake?

What types of trials do Christians face?

What does it mean to take up my cross?

What is the enemy's role in suffering?

What types of suffering are sharing in Christ's suffering? What types are not?

How do believers prepare for the times ahead?

What is one thing you learned that you did not know before?

What questions do you still have about this subject?

UNIT FIVE: GROUP EXERCISES

Using the Exercises from Unit Five's classes, have each person in the group ask the Lord to guide them about sharing a **personal** and **current** example.

Choose from ONE of the following:
- From Son of David - Son of Man: One way that following Jesus right now is different than they were expecting.
- From Enemy Tactics: One way that the evil one is attacking them or their faith right now.
- From Help My Unbelief: One way that God is currently challenging them to overcome their unbelief.
- From Count the Cost: One way that they are paying a cost for following Jesus in their life right now.

After each person shares, listen to the Holy Spirit for any words of encouragement and pray for them as a group.

Please be respectful and keep the information they shared confidential within the group. Do unto others as you want done to you.

UNIT SIX:
CHRISTLIKENESS & COMMISSION

KEY SCRIPTURE VERSE FOR UNIT SIX
I press on toward the goal to win the prize for which God has called me heavenward in Christ Jesus. All of us, then, who are mature should take such a view of things. And if on some point you think differently, that too God will make clear to you. - Philippians 3:14-15

CLASS 1: LIVING BY FAITH
1 Reading, 1 Scripture Reading, 1 Exercise
God's desire is for us to know and believe Him in each area of our own lives so that we are not following the ways of this world but trusting in Him like little children. As we set out to tell others to trust God, He says to us, "You first."

CLASS 2: CHRISTLIKENESS (BEING)
2 Exercises, 1 Worksheet
Jesus is our example of flesh and blood life lived by the power of God's Spirit and according to God's will. We are called to be like Him in character, wisdom, and approach.

CLASS 3: COMMISSION (DOING)
1 Reading, 1 Worksheet, 1 Exercises
Jesus commissioned all of His followers to make disciples and participate in the work of His Kingdom. Each one of us has been called as a witness and a minister of the Most High God.

CLASS 4: MATURITY (FULLNESS)
1 Reading, 1 Exercise, 1 Evaluation
Spiritual maturity looks like the life of Jesus and daily obedience to His teachings and commands. All believers are called to maturity and to helping others to become mature.

KEY QUESTIONS

GROUP EXERCISES

You First: Living by Faith

Jesus said that the Law and the Prophets could be summarized in two commandments, which are to love the Lord your God with all your heart, soul, mind, and might, and to love your neighbor as yourself. (See Matthew 22:37-39; Deuteronomy 6:5; Leviticus 19:18.) Jesus fulfilled the Old Covenant and the Law of God in perfect righteousness and obedience. Therefore, we no longer have to strive to measure up to God's standard in order to receive His love and be blessed by Him.

This said, Jesus gave a new command to us who follow Him, "Love one another as I have loved you." (See John 13:34, 15:12-17.) With this, He entirely changed the configuration and flow of love and blessing. Under the old system, adherents exhaust themselves attempting to love God with all their heart and then, as if there is anything left after using all of their heart, to love others as themselves. But, in the new way of Christ, we as believers receive love unconditionally, freely, and bountifully from God and then are full and able to freely give out what we have received from Him.

This is part of what I call God's **you first** policy. We cannot give out what we have not received for ourselves. God spoke from Heaven in an audible voice in order for His Son (and everyone else around) to unquestionably know of His love and approval. (See Matthew 3:17, 17:5; Mark 11:1; Luke 3:22, 9:35.) In the same way, because of what Jesus did for us, we can be assured of God's love for us before we have done anything to deserve it. (See Ephesians 2:8-9.) But, in order for us to love others as Jesus loves us, we have to let Him love us first.

In fact, Jesus tells His followers to abide in His love. (See John 15:1-9.) This means leaving the old behind being led by the Holy Spirit within us. It means *waiting* for God's guidance and *trusting* that He is working all things out for our good. (See Romans 8:1, 14, 28.) It means *being held and kept* in His presence so that we can receive the fullness of all that He has for us.

Abiding can be hard work because we have to resist the temptations and ways of this world and our flesh in order to remain in Christ. This said, it is the only work that God requires of us.

> *John 6:29 NLT: Jesus told them, "**This is the only work God wants from you: Believe** in the one he has sent."*

For this reason, we need to do whatever is necessary to rearrange our lives and our priorities in order to abide. This may mean spending time in God's presence and keeping Him first in our lives even if this causes other priorities to receive less of our attention and energy. It may mean reading and meditating on His Word rather than watching television or reading other books. It means doing anything that helps us to know God's love and hear His voice, even at the expense of everything else in our lives.

As we abide, every hindrance is removed, wounds are healed, wrong thinking is replaced with truth, all fear is expelled, and we stop striving for acceptance from anyone other than the One who already accepts us and who is the only One that really matters. This makes us free to love and frees us up to obey God's voice and truly fulfill His purposes.

Simple Obedience

Before we can tell other people to obey God, He says to us, **you first**. Sometimes, our approach to obedience can become overly passive in the name of "God's sovereignty" thinking that God has predetermined His will and it is both totally inescapable and unaffected by the choices of man. Other times, we can think that doing God's will lies entirely on our ability to obey Him perfectly or the rest of eternity could be altered by our decisions. Another method is to make our own plans and then ask God to bless what we do.

None of these reflect the relationship of Father and child cooperating to bring about God's will on the earth. To put it plainly, God does have His will, and He gives us free will to cooperate with Him or not. God's will was Eden. Adam's free will messed it up. (See Genesis 3) Jesus, on the other hand, surrendered His free will in order to do only what the Father wanted. On a daily basis and even a moment-by-moment basis, Jesus said and did only what He heard and saw His Father doing by living in obedience to the Holy Spirit. (See John 4:34, 5:19, 6:38, 12:49.)

God doesn't really need our help. He wants our cooperation as His children as He fulfills His eternal plans in all the earth. Sometimes, it seems that He tells us everything because we are His friends and other times, it seems that we are on a need-to-know basis because if He told us everything our minds would explode. This said, when we trust that He loves us and is working for our good and the good of others, we are free to obey even when we don't know exactly what He is doing. In fact, we stop trusting in ourselves and our own ways and truly begin to know to the depths of our being that God is real and He is good to us. Through this, our mind, will, and emotions are changed to be like Jesus as we keep our attention on Him and press into deeper levels of knowing and doing God's will for our lives.

> *Romans 12:2: Do not conform to the pattern of this world, but* **be transformed by the renewing of your mind.** *Then you will be able to test and approve what God's will is--his good, pleasing and perfect will. (See also James 3:15-17; Galatians 5:19-23)*
>
> *Philippians 2:13: for it is* **God who works in you to will and to act in order to fulfill** *his good purpose.*
>
> *2 Corinthians 3:18: And we all, who with unveiled faces contemplate the Lord's glory, are* **being transformed into his image** *with ever-increasing glory, which comes from the Lord, who is the Spirit.*

Obedience is simple. All we have to do is listen to God and do what He says. We obey God by submitting to God's will and ways of doing things even at the expense of our desires, pride, plans, timing, reputation, and way of doing things. (See Hebrews 5:8, 12:3-11; James 1:4; Romans 5:3-5) God knows the end from the beginning and often uses supernatural or miraculous methods of executing His plans because His ways are a lot higher than ours and have a holy and eternal objective. (See Isaiah 55:8-11) For this reason, He often leads us in ways that make absolutely no earthly sense whatsoever in order to demonstrate His love, mercy, and power and so that His name is exalted.

When we do what God asks of us, nothing more and nothing less, we can obey and walk away because we are not responsible for the results...God is. When we have followed the promptings of the Holy Spirit, we can have a clear conscience and be confident that we have done what God asked of us, even if we do not see tangible change right away. We do not have to look for recognition, approval, or anything in return from those whom we serve.

When situations and people tempt us into old behavior patterns and we want to confront them in their sin and selfishness, desiring secretly in our hearts to crucify them, God says to us, **you first**. God never leads us in hypocrisy. Before we can rebuke anyone for their faults, we must consider our own flesh, selfish ambitions, and preferences to be as good as a dead sacrifice on the altar of God. This way, we will not be offended by the flesh of others so that we can truly love them.

Simple Love

All of us want the love of other people but again, God says to us, **you first**. First we have to learn to love others whether they love us back or not. God's kind of love is merciful. It is not unkind, rude, or jealous. It does not hold a grudge, keep track of how many times people say or do stupid things, or demand loyalty. He just loves.

As we set out to love, undoubtedly, unlovable people cross our paths and it seems that they have been placed there for the singular purpose of aggravating us and revealing to the world just how poorly skilled we are at being like Jesus. But, this is exactly the time for us to overlook their offenses and even to bless them. (See Matthew 5:39-48.) That aggravating person is dead in Christ's death (just like we are), and their sins have already been judged (just like ours have been). This means that we don't have a right to judge them because God already has. If they are a believer, then they are a new creation in Christ even though they may not be behaving like one. What they need is encouragement to know who they really are as a child of God. If they are not a believer, then they are still someone for whom Christ died, and what they need is to hear how much He loves them.

Love is simple, but it is not easy. It can be hard to know what love looks like sometimes. The right approach to loving one person could be a disservice to another depending on where they are in life and what God has purposed for them. (See 1 Thessalonians 5:14.) Sometimes love is allowing ourselves to be treated like a doormat while, at other times, love is rebuking a bully. Sometimes love rushes in to help, and other times love does not.

The only way for us to truly love the way that Jesus loves is to be led by the Holy Spirit the way that He was. As we do so, we discover that love is not catering to spoiled impulses and preferences, enabling or endorsing error, encouraging fleshly lusts or worldly desires, or serving needs towards false ambitions. Love is not turning people into our discipleship projects, conforming them to our image or the patterns of our culture, or creating false dependencies. Love is pointing people to the Father and extending mercy and grace to them as their imperfections are revealed. Love is helping others to stand firm in God's will, plan, and path for their life no matter how hard it gets and leaving them in God's hands when necessary so that their faith is firmly established in Him alone. (See Hebrews 3:13, 10:24; 1 Thessalonians 5:11.) Love is never giving up or losing hope that a person we love can be saved and set free from the pain and torments that afflict them so that they can be transformed into all that God has designed them to be.

In the world's kind of love, there is fear and hidden selfishness such as, "Will they love me back?", or "What if I get hurt by loving so much?" But God's kind of love can be selfless because our love does not depend on anything or anyone other than our relationship and our trust in God—our loving Heavenly Father.

Simple Trust

Each of us have to trust God for ourselves. This is another part of God's **you first** policy. We have no business telling anyone else to trust Him if we do not trust Him first for ourselves.

Sometimes trusting God is as unsophisticated as believing that He is a rewarder of those who seek Him even if we feel like we do not know what we are doing. (See Hebrews 11:6.) Other times, it means completely taking our hands off of a situation in order to get out of God's way and allow Him to work it out according to His will. (See John 6:29; Zechariah 4:6.) Then again, there are times that God asks us to wholeheartedly jump into doing something completely foreign to us so that we depend entirely on Him as we do it. (See 2 Corinthians 1:9.)

> Proverbs 3:5-6: **Trust in the LORD with all your heart and lean not on your own understanding;**
> in all your ways submit to him, and he will make your paths straight.

Truth be told, when we start truly relying upon God in deeper levels of trust and obedience, it seems that He leads us straight into situations which appear to be the exact opposite of what He promised us. I call this "a walk with the Lord through the valley of the shadow of death." (See Psalm 23:4.) The path of true greatness and glory includes being willing to be nothing so that God can truly be everything in our lives.

He often leads us through obscurity, failure, humiliation, isolation, and various other trials so that we learn to rely upon Him and His faithfulness to bring about what He promised rather than relying on our own strength, abilities, intellect, or skills. When we have become like children and have learned not to trust in our own knowledge of good and evil, we can receive the Kingdom of God. (See Matthew 18:3.) When we have endured through God's **you first** policy of preparation, we will fear no evil because we have learned to trust God in all things.

Cut to the Heart

Before any of us can do much of anything for God, we must submit ourselves to His **you first** policy. In fact, God's desire has always been for people to worship Him in Spirit and in truth, not through religious observance and outward circumcision but because of circumcision of their hearts. (See John 4:24.)

> *Deuteronomy 10:16:* **Circumcise your hearts**, *therefore, and do not be stiff-necked any longer. (Also Deuteronomy 30:6; Jeremiah 4:4, 9:25-26.)*

> *Philippians 3:3: For it is* **we who are the circumcision**, *we who* **serve God by his Spirit**, *who* **boast in Christ Jesus**, *and who put* **no confidence in the flesh**. *(Also Romans 2:28-29.)*

Since the day of Pentecost, people near and far have been "cut to the heart" when they hear the Gospel of Jesus Christ. Some, like the 3,000 people who repented after hearing Peter's Pentecost day speech, were cut to the heart and became believers. Others, like the religious people listening to Stephen's speech, were cut to the heart in anger and indignation.

> *Acts 2:37: When the people heard this, they were* **cut to the heart** *and said to Peter and the other apostles,* "**Brothers, what shall we do?**"

> *Acts 7:51, 54 KJV: "You stiff-necked people!* **Your hearts and ears are still uncircumcised.** *You are just like your ancestors:* **You always resist the Holy Spirit!**... *When they heard these things, they were* **cut to the heart**, *and they gnashed on him with [their] teeth.*

As God calls us to His **you first** process, we will either be humbled and willing to do whatever it takes to repent, change, and serve Him or we will be incensed, and resistant in our own self-righteousness. When we are cut to the heart for Christ, it is because we have received revelation from God that Jesus is who He says He is. It is exhilarating and humiliating at the same time because it is like realizing with full assurance that something that we have been in denial about for a long time is actually true. It is recognizing that we have been wrong all along about Jesus and that we do not deserve the grace that He has never stopped extending to us.

The prophet Ezekiel had a vision of a man dressed in white linen who placed the mark of God on the people who were cut to the heart in grief over the horrendous lack of regard for God in Jerusalem. God's prophet Jeremiah was so deeply cut to the heart for God's people that he is commonly called the weeping prophet. Jesus had so much compassion because of His circumcised heart that some people thought He might be Jeremiah reincarnated. (See Matthew 16:14; Luke 9:8, 19:41; John 11:33-35.) Now, God cuts us to the heart by filling us with His love for people and dismay over their separation from God. This motivates us to serve Him and draw them into His Kingdom.

Have you been cut to the heart yet? If you want to do great things for God and His Kingdom then, God is calling you and saying, "**you first**."

www.manifestinternational.com

Living by Faith
Scripture Reading & Worksheet

Read each of the following passages and then use the chart below for study and reflection.

- Hebrews 11
- Proverbs 3:5-6
- James 2:14-26
- Luke 1:26-38
- Matthew 21:21-22
- Philippians 4:13
- Mark 9:23
- 2 Corinthians 1:3-12

Insights this gives me about the life of faith:	
3 Highlights or Significant Points: 1. 2. 3.	**3 Questions I have about living by faith:** 1. 2. 3.
How God is calling me deeper in trusting Him over my own understanding:	
Areas of my life God is asking me to trust Him with: Finances Family Marriage/Romance Work/Career Social/Friends/Fun Health/Sickness Location/Living Place School/Education	
Excitement and/or concern I feel about stepping out in faith:	
Practical steps of faith God is asking me to take in my life right now:	

Basic Training Exercise

FROM FAITH TO FAITH

Romans 1:16-17 ESV - For I am not ashamed of the gospel, for it is the power of God for salvation [deliverance, healing, sustenance/provision, life] to everyone who believes, to the Jew first and also to the Greek. For in it the righteousness of God is revealed from faith for faith, as it is written, "The righteous shall live by faith."

DESCRIPTION

Through our faith in Jesus, and what He did for us through His death and resurrection, we have been made righteous before God. Therefore, have free access into all the benefits of being in right standing with God. We receive all these benefits by faith.

By definition, in the Romans verse above, the word used for salvation includes salvation, deliverance, healing, and sustenance/provision. Therefore, the Gospel of Jesus Christ is the power of God on our behalf for every problem we will ever face.

It is God's desire for us to trust Him and live by faith in every area of our lives. We bring God glory when we allow Him to move on our behalf in ways that only He can. This said, similar to training muscle groups of our bodies, we may have exercised our faith in one area but remain weak in another. Plus, even when we feel that we are standing strong in faith, there are always new levels of trust that the Lord desires to take us to so that He can receive greater glory in our lives.

Therefore, to practice From Faith to Faith is about building our faith in God and what He did and desires to do for us by turning over new areas of our lives to a deeper commitment of trusting Him.

PRAYER

Father, I believe that I am righteous before you because of the work of Jesus. Increase my faith in more areas of my life so that I can bring you greater glory. Show me how to exercise my faith by trusting you more in all things. In Jesus' name, Amen.

Basic TRAINING
SPIRITUAL EXERCISES

PURPOSE:

To grow in faith and application of trusting God in our lives.

To increase in obedience and understanding of God's will and ways.

To identify and prune our lives of areas of faithlessness.

SPIRITUAL FRUIT:

Faith and faithfulness.

Deeper experience of God's ways and work on our behalf.

Repentance from self-reliance over trust in God.

Purified motives and approach to life.

PRACTICE

1. Ask God to reveal to you an area where He desires for your faith to grow. (We'll call it your Focus Area.)
   - For example, living by faith in His salvation, deliverance, healing, sustenance/provision, sanctification, miracles, or any other situation in your life right now.

2. For ten (10) days, consciously, deliberately, and totally submit your Focus Area to God. (Ten represents total.)
   - Pray, "Father, I turn _____ over to you. I place my trust in you and your ways above my own thoughts, abilities, and resources. Guide me in the way you want me to go. In Jesus' name, Amen."

3. Ask the Lord to give you one or two Scriptures to believe in and build your faith upon for your Focus Area. (Note: Using only one or two will help you center your faith.)
   - Read these Scriptures out loud every morning when you wake up and every night before you go to bed. Read them throughout the day whenever you are able.
   - Spend at least ten (10) minutes per day in prayer about your Focus Area. In your times of prayer, alternate between quoting your Scriptures and praying in tongues. Also, try singing your Scriptures and singing in tongues.

4. Over the course of the ten days, allow the Lord to build your faith in Him for your Focus Area.
   - Renounce presumption that you understand God's ways.
   - Listen to any guidance He gives you. Do what He says.
   - Resist the wisdom of this world. Resist the lies of the devil.

5. After the ten days is completed, take note of the following:
   - What did God do in your situation?
   - How do you see things differently than you did before?
   - In what ways were you tempted to believe lies from the enemy or trust in your own strength?
   - How does knowing that you are righteous in Christ help you to trust God with situations in your life?

ADDITIONAL SCRIPTURES:

Hebrews 11:1, 6

James 2:17-18

Colossians 2:8

1 Corinthians 1:24, 2:5

Proverbs 3:5-6

Genesis 15:6

Habakkuk 2:4

John 6:29

Jude 1:20

NOTES: _____

CORNERSTONE – UNIT 6.2

CHRISTLIKENESS (BEING)

3 Exercises on the following pages.

Basic Training Exercise

DEVOTIONAL READING

Basic TRAINING
SPIRITUAL EXERCISES

Song of Songs 7:10-12 NIV - I belong to my beloved, and his desire is for me. Come, my beloved, let us go to the countryside, let us spend the night in the villages. Let us go early to the vineyards to see if the vines have budded, if their blossoms have opened, and if the pomegranates are in bloom—there I will give you my love.

DESCRIPTION

Devotional Reading is about building our relationship with God by encountering Him through His Word. While it is valuable to take times for pure Bible study and scrutinizing, Devotional Reading is for the purpose of experiencing God's love and loving Him back.

As an example, consider a wife who spends time learning about her husband's likes and dislikes so that she can do what is pleasing to him. Compare this to a wife who spends time with her husband, listening to him, hearing of his affection for her, and expressing her love for him. This is the difference between reading for study and reading out of devotion.

To practice Devotional Reading includes approaching the Scriptures with our heart rather than for intellectual understanding.

CONSIDERATIONS

In your life with the Lord, have you tended toward study of the Scripture or devotional reading? Why do you think that is?

How has God used the Scriptures to speak to you in the past? What did you do about it? How has this changed your way of doing things?

In what ways do you think approaching God's Word *only* for devotion could be beneficial? Harmful?

In what ways do you think approaching God's Word *only* for study could be beneficial? Harmful?

What do you think is the right balance between Bible Study and Devotional Reading? How does one maintain this balance?

PURPOSE:

To encounter God through His written Word.

To allow the Word of God to penetrate our heart and consequently, our lives.

To listen to God's voice.

SPIRITUAL FRUIT:

Increased focus on God's voice.

Deeper love for God.

Greater experience of God's love for us.

Developing skill in hearing God's voice.

Softening of our hearts in Christ's likeness.

Alignment with God's will, perspective, and purpose.

PRAYER

Father, thank you for your love. Help me to understand your love for me and to express how my heart feels about you. Speak to me now through your Word so I can hear your voice speaking to my heart. In Jesus' name, Amen.

PRACTICE

1. Slow yourself down. Take a breath. Offer yourself to God.
   - Bring a notebook to write things down as desired.

2. Ask the Holy Spirit to help you select one passage of Scripture to use for Devotional Reading. (Psalms tend to be particularly good for this.) Some good passages include:
   - Psalms 1, 5, 8, 23, 27, 37, etc; The Song of Songs
   - Exodus 15; Deuteronomy 8; Isaiah 54, Isaiah 60, etc.
   - John 8:3-11; John 15:1-17; Luke 1:28-55, etc.
   - Ephesians 3:16-20; 1 Corinthians 13; Romans 8, etc.

3. Invite the Holy Spirit to speak to you as you read the passage one time all the way through – slowly.
   - In general, describe what this passage is about.
   - How is this relevant to your life right now?
   - How did this passage make you feel? For example, happy/sad, sympathetic/angry, loved/condemned, etc.
   - Tell the Lord how you feel. Listen for how He responds.

4. Read the passage again - slowly. This time, as you proceed towards the end of the passage, prayerfully linger on anything that the Lord seems to be highlighting to you.
   - If you were to summarize one thing that God revealed to you from this passage, what would it be?
   - How does this reveal or demonstrate God's love for you? Or His mercy, compassion, faithfulness, goodness, etc.

5. Use the revelation God has given you of His love to express your devotion to God.
   - You can use spoken words, writing/journaling, singing, or drawing/painting, etc. as you feel inspired.

NOTES: _____

ADDITIONAL SCRIPTURES:

Psalm 119: 36

John 15:1-17

1 Corinthians 13

2 Timothy 3:16

2 Peter 1:20-21

Hebrews 4:12

Psalm 119:97

Deuteronomy 29:29

Psalm 119:103

Psalm 18:30

Psalm 119:15-18

Category: Listening to God

Basic Training Exercise

DIVINE NATURE

2 Peter 1:3-4 NIV – His divine power has given us everything we need for a godly life through our knowledge of him who called us by his own glory and goodness. Through these he has given us his very great and precious promises, so that through them you may participate in the divine nature, having escaped the corruption in the world caused by evil desires.

DESCRIPTION

God has given us what we need in order for us to be like Him. Godliness is the reason He created mankind – to reflect His image and His likeness. But since Adam, no one except Jesus has been able to do this fully.

When we believe Jesus, the Holy Spirit dwells in us. This is the same Spirit of the Lord that came upon Mary, causing her to conceive and give birth to the Son of God. The same Spirit that dwelt inside of Jesus to guide Him in a perfect and sinless life now dwells inside of us. We have divine nature inside us.

From the moment the Holy Spirit enters our hearts, a conflict begins between this divine nature and our own corrupt and fleshly desires. As we allow ourselves to be led by divine nature instead of our flesh, we become more and more like Jesus. The Spirit of the Lord within us will give us strength to resist our own urges and replace them with righteous thoughts and actions. The more the Holy Spirit transforms us in this way, the more of God's image we reflect.

Practicing participation in Divine Nature is about becoming increasingly conscious of the Spirit of God dwelling within us and choosing to obey His leadings as superior to our own inclinations.

PRAYER

Father, thank you for placing your Holy Spirit inside of me to help me become like Jesus. Help me submit to your guidance from within and strengthen me with your power for godliness. In Jesus' name, Amen.

Category: Divine Nature

ALL RIGHTS RESERVED © 2018 Wendy Bowen

www.manifestinternational.com

Basic TRAINING
SPIRITUAL EXERCISES

PURPOSE:
To become increasingly godly and reflect God's image.

To be led by the Holy Spirit in righteous and pure thoughts.

To be empowered by the Holy Spirit for right words and actions.

SPIRITUAL FRUIT:
Holiness. Christlikeness. Godliness.

Increasing in the fruit of the Spirit listed in Galatians 5:22-23.

Growing evidence of our calling and election through the attributes listed in 2 Peter 1:5-7.

TALK WITH GOD

Jesus was perfect in all of His thoughts, words, and actions. How does this increase your respect and worship for Him? Tell Him about it.

How have you experienced the conflict between your own desires and what the Holy Spirit within you desires? In your life so far, who has been winning this conflict?

How does knowing that Jesus dwells inside you change your concept of approaching godliness? How does God want you to put this into practice in your life?

How is God inviting you to participate more deeply in His divine nature? What area of your thoughts, words, and actions does Jesus want you to reform right now?

Do you think it is possible for a person to be so renewed by the Holy Spirit that they do not sin? Why or why not? What is God's desire in this?

PRACTICE

1. Use the Talk with God points above to have a conversation with God about participating in Divine Nature. Listen to what He shares and put it into practice.

2. As you go through your day, find a way to regularly remind yourself that Jesus dwells inside of you. When you remember, take a moment to re-center your thoughts on Him. Allow Him to guide and strengthen you from within.

3. As you engage with others, remember that the Spirit of the Lord dwells inside of you. Turn yourself over to His guidance. How is Jesus engaging with this person? What is Jesus saying to them? It it is not "what would Jesus do?" but "what is Jesus doing right now?" ... through you!

4. Journal to Jesus about the areas of your life or times of day when it seems to be more challenging to obey the Holy Spirit rather than your flesh. Seek the Lord for His insight and assistance with this.

NOTES:

ADDITIONAL SCRIPTURES:

Ephesians 4:23-24

2 Peter 2:20

1 John 3:9

1 John 5:18

Titus 3:5

Romans 7:14-20

Romans 8:1-15

Hebrews 1:3

Galatians 5:17-22

Category: Divine Nature

ALL RIGHTS RESERVED © 2018 Wendy Bowen

www.manifestinternational.com

PROCESS WORKSHEET
SUFFICIENCY

www.manifestinternational.com

INSTRUCTIONS

God is all sufficient and almighty. As His children, His desire is for us to depend on Him for all we need. In fact, Jesus said that unless we become like little children, we cannot inherit the Kingdom of God. This said, relying on an invisible God can often be more challenging for us than relying on ourselves or our own methods.

Use this worksheet as a guide for allowing God to shed light on your level of self-sufficiency vs. finding sufficiency in Him. Pray through and write down a summary of each of the following points.

1. **How much do you rely on your own abilities in the following areas? Rate each area from 1 to 5.**
   1 = I do not rely on this – 5 = I rely on this heavily

   > Ability to Work: Work-ethic, willingness to work hard, do whatever it takes… _____
   >
   > Ability to Provide: Capacity for making money, having enough, making things stretch/last… _____
   >
   > Social Skills: Use of your personality, looks, humor, or charisma to appeal to others… _____
   >
   > Personal Expertise: Areas of skill, capability, knowledge, know-how, experience/wisdom… _____
   >
   > Personal Strength: Bodily strength, emotional strength, spiritual strength, ability to "handle it"… _____
   >
   > Use of Technology: Use of technological tools to resolve issues independently… _____
   >
   > Use of Treatments: Use of methods, routines, practices, medicines, remedies that work for you… _____

2. **In what ways is your sense of security reliant upon your ability to do things for yourself?**

   > Do you have anxiety or fears about not being able to take care of yourself?
   >
   > Describe a time when you were not able, capable, or strong enough to take care of yourself or a situation in your life. What was that like for you? Did you enjoy it or find it challenging? How so?
   >
   > What do you think are some potential dangers of self-reliance and/or self-sufficiency?

3. **In what ways does your sense of security depend on other people? On experts or authorities?**

   > How much do you rely upon your spouse, parents, family, friends, or social groups for your needs?
   > - Share a time when you felt secure because of other people.
   > - Share a time when your reliance on other people proved to be problematic or disastrous.
   >
   > How much do you rely on of the guidance/approval of professionals, experts, authority figures, ministers, or people who know God better than you?
   > - Share a time when you felt secure or safe because of the counsel of a professional or "expert."
   > - Share a time when an "expert," authority figure, or person you revered led you in the wrong direction.
   >
   > What do you think are some potential dangers of trusting in other people, even experts?

4. **In what ways are you at ease because of your beliefs, principles, and/or following the rules?**

   > How does knowing you are "being a good person" or "doing the right thing," help you to feel secure?
   >
   > Do you believe God blesses you more for being good? Punishes you for not doing the right thing?

- Share a time when you felt that God blessed you because you had been obedient.
- Share a time when you became angry/upset because God blessed someone you considered bad/wrong.

What do you think are some potential dangers of self-righteousness?

5. **How did Jesus demonstrate for us the life of reliance upon God in all things?**

   > Jesus said, "By myself I can do nothing," or "I say only what the Father tells me," or "I do nothing on my own initiative." (See John 5:19,30, 8:28, 12:49) What did He mean?

   List at least three examples of how Jesus had to live by faith. In what ways did He rely on God?

   1. _____
   2. _____
   3. _____

   How do these examples of Jesus' dependence on the Father reveal how God wants us to rely on Him as His sons and daughters?

6. **What would it be like to trust God with every aspect of your life?**

   > What concerns, fears, or anxieties rise up in you at the thought of trusting God in all things?

   How do you think your life would be different if you gave up control in order to do only what God said?

   Is there a particular area of your life that Jesus is asking you to trust Him with right now? How so?

   In what ways have you been striving to perform or earn something apart from the Lord?

7. **How is Jesus asking you to trust and rely on His sufficiency in your life right now?**

   > How is God calling you to rest? Trust in His provision? How is He calling you to co-labor with Him rather than just laboring?

   (See Isaiah 55; Matthew 7:11; Matthew 11:28-30; Luke 12:22-32; Romans 4:3-5; Mark 8:36.)

   How is God asking you to do and speak only what He reveals by His Spirit rather than your own personality or approach to people?

   (Consider 1 John 2:27; Luke 12:12; John 6:29 & 63; Romans 8:7-8 & 32.)

   How is God asking you to trust His expertise and strength rather than "handling" things yourself, or trusting in experts, or trusting in principles/rules?

   (See 1 Corinthians 1:12; 1 Corinthians 3:18-23; Luke 18:9-14; Galatians 3:2-3; Revelation 3:17)

   How does God want you to turn to Him as the One to resolve your issues, answer your questions, give you direction, and heal your body, soul, and mind?

   (Consider 1 Peter 2:25; 2 Corinthians 1:9; John 14:26; Hebrews 11:6.)

8. What are your next steps for trusting in God's sufficiency for your life?

COMMISSION: YOU WILL BE MY WITNESSES

Ever since Adam's error, God has employed witnesses to testify about who He is, what He has done, and what He will do in times to come. Adam and Eve, eyewitnesses to Eden, testified about God, being in relationship with Him, and about the promise of a Son who would crush the head of the serpent. (See Genesis 2–3.) Enoch walked with God, prophesied, and his supernatural life was, in itself, a testimony. (See Genesis 5:21-23.) Noah was a preacher of righteousness who built an ark because he believed what God told him about the judgment that was to come on the world in his day. (See Genesis 6:9-22; 2 Peter 2:5.) Later, when it seemed that all hope was lost and no one in the world worshipped or acknowledged God, God called upon Abraham to live a life of faith as a witness of the one true God. (See Genesis 12:1-4) Later, when God led the nation of Israel out of slavery, the miracles, signs, and wonders done in Egypt and the parted waters of the Red Sea testified to all the surrounding nations that the most powerful God of all creation was with His chosen people. (See Exodus 15:14-16, 18:1; Joshua 2:10.) The Laws of God were given to Israel to govern them so that they would be a living testimony as witnesses with first-hand experience of the Most High God's holiness, justice, and power. (See Exodus 19:4-6; Deuteronomy 4:5-6, 33-35; Isaiah 43:10, 12, 44:8.) Jesus came to testify of God's Kingdom, God's righteous day of judgment to come, and the opportunity to receive mercy by grace through faith in Him. After the resurrection, Jesus commissioned His disciples as His witnesses to all the nations of the earth.

> *Luke 24:46-48: He told them, "This is what is written: The Messiah will suffer and rise from the dead on the third day, and repentance for the forgiveness of sins will be preached in his name to all nations, beginning at Jerusalem.* **You are witnesses of these things.**"

> *Matthew 28:18-20: Then Jesus came to them and said, "All authority in heaven and on earth has been given to me.* **Therefore go and make disciples of all nations,** *baptizing them in the name of the Father and of the Son and of the Holy Spirit, and* **teaching them to obey everything I have commanded you.** *And surely I am with you always, to the very end of the age."*

> *Acts 1:8: But you will receive power when the Holy Spirit comes on you;* **and you will be my witnesses in Jerusalem, and in all Judea and Samaria, and to the ends of the earth.**"

The same command remains for us today. Each one of us has been commissioned by Jesus to declare the good news of Jesus Christ so that everyone can hear and believe. (See Romans 10:8-17.) We have a responsibility to deliver God's message and, significantly, Jesus will not return until we have accomplished our task as His witnesses to the whole world.

> *Matthew 24:14: And this* **gospel of the kingdom will be preached in the whole world** *as a testimony* **to all nations,** *and* **then the end will come.**

MY WITNESSES

In a legal sense, a witness is "one who affirms what they have seen, heard, or experienced." In a court of Law, a witness testifies for or against someone or something based on what they know about that person or situation. For example, Jesus left His home in heaven as God's witness in order to testify about what He had seen, heard, and experienced of the Kingdom of God. Now, He sends His disciples out as His witnesses to share with the world what we have seen, heard, and experienced of Jesus.

As we have discussed, this means that witnessing for Christ starts with being cut to the heart in our own lives. We cannot share with others what we do not know for ourselves. God hates hypocrisy and knows that it is easy to refute the testimony of a witness who lacks integrity. The way we live our lives shares a thousand testimonies even when we never speak a word, and even when we are not teaching, preaching, sharing our testimony, or deliberately making disciples.

Moreover, a transformed person simply can't help but tell everyone about Jesus! A true witness for Christ does not consider Jesus' commission to be a work assignment or intolerable burden of responsibility. When our lives have been changed by Jesus Christ, we are always prepared to share the story of how Jesus Christ has changed our lives by His salvation, no matter what happens to us! (See 1 Peter 3:15.)

This is what happened with the first followers of Jesus. Every single one of the first 120 believers in Jerusalem was someone whose life had been dramatically changed by Jesus Christ. This group contained ordinary fishermen who had walked with Jesus while He performed miracles, men and women whom Christ had healed from sickness and freed from demonic oppression, Jesus' mother Mary, who still remembered Jesus' divine conception by the power of the Holy Spirit, Jesus' half-brothers who had not previously believed that Jesus was the Christ, and other disciples who had seen and heard the resurrected Jesus with their own eyes and ears. (See Acts 1:13-15, 2:1, 10:41; 1Corinthians 15:3-7.) These believers could not return to life as usual after the resurrection of Christ. Their purpose in life was permanently altered as the great commission became their eternal assignment.

> *Acts 4:19-20: But Peter and John replied, "Which is right in God's eyes: to listen to you, or to him? You be the judges! As for us,* **we cannot help speaking about what we have seen and heard.***"*

> *Acts 5:30-32:* **The God of our ancestors raised Jesus from the dead**--*whom you killed by hanging him on a cross. God exalted him to his own right hand as Prince and Savior that he might bring Israel to repentance and forgive their sins.* **We are witnesses of these things**, *and so is the Holy Spirit, whom God has given to those who obey him."*

Throughout the Book of Acts and beyond, the word of God's redemption through Jesus Christ spread throughout the world. God added masses of people to His Kingdom through their faith in His Son.

> *Acts 2:41, 47b: Those who accepted his message were baptized, and* **about three thousand were added to their number that day.** *... And* **the Lord added to their number daily** *those who were being saved.*

> *Acts 4:4: But* **many who heard the message believed***; so the* **number of men who believed grew to about five thousand.**

> *Acts 6:7:* **So the word of God spread. The number of disciples in Jerusalem increased rapidly**, *and a large number of priests became obedient to the faith.*

> *Act 11:21: The Lord's hand was with them, and* **a great number of people believed and turned to the Lord.**

> *Acts 12:24: But the* **word of God continued to spread and flourish.**

> *Acts 19:20: In this way* **the word of the Lord spread widely and grew in power.**

This said, not everyone will receive the Gospel message. When Jesus proclaimed the Kingdom of God, He often finished His teaching by saying, "if anyone has ears to hear, let them hear!" He knew that not everyone who has natural ears has the ability to hear what the Spirit of the Lord is saying.

Moreover, when Jesus sent His disciples to testify about Him, He prepared them for those who would reject the message of the Kingdom of God by telling them to "shake the dust off of their feet." This is a sign of judgment and cannot be taken lightly as we remember that the foremost objective of witnessing is to wash people's feet from the dust and wickedness of this world, not to shake dust back at them. (See John 13:1-20.) Christ's disciples were Jewish and knew that when a Jew left a Gentile town or city, they would literally shake the dust off their feet to symbolically demonstrate their holiness and separation from the error of the Gentile's worldly ways. Because of this, they understood that when someone rejected the good news of the Kingdom, they shook the dust off of their feet to visibly express the rejecter's error.

> Matthew 10:14-15: **If anyone will not welcome you or listen to your words**, leave that home or town and **shake the dust off your feet**. Truly I tell you, **it will be more bearable for Sodom and Gomorrah on the day of judgment** than for that town. (Also Mark 6:10-11; Luke 9:5.)

Even if people do not listen to us, it is still our responsibility to, "GO." We must share the love of God through Jesus Christ with all people everywhere. As an example of this duty, in the Old Testament, God called upon the prophet Ezekiel to declare to an exiled people a message of hope through repentance from sin. Ezekiel was accountable to God for sharing the message but not for how people responded to it. If Ezekiel shared the message and the people did not repent of their sin, then their sin was on their own head because they had been given the opportunity to believe and chose not to. However, if Ezekiel did not share the message with the people, then God held their sin against Ezekiel. (See Ezekiel 33:1-9.)

As disciples of Christ, we have a responsibility for proclaiming the Gospel to all nations. We are not responsible for how people respond to the message. It is God who grants repentance to those whom He has chosen.

> Acts 11:18: When they heard this, they had no further objections and praised God, saying, "So then, **even to Gentiles God has granted repentance that leads to life**."

> Acts 13:48: When the Gentiles heard this, they were glad and honored the word of the Lord; and **all who were appointed for eternal life believed**. (See also 2Timothy 2:19.)

> 2Timothy 2:25: Opponents must be gently instructed, **in the hope that God will grant them repentance leading them to a knowledge of the truth**.

The Apostle Paul alluded to the connection between Ezekiel's accountability to God the obligation of witnessing for Christ when he declared himself to be innocent of everyone's guilt because he had faithfully preached the whole counsel of God to them. (See Acts 20:26-27.)

MAKE DISCIPLES

Along these lines, it is important to recognize that the commission of Jesus is not, "Go and make people say a prayer to receive eternal salvation," but, "Go and make disciples by teaching them everything I have taught you." God is not after converts, prayers, and professions of faith without circumcised hearts. God is looking for transformed lives of people who will repent of their own ways in order to reveal His nature and power to the lost and dying world. The Apostle Paul referred to this as drawing people into the obedience of faith. (See Romans 1:5, 16:26.)

In fact, the word Jesus used for *make disciples* means, "to follow the precepts, to enlist as a scholar, to teach or instruct." As such, making disciples is helping people apply God's **you first** policy in their own lives by aligning their lives with the teachings and commands of Jesus. This said, the way that each disciple of Christ makes other disciples of Jesus will vary based on how God has designed and called us. Throughout the Book of Acts and beyond, the Holy Spirit revealed Christ's chosen apostles, prophets, evangelists, shepherds, and teachers. (See Acts 1:2, 5:29, 11:27, 13:1, 15:32, 20:28, 21:8, 10.)

*Ephesians 4:7, 11-13: But to **each one of us grace has been given as Christ apportioned** it. ... So **Christ himself gave the apostles, the prophets, the evangelists, the pastors and teachers, to equip his people for works of service**, so that the body of Christ may be built up **until we all reach unity in the faith** and in the knowledge of the Son of God **and become mature**, attaining to the whole measure of the fullness of Christ.*

Even today, every believer is a gift from Christ to the rest of the Body which corresponds to these types of ministries. Each ministry reflects a different aspect of Christ's mission but has the same purpose – to make disciples by drawing others to spiritual maturity and unity with one another. God desires for us to be a living, breathing, walking, talking demonstration of His grace through Jesus Christ. Simply put, the aim of the Christian life is *Christlikeness*, both individually and corporately as a witness for Christ to all creation.

*Ephesians 3:10-11: **His [God's] intent was that now, through the church, the manifold wisdom of God should be made known to the rulers and authorities in the heavenly realms**, according to his eternal purpose that he accomplished in Christ Jesus our Lord.*

BY TEACHING, PREACHING, TESTIFYING

Throughout the Book of Acts, believers everywhere testified about the resurrection of Jesus. Their focal point was not on the cross of Christ or His suffering but on His resurrection to eternal life. The resurrection confirms God's choice and acceptance of Jesus' offering of atonement for the sins of the world. Amen!

*Acts 4:2, 33a: They were greatly disturbed because the apostles were teaching the people, **proclaiming in Jesus the resurrection of the dead**.... With great power the apostles **continued to testify to the resurrection of the Lord Jesus**.*

Also Acts 2:24,32, 3:15, 4:10, 5:30, 10:40, 13:30, 17:31, 23:6.

The Gospel message was shared in various ways depending on who was speaking and who was listening. Primarily, this was done through teaching, preaching, and testifying. Simply put, teaching is instruction from the Scriptures in the knowledge of God through Jesus Christ; preaching is sharing the good news of Christ's salvation; and testifying is sharing a personal story or experience of the transformative power of God through Jesus. Jewish people who knew the Scriptures typically wanted evidence from the Word of God to prove that Jesus is the Messiah and some kind of supernatural confirming sign from God to prove it. Gentiles were most often looking for wisdom or higher understanding so that they could live a better life. (See 1 Corinthians 1:22.) The message of the gospel was tailored to the audience so that the hearers could believe and be saved but without compromising God's message or intent.

*1 Corinthians 9:19-22: Though I am free and belong to no one, **I have made myself a slave to everyone, to win as many as possible**. To the Jews I became like a Jew, to win the Jews. To those under the law I became like one under the law (though I myself am not under the law), so as to win those under the law. To those not having the law I became like one not having the law (though I am not free from God's law but am under Christ's law), so as to win those not having the law. To the weak I became weak, to win the weak. **I have become all things to all people so that by all possible means I might save some**.*

An example of Paul's **teaching**, was in Pisidian Antioch. In the Jewish synagogue after the customary Scripture reading, Paul stood up and taught from the Scriptures that Jesus is the promised Messiah of Israel. Paul addressed his fellow Israelites as children of Abraham and God's special people by birth. (See Genesis 12-25.) From the Scriptures, He refreshed their memory about the events from the time of their exodus from Egyptian slavery to the time when God promised David that the Messiah of Israel would come from his descendants and would rule on God's throne for all eternity with an everlasting dynasty. (See 2 Samuel 7.) Then, Paul pointed to John the Baptist as Jesus' forerunner (in the spirit of Elijah), who announced the coming of the King and the Kingdom of God and how in fulfillment of all the prophecies, the religious leaders crucified Him. (See Isaiah 40:3; 53.) But God, by His power, had raised Jesus from the dead giving irrefutable proof that Jesus is the Messiah of Israel and the King above all kings who reigns forever. This is good news! The Messiah that all Israel had been waiting for had come and, through faith in Him they could have a right relationship with God, something that they had never been able to attain through obedience to the Law. Other examples of this kind of teaching of the Gospel include the speeches of Peter and Stephen, Philip's teaching to an Ethiopian eunuch, and Apollos refuting opponents with the Scriptures. (See Acts 2, 3, 7, 8:26-40, 13:16-41, 18:27-28.)

As an example of Paul's **preaching**, in both Lystra and Athens, Paul spoke to Gentiles who did not have any Scriptural knowledge of the one true God but needed to hear the Gospel to be saved. The people of Lystra worshipped many idols and believed in the power of the gods. The people in Athens also had idols but emphasized epicurean or stoic philosophy. Epicureans were materialists who believed that the world was ruled by chance and, accordingly, their approach to life was, *eat, drink, and be merry*. Stoics believed that the world was ruled by fate which was out of their control and, therefore, their aim was to live with minimal emotion and in alignment with the laws of nature while their mindset was, "what will be will be." Paul tailored his message in these places to refute their existing beliefs and tell them about Jesus.

> *Acts 14:15b-17:* **We are bringing you good news**, *telling you to* **turn from these worthless things [idols] to the living God,** *who made the heavens and the earth and the sea and everything in them. In the past, he let all nations go their own way. Yet he has not left himself without testimony: He has shown kindness by giving you rain from heaven and crops in their seasons; he provides you with plenty of food and fills your hearts with joy."*

> *Acts 17:23, 30-31: For as I walked around and looked carefully at your objects of worship, I even found an altar with this inscription: to an unknown god. So you are ignorant of the very thing you worship--and* **this is what I am going to proclaim to you.** *... In the past God overlooked such ignorance, but* **now he commands all people everywhere to repent.** **For he has set a day when he will judge the world with justice by the man he has appointed. He has given proof of this to everyone by raising him from the dead.**

In both instances, Paul highlighted God's role as Creator of the Universe. Paul highlighted God's loving provision of rain, crops, sustenance, and life as the obvious sign of God's existence and of His goodness towards all that He created. (See also Romans 1:19-20; Matthew 5:43-48.) Paul informed them of how every person in every nation on earth is descended from Adam, whom God had created, and how God loves all people in spite of the fact that they do not know Him or worship Him. Paul stressed God's authority and control over all the nations of the earth throughout the entire course of history, indicating that God is the true eternal Judge of all. Paul preached the resurrection as proof that God has appointed Jesus Christ as the eternal Judge, and that He will return to administer justice, including everlasting life to those who have believed and everlasting wrath to those who have not believed. Notably, Paul did not bash people or their beliefs. He used what they believed to be true as a segue into revealing the superiority of Jesus Christ as the one true God's Chosen One and only Son.

Examples of Paul's testifying can also be found in the Book of Acts. (See Acts 22:3-21, 26:1-23.) Paul did not shrink back from sharing the full story of how off course he had been before he believed Jesus and how God, in His great mercy, had intervened in his life. Additionally, there are countless other examples in the Scriptures including all the stories that are not told of how Jesus changed people's lives.

> *John 9:25: He replied, "Whether he is a sinner or not, I don't know.* **One thing I do know. I was blind but now I see!**"

> *John 4:28-29, 39: Then, leaving her water jar, the woman went back to the town and said to the people, "***Come, see a man who told me everything I ever did.*** Could this be the*

*Messiah?" ... Many of the Samaritans from that town **believed in him because of the woman's testimony**, "He told me everything I ever did."*

*John 21:25: **Jesus did many other things as well**. If every one of them were written down, I suppose that even the whole world would not have room for the books that would be written.*

TO THE END OF THE AGE

Until Jesus returns, our commission from Him is to make disciples for His Kingdom out of every nation, tribe, and tongue. People everywhere need to hear the word of what Jesus has done for us to spare us from the wrath of God and the day of judgment that is yet to come. People everywhere need to repent from their sins and turn to Jesus for their salvation. There is no other way to be saved. (See Acts 4:12.)

*Acts 26:16-18: Now get up and stand on your feet. **I have appeared to you to appoint you as a servant and as a witness** of what you have seen and will see of me... **I am sending you to them to open their eyes** and **turn them from darkness to light**, and **from the power of Satan to God**, so that they may receive forgiveness of sins and a place among those who are sanctified by faith in me.*

*Act 2:38-40: Peter replied, "**Repent and be baptized, every one of you, in the name of Jesus Christ for the forgiveness of your sins**. And you will receive the gift of the Holy Spirit. The promise is for you and your children and for all who are far off--for all whom the Lord our God will call." With many other words he warned them; and he pleaded with them, "**Save yourselves from this corrupt generation**."*

No matter what happens to us or what opposition we face, our assignment from the Lord remains until everyone whom God has chosen for eternal life has heard and put their trust in Jesus.

*Acts 5:20: "**Go**, stand in the temple courts," he said, "**and tell the people all about this new life**."*

*Acts 18:9-10: One night the Lord spoke to Paul in a vision: "**Do not be afraid; keep on speaking, do not be silent**. For I am with you, and no one is going to attack and harm you, because **I have many people in this city**."*

MY TESTIMONY WORKSHEET

MY STORY OF HOW JESUS SAVED ME

Briefly share how Jesus first made Himself real in your life and how He has changed you.

FORGAVE MY SIN:
List some specific things you know God has forgiven you for.

REDEEMED ME FROM THE CURSE:
List some specific challenges or family/generational patterns God has delivered you from.

FREED ME FROM EVIL (BE SPECIFIC):
List some specific influences of darkness God has freed you from.

HEALED MY BODY/MIND/HEART (BE SPECIFIC):
List some specific sickness or infirmities God has healed for you.

Basic Training Exercise

COME AND SEE

Basic TRAINING
SPIRITUAL EXERCISES

John 4:28-30, 39-42 NIV - Then, leaving her water jar, the woman went back to the town and said to the people, "Come, see a man who told me everything I ever did. Could this be the Messiah?" They came out of the town and made their way toward him.... Many of the Samaritans from that town believed in him because of the woman's testimony, "He told me everything I ever did." So when the Samaritans came to him, they urged him to stay with them, and he stayed two days. And because of his words many more became believers. They said to the woman, "We no longer believe just because of what you said; now we have heard for ourselves, and we know that this man really is the Savior of the world."

DESCRIPTION

When disciples of John the Baptist asked Jesus about following Him, His response was, "Come and see." Later, after Jesus prophetically discerned the secrets of a Samaritan woman's life, she went back to her village and told everyone to "come and see" the Prophet she had encountered. She knew He was the King and Messiah they had been waiting for.

Sharing our testimony of how Jesus has touched our lives can be powerful by itself. This said, it is also beneficial to accompany our sharing of our story with a demonstration of God's Kingdom. Once they come to see and hear for themselves, they will have had an experience that they cannot easily forget. This could prove to them that Jesus is real and change their faith.

Therefore, practicing this Come and See exercise is about sharing our own story of encountering Jesus while also taking it to the next step of engaging the people we share with in the Kingdom of God.

PRAYER

Father, thank you for the ways that you have made yourself real to me. Help me to share my experience of you with others so that they can encounter your Kingdom and goodness. In Jesus' name, Amen.

Category: Evangelism

PURPOSE:

To effectively share our experience of Jesus with others and invite them to their own faith in Him.

To demonstrate the Kingdom of God to those who may not have experienced it yet.

To shine as light in the darkness so that people can come to know Jesus.

SPIRITUAL FRUIT:

Confidence in sharing our faith with others.

Growing in our ability to demonstrate God's Kingdom.

Recognizing what Jesus has done in our lives.

Increasing in being the light of the world to those who are in darkness.

CONSIDERATIONS

How did you first come to know Jesus? What is your salvation testimony? What has Jesus done so far for you?

In what ways has Jesus revealed His Kingdom and power to you? Did He manifest Himself to you in some way? Have you been healed or received a personal prophetic word? Has He changed your character? Were you "blind but now you see?"

How can you share your experience of Jesus with unbelievers in a way that is relevant to their lives?

How are you personally equipped to demonstrate God's Kingdom? (i.e. prophesying, healing, casting out demons, demonstrating Kingdom character in love, joy, and kindness?)

Why is it important to demonstrate the Kingdom of God to people? How can you become better equipped to do so?

PRACTICE

1. Ask God if there is anyone who may not know Jesus yet that He desires for you to share His Kingdom with.

2. Tell them something about your experience with Jesus. Be led by the Holy Spirit so it is tailored by the Lord for them.

3. Use the following as a guide for revealing God's Kingdom:

If you are not yet equipped in the works of God's Kingdom:
- Is there a church, ministry, prayer group, or worship night you could invite them to where the true Gospel is proclaimed and the Kingdom is manifested?

If you are equipped in the works of God's Kingdom:
- How does God want you to demonstrate the Kingdom to this person? Ask them if you can pray for them. Is God giving you a prophetic word for them? Do they need healing for anything? Follow where the Lord leads you.

If you are advanced in the works of God's Kingdom:
- Invite them to tag along with you as you minister to others. Jesus openly demonstrated His approach to curious followers and they saw, heard, and believed.

NOTES:

ADDITIONAL SCRIPTURES:

John 1:35-42

Matthew 10:7-8

Luke 10:17-20

Acts 10:38

Matthew 8:16

1 Corinthians 14:24-25

Category: Evangelism

CORNERSTONE – UNIT 6.4

Towards Maturity
Scripture Reading & Worksheet

Read each of the following passages and then use the chart below for study and reflection.

- Matthew 5:43-48
- Philippians 3:8-16
- 1 Corinthians 3:1-15
- 1 Corinthians 2:6-16
- 2 Timothy 3:16-17
- 2 Timothy 2:20-26

General Summary of These Passages:	
Main Themes & Common Message:	**Key Verses:**
3 Characteristics of Christian Maturity:	**3 Questions you still have about this:**
1.	1.
2.	2.
3.	3.
How does this change your impression of what the Christian life is really about?	
How is God asking you to respond to these passages in your life today?	

Basic Training Exercise

PRESSING ON TO SUCCESS

Philippians 3:12-14 NIV – Not that I have already obtained all this, or have already arrived at my goal, but I press on to take hold of that for which Christ Jesus took hold of me. Brothers and sisters, I do not consider myself yet to have taken hold of it. But one thing I do: Forgetting what is behind and straining toward what is ahead, I press on toward the goal to win the prize for which God has called me heavenward in Christ Jesus.

DESCRIPTION

Jesus is God's image of perfect success. Yet, His life did not match the world's view of triumph. Instead, Jesus willingly laid down His life to fulfill God's purpose. When He tells His followers to take up our cross and follow Him, He means denying ourselves as He did, including letting go of our own opinions, desires, cultural norms, preferences, and concepts of success.

For example, when measured by certain standards, the Apostle Paul had much to boast about. However, Paul knew that the world's standards of measurement are worthless in the sight of God. Paul had one objective in life and it was to know Jesus and be like Him, no matter the cost to his life, ego, or agenda. Pressing on to Success is about entering into a deeper commitment to following Jesus, surrendering ourselves to God, and moving towards His purposes for our lives, no matter the cost.

STUDY/MEDITATION

Read Philippians 3:4-14 slowly and prayerfully. Read it two or three times, asking the Holy Spirit to speak.

How did the Apostle Paul's image of success change when He came to know Jesus?

What was Paul's aim in life with the Lord? What was his burning desire?

What did Paul have to lose, give up, or walk away from in order to follow Christ?

Why was Paul willing to give up these things?

Category: Self-Denial

Basic TRAINING
SPIRITUAL EXERCISES

PURPOSE:

To detach from, let go of, cut off, release, and repent of anything hindering my walk with Jesus and attaining His likeness.

To silence the past and look onwards to the future in the new mercies of God.

To take steps necessary for the advancement of God's Kingdom purpose for my life.

SPIRITUAL FRUIT:

Increased freedom to obey God today.

Advancement in God's purpose for your life.

Alignment with God's perspective and purpose.

Restored focus on Christ.

PRAYER

Father, thank you for sending Jesus to be the perfect example of pressing on in your purposes. Help me by your Spirit to forget the past and take new steps of faith towards all you have for me. In Jesus' name, Amen.

TALK WITH GOD

In your life right now, in what ways/areas is Jesus asking you to "forget what is behind" and press on to follow Him?

How are your standards of success or failure affecting your obedience to God? How is your boldness for God affected by your self-image, fears, or insecurities?

Are your desires, opinions, preferences, behaviors, or cultural norms hindering your advancement in God's purposes? If so, which ones? What does God say about these things?

Are there material objects or relationships that God is asking you to let go of? How is He asking you to go about doing this?

PRACTICE

1. Write down your past or present definition of success and its attributes. What does success look like to you? How do you measure success?

2. Write down what you believe God's idea of success is.

3. Compare your definition and God's view of success.
   - How does your view differ from God's?

4. Write a new definition of success for your life.
   - Ask Jesus to refresh your focus on His desires for your life.
   - Ask Him if there is anything from your past that you need to let go of or give/throw away. (It could be a past trophy, a sentimental object, or an old mindset, etc.)

5. Ask God what steps of faith He is calling you to take as you pursue Christ and His likeness. Do what He says.

NOTES:

_____

ADDITIONAL SCRIPTURES:

Colossians 2:13-15
Matthew 16:23-26
Luke 14:26
Romans 8:38-39
1 Corinthians 9:24
John 12:25
Luke 9:51

Category: Self-Denial

COMMANDS OF JESUS - EVALUATION

"IF YOU LOVE ME, KEEP MY COMMANDS." JOHN 14:15

1 = Not obeying/Not enough   *2 = Some/Partial Obedience*   *3 = Regular Obedient Application*

Repent	1	2	3	Hearing Jesus/Listening carefully	1	2	3
Believe	1	2	3	Not judging	1	2	3
Following Jesus	1	2	3	Not condemning	1	2	3
Rejoicing at Persecution	1	2	3	Forgiving repeatedly	1	2	3
Reconciling with adversaries	1	2	3	Taking planks out of own eyes	1	2	3
Cut hand & Pluck eye (cut out sin)	1	2	3	Helping others with speck in eyes	1	2	3
No taking oaths	1	2	3	Not putting pearls before pigs	1	2	3
Not resisting evil person/people	1	2	3	Asking, Seeking, Knocking	1	2	3
Turning other cheek	1	2	3	Doing unto others as you want to you	1	2	3
Giving more than demanded	1	2	3	Entering through narrow gate	1	2	3
Going extra mile	1	2	3	Every effort through narrow door	1	2	3
Giving to everyone who asks	1	2	3	Watching out for false prophets	1	2	3
Loving enemies & persecutors	1	2	3	Receiving healing (Be clean, loosed)	1	2	3
Blessing those who hate you	1	2	3	Letting dead bury the dead	1	2	3
Be perfect/merciful as God is	1	2	3	Showing mercy, more than sacrifice	1	2	3
Doing good deeds in secret	1	2	3	Praying for laborers	1	2	3
Giving in secret	1	2	3	Proclaiming Kingdom	1	2	3
Few words in prayer (no babbling)	1	2	3	Healing sick, casting out demons, etc.	1	2	3
Praying the Lord's prayer	1	2	3	Freely receiving & giving	1	2	3
Fasting without show	1	2	3	Shaking dust off feet	1	2	3
Not storing treasures on earth	1	2	3	Not rejoicing in spiritual power	1	2	3
Storing treasures in heaven	1	2	3	Being wise as serpent, harmless as dove	1	2	3
Not worrying about your life	1	2	3	Not worrying about what to say	1	2	3
Heart not set on food or clothes	1	2	3	Speaking out what Jesus has revealed	1	2	3
Seeking Kingdom First	1	2	3	Not fearing man, fearing only God	1	2	3
Not worrying about finances/$$	1	2	3	Not supposing peace, but sword	1	2	3
Guarding against greed	1	2	3	Not stopping false teachers	1	2	3
Coming to Jesus for rest	1	2	3	Believing God	1	2	3
Learning of Jesus	1	2	3	Believing also in Jesus	1	2	3
Denying self, taking up cross	1	2	3	Keeping commands of God	1	2	3
Having no fear	1	2	3	Not separating marriages	1	2	3

Being aware of yeast: religion	1	2	3	Watching out that no one deceives you	1	2	3
Being aware of yeast: unbelief	1	2	3	Being ready for service	1	2	3
Being aware of yeast: worldliness	1	2	3	Not taking place of honor for self	1	2	3
Paying taxes to Caesar	1	2	3	Taking lowest place	1	2	3
Coming to God like a child	1	2	3	Not inviting friends to banquet	1	2	3
Going to those who sin against you	1	2	3	Inviting those who cannot repay	1	2	3
Selling possessions, giving to poor	1	2	3	Hating own life (compared to Jesus)	1	2	3
Being a servant of all	1	2	3	Hating family (by comparison)	1	2	3
Loving God	1	2	3	Using wealth to make heavenly friends	1	2	3
Loving neighbor as self	1	2	3	Hating money	1	2	3
Not chasing Kingdom, anointing	1	2	3	Rebuking those in sin	1	2	3
Being ready for Jesus' return	1	2	3	Not fearing end times wars and battles	1	2	3
Keeping watch for Jesus' return	1	2	3	Remembering Lot's wife	1	2	3
Showing mercy (Good Samaritan)	1	2	3	Praying to not fall into temptation	1	2	3
Generously giving to the poor	1	2	3	Being born again by the Spirit	1	2	3
Feeding the hungry, thirsty	1	2	3	Not turning God's house into marketplace	1	2	3
Taking in strangers	1	2	3	Worshipping in spirit and truth	1	2	3
Clothing the naked	1	2	3	No excuses (take up mat and walk)	1	2	3
Caring for the sick	1	2	3	Stop sinning, sin no more	1	2	3
Visiting prisoners	1	2	3	Not working for food that spoils	1	2	3
Taking Communion rightly	1	2	3	Not judging by appearances	1	2	3
Going to all nations (fulfill calling)	1	2	3	Judging with right judgment	1	2	3
Making disciples	1	2	3	Obeying teachings of Jesus	1	2	3
Baptizing others into faith	1	2	3	Obeying commands of Jesus	1	2	3
Teaching the teachings of Jesus	1	2	3	Washing feet of others	1	2	3
Feeding God's sheep, lambs	1	2	3	Doing the works as at first (first love)	1	2	3
Waiting on God	1	2	3	Not afraid of suffering	1	2	3
Witnessing for Jesus	1	2	3	Being faithful even unto death	1	2	3
Doing the works of Jesus	1	2	3	Holding on to what you have	1	2	3
Abiding in Jesus, remaining	1	2	3	Waking up! Re-Strengthening to finish	1	2	3
Loving one another as Jesus loves	1	2	3	Being earnest	1	2	3
Laying down life for others	1	2	3	Being hot or cold	1	2	3

Unit Six – Key Questions
Christlikeness & Commission

Use this worksheet to test your grasp of the material and exercises of Unit Six.

What does spiritual maturity look like?	
What is God's will for me?	**What does it look like to live by faith?**
How did Jesus live? How does He want me to live this way?	**What is the obedience of faith?**
What does it mean to make disciples? How does God want me to do this?	**How does God want me to grow to spiritual maturity?**
What is one thing you learned that you did not know before?	**What questions do you still have about this subject?**

UNIT SIX: GROUP EXERCISES

Have each member of the group share one way that God is currently challenging them to live by faith or obey the commands of Jesus more. Ask them to articulate how they intend to begin to step into this in obedience. (i.e. Being or Doing.) Pray for them as they step out in faith.

AND/OR
As a group, discuss what the marks of spiritual maturity are for an individual or for a group of believers. Talk about how this impacts God's purpose for your group. (i.e. the way you meet, what you do, etc.)

AND/OR
Pair up two-by-two and use the Come and See Exercise to go out in your city and tell people about Jesus.

ABOUT THE AUTHOR

Wendy Bowen has lived entirely by faith for many years in the *literal* application of what is today known as the Manifest International Approach, (see manifestinternational.com/approach) God has never failed her. She proclaims Jesus, the whole counsel of God, and spreads the message of God's faithfulness all over the world. She equips followers of Jesus to live by faith in these end-times so as to endure to the end and be saved.

www.manifestinternational.com

Manifest
INTERNATIONAL
We Live to Manifest Our King

www.ingramcontent.com/pod-product-compliance
Lightning Source LLC
Chambersburg PA
CBHW080439110426
42743CB00016B/3218